*To the family I was born into
and the family who now harbour me.*

'Far from being the basis for good society, the family,
with its narrow privacy and tawdry secrets,
is the source of all our discontents.'

Edmund Leach

Foreword

Thanks to Una Whelan, a painstaking editor as usual, and to Danny McCarthy and Nicola Sedgwick for their encouragement. To Ian O'Flaherty for the inspiration. To Dave Conachy, Emma Blain, Willie Brennan, Peter Gallagher, Patricia Redlich, Patricia Devine, Martin Fitzpatrick, Paul Allen. To Sam Smyth, John Downing, John Dunne, Stephen Collins, Ivor Kenny, Ken Whelan, Eugene Masterson, Ralph Riegal, Claire McGovern, Gene Kerrigan and all the other reporters whose books and articles I used to research this book. To Independent News & Media and to Ian O'Flaherty for the photographs.

Acknowledgements

Four line extract from the poem *This Be The Verse* by Philip Larkin from *High Windows* published by Faber and Faber; Extract from *The Other Side Of The Rainbow* by Máire Brennan published by Hodder and Stoughton UK.

Contents

Chapter 1

Insights

Ireland is a land of feuds. 'The Irish are a fair people; they never speak well of one another,' said the writer Samuel Johnson. He had a point. Talk of a United Ireland has always been something of a misnomer – the Irish have never been united.

In the twilight of the Gaelic civilisation rival chieftains and their clans fought with each other over everything from territory and wives to cattle and gold. While they were squabbling and conducting ancient feuds with their neighbours and relations they didn't see the real threat coming from Strongbow and the Norman conquest.

Little has changed since. The Civil War pitted comrades against each other and even families split. The state itself is founded on this political feud, which continues to this day. What side your great grandfather or grandmother took in the Civil War still determines many people's political allegiances in the twenty-first century.

'The first item on the agenda of any Irish political movement,' said the writer Brendan Behan, 'is "the split".'

Dublin, a literary city, was always famous for the feuds between its writers and artists. It was as if the city itself was too small to contain their great egos. George Moore, the great Irish writer, carried on a lifelong feud with many other writers in the city, particularly with Oliver St John Gogarty, a real person who gained immortality as James Joyce's Buck Mulligan. Moore was a cantankerous individual who insisted on saying the Angelus each day in the reading room of the St Stephen's Green Club just to annoy the majority of the members who were Anglo-Irish Protestants.

James Joyce himself carried on a lifelong literary feud with Dublin, the city that enthralled and inspired him.

The rollicking Brendan Behan took a libel action against the poet Patrick Kavanagh over some perceived slight in a book review. He won the case but was awarded derisory damages.

To this day feuding continues in literary Dublin with Ulick O'Connor and Hugh 'Jack' Leonard wasting no opportunity to snipe at one another. At a party in the home of writer Colm Tóibín, the playwright Tom Murphy dumped a plate of curry on his adversary Michael Colgan of the Gate Theatre. But what are a few literary insults, one way or another?

A row over a border between two fields has ruined family relationships with years of expensive litigation and destroyed friendships with pig-headedness and greed.

So it is that all rows are local. And the more local the row, the more bitter the feud becomes. But of all the feuds the most bitter is the family feud. Normal, level-headed people lose their reason and even the smallest detail becomes a matter of utmost importance and significance in a warring family. A slight by a sibling, intended or not, is mulled over at great length and if there is a wrong meaning to be taken from a gesture it will be taken; if something innocuous is regarded as a slight then a slight it becomes. So we join the great mass of seething familial rows in all their glory, rows over sex, money or power.

The psychiatrist and broadcaster Anthony Clare declared that when somebody trades their private life in public it can be very dangerous for them, and for those around them. He said this in the context of Terry Keane's betrayal of former Taoiseach, Charles Haughey. 'If you talk about private things publicly, how can somebody engage in a private relationship with you again? What kind of intimacy can you have?'

When families fight they usually end up in court. It is there that their private feuds become public property. And that is the end of the family relationship; for most families it is a step too far and there is no way back.

But, often, feuding families are so bitter that they want to fight it out in public, letting the full glare of publicity shine a light into the darkest corners of the family cupboard. They don't seem to realise that the glare will illuminate all the family skeletons, including their own.

Frequently, though, a feud has its roots elsewhere. Family members may appear to be squabbling about business but the reality is that their bitterness and disputes go back through the years to childhood slights and betrayals that are hidden deep in the subconscious.

'The problem with family feuds is that it is personal. The battle may be about property, inheritance, or even corporate strategy, but it's never just business. It's never even just about money. Family feuds are always about scoring points, very personal points,' says Patricia Redlich, the well-known social commentator and psychologist who writes a column in the *Sunday Independent*.

'The family is the place that nurtures us. It's also the emotional battleground par excellence. Nobody can get to us like a brother, mother, sister or father. That's because members of a family compete with each other. We compete with each other for our parents' attention. Mother competes with us for father's attention, and father does likewise in order to get enough of mother's time. It's a war zone. And that's when the family is functioning reasonably well!

'Competition within the family is how we learn to be the way we are. We define ourselves in terms of how we fit into the family pecking order. That's what shapes our personalities. Each blow we take in that tough exchange really hurts, because all this happens when we're young and vulnerable. We never forget. And we're always fearful, because they know our weakness, and have the power to exploit it.

'So when there's a battle between family members, it's not just about the item on the official agenda. It's always also about every painful experience we ever had in that family which nurtured us, but which also, of necessity, was the pain-ridden scene of so many emotional struggles as we slowly found out who we are, and how life works. It is the force of that pain which makes family feuds so ferocious,' she says.

Even the bitter experiences of other families do not deter a family from descending into a public display of their pain, anguish and disappointment with each other.

'Like civil war, siblings' squabbles are less inhibited and more vicious than disputes between strangers,' said Sam Smyth in his book *Thanks a Million Big Fella*, the acutely observed classic which tells the story of the fall of Michael Lowry and the war between Ben Dunne and his sister Margaret Heffernan over control of the Dunnes Stores retailing empire.

'When relatives fall out, the hurt is greater, the wounds are deeper and they take longer to heal. Less privileged families may disagree over who gets what piece of furniture after the death of a parent, but the very rich are different.

'They have the means to hire lawyers as proxy warriors and instruct them to be as ruthless and cruel as their professional ethics permit. It allows enough latitude to license torment in legal battles between kith and kin. But it is too easy to blame the lawyers for the malice of their clients: ultimate responsibility lies with the people who instruct them and pay the bills.

'Lawyers with a reputation for inflicting the most pain on their clients' opponents are in heavy demand and it is reflected in the fees they charge. Rich people with legal problems never ask their friends if they can recommend a cheap, mild-mannered lawyer,' says Smyth.

As it happens the battles of Ben Dunne and his sister Margaret Heffernan gave a unique insight into the secret world of an Irish private family company. What emerged wasn't very pretty and it wasn't very dignified. Nearly fifteen years after the event Ben Dunne, a big bear of a man with a genial smile who has swapped a life of secrecy for a high public profile, was asked about his relationship with Margaret, who had ousted him from the family firm.

'Normal,' he answered.

'Good?' asked the interviewer, Ursula Halligan, on TV3.

'Normal,' he answered.

Ben Dunne went on to compare the relationship as akin to a couple who had a messy divorce. Normal was the best they could expect. They met occasionally in restaurants he said, but as far as having anything in common the two family members had fallen out so badly that there was no longer any chance of anything other than a purely formal relationship.

For the disinterested observer it might seem that a company like Dunnes Stores, worth hundreds of millions, has enough for everyone. Why fight about it? For the very rich it is not really about the money at all. It is about the past, it's about power. Ultimately it is about the will to win. The cost in terms of money or collateral damage is almost immaterial.

'Conflicts are par for the course in family business,' said Philip Smyth, a family business consultant with BDO Simpson Xavier. 'Family businesses need structures that enable stakeholders to discuss conflict in a dispassionate way where people aren't involved in shouting and screaming – doing a lot of talking and very little listening.'

But sometimes people prefer the shouting and screaming to bringing in a bunch of dry accountants to settle their disputes. They want the emotional satisfaction of revenge and it can take many forms.

Terry Keane, the gossip columnist and mistress of Charles Haughey, had a few accurate observations about the human condition and why families end up feuding.

'Oh no, I wouldn't have wanted to be his wife at all. I would never have married a man like Charlie; he was a bounder, a loveable rogue, tremendously sexy. You plan a marriage, you don't plan an affair. I never planned to fall in love with Charlie Haughey and I would never have changed my name for him. I enjoyed being his mistress; I enjoyed the role.

'You see, as a mistress you get the best side of someone; they're dressed up, going somewhere nice to meet you and anticipating having a bit of fun. You are not talking about school reports or the bathroom leaking. Being a mistress is a rarefied sort of relationship. It's not real in some ways. It is conducted in romantic places as a kind of fantasy scenario. Everything is set up to avoid the nitty-gritty of every day. Being a mistress is love without responsibility.'

Being part of a family, and particularly a family business, is all about the 'nitty-gritty' and when personalities clash the encounter gets lost in the family history rather than rational decision making.

When motherhood intrudes it can be devastating, as Susan McLaughlin illustrated some years ago. Susan McLaughlin, the wife of wealthy Dublin stockbroker and businessman Kyran McLaughlin, could accept that he had left her for a younger woman. The multimillionaire businessman, described by the profile writers as 'arrogant', had left her very well provided for when he left home after an acrimonious marriage.

But when Mrs McLaughlin discovered that her husband's lover was about to bear his child she didn't throw a tantrum, splash his car with paint or seek to embarrass him in front of her children. What she did was far more devastating.

The attractive 'forty-something' decided on revenge that was low key, but far-reaching in its implications for her powerful husband.

In the attic of their rambling mansion she found a filing cabinet of highly sensitive financial documents. She handed them over to the Moriarty Tribunal which was then sitting in Dublin investigating off-shore tax evasion and what were known in important Dublin business circles as the Ansbacher Accounts.

The lawyers at the Moriarty Tribunal found some very interesting reading, including a highly incriminating piece of financial advice entitled 'A Note to John Furze' which was something of a classic in its own way. John Furze was the Cayman Islands banker who was involved with a Dublin financial wizard called Des Traynor. Between them they were the financial engineers behind the Ansbacher Accounts.

(Conspiracy theorists have long noted that both died relatively young and fairly suddenly in circumstances that were not always as clear as they seemed.)

As it happened Kyran McLaughlin hadn't written 'A Note to John Furze' but the fact that it was found in his attic was devastating for the businessman. He had to resign as joint managing director of the Dublin financial firm of Davy Stockbrokers and he was suddenly in the spotlight of the tribunal investigating corruption at the highest level in Irish society. Revenge for Susan McLaughlin was sweet indeed.

Every family has its feuds, but most of us patch them up and get on with it. But it can be more difficult for the rich and famous.

The actor Daniel Day-Lewis has been conducting a long-standing and seemingly bitter feud with his uncle, Jonathan Balcon. Apparently Balcon, a retired British Conservative councillor, had dared in an interview to criticise Day-Lewis over his personal life after he had broken up with his lover Isabelle Adjani by way of a long-distance phone call, even though she was seven months pregnant with his child at the time.

'An uncle of mine felt the need to give an interview a few years ago. He took a moral stance on my actions. That was laughable. He is probably one of the most amoral people I have ever encountered. That man has always been a joke in our family,' said Day-Lewis in retaliation. His uncle was 'a bully, a fraud and a hypocrite,' he said.

'If he had been younger I'd have taken him to the market place and smacked him,' said the star of the film *Gangs of New York* and *My Left Foot* who lives in an opulent home named Castle Kevin near Annamoe, Co Wicklow.

According to Uncle Jonathan he had been asked a question about the star and had given an honest answer.

'To harbour this grudge for such a long time is just quite ridiculous and if I could afford to sue him over the word 'fraud' – or be bothered – I would. But then to be honest with you I'm a bit bored with the whole thing. It's very sad and, again, pathetic.'

But the word 'sue' is an important element in family feuds. Where there is money and animosity there will generally be lawyers and after that it isn't very long before the whole mess is being trotted out in court. And that can even happen to the lawyers themselves.

One such person who found himself on the wrong side of a family feud was the well-known Limerick solicitor John Devane. He is known as a litigious lawyer who has handled very profitable cases involving everything from suing the state over army deafness to representing prisoners who claim their human rights have been infringed by having to 'slop out' in prison.

The handsome fees he earns has allowed him to invest in property and he let one of his houses, a property in Castletroy, Limerick to his sister Marie. But when he tried to get her out of the house in January 2005 so that he could sell it he got a bit of his own medicine. She turned into 'the sister from hell' he told a Limerick court.

Forty-three-year-old John Devane of Ardnacrusha, Co Clare had served a notice to quit on his sister, but when the auctioneers arrived she asked them not to embarrass her by putting up a 'For Sale' sign on the house she was renting from her brother. They agreed and left.

A couple of days later, on January 18, 2005, John Devane called to the house to 'talk to her' and cut off the electricity supply. According to him she started screaming and shouting at him when he entered the house. According to his sister he hit her and during the assault she sustained bruising to her arms and thighs. The gardaí were called out to settle the brother and sister dispute.

'She's a drama queen at the best of times,' said Mr Devane, denying the accusations of assault.

The family feud was thrashed out at a sitting of Limerick District Court where Judge David O'Riordan decided that he had 'a doubt in my mind' over the assault and he dismissed the charges.

While family feuds may be very negative for the people directly involved there can be a positive side. The Dassler brothers Adolf and Rudolf from the small Bavarian town of Herzogenaurach set up a sportswear firm in the 1920s and became the first company to make footwear purely for sporting purposes. When Jesse Owens won a golf medal in the 1936 Olympics in Berlin it was bad for Germany but good for the brothers, whose sports shoes he was wearing.

In her book *Pitch Invasion* Barbara Smit reveals how the brothers, once the best of friends, fell out and their acrimonious split in 1948 not only divided the Dassler family but the entire town where they lived. In the process, however, it created two world-class businesses, Adidas formed by Adi Dassler, and Puma formed by his brother Rudi Dassler.

Although all that negative energy went into success, today, more than half a century later, the town remains divided and the executives working for the two companies carry on the feud which first split the family nearly sixty years ago.

Family feuds are not exclusively the preserve of the rich and famous – although money plays its part when most families squabble. Niamh O'Connor told the slightly macabre tale in the *Sunday World* of a Dublin taxi driver who was brought to court for robbing flowers and memorials put on his mother's grave by his sisters.

Burly taxi man Christy Flood's obsession with his mother's grave led to a bitter family feud with his being accused of 'waging war' against his sisters Sharon and Ann.

It all stemmed from his mother's house in north Dublin, which she had promised to leave to him. He even produced a will which verified the claim. But it appears his mother didn't have title deeds to the house which in fact was owned by Fingal County Council. When their mother died it wasn't Christy Flood who got the house, but his sister Sharon, who bought it off the council. But now she's had to transform it into a fortress with CCTV cameras and other security devices to keep her brother away.

Christy was so incensed that his sister got the house he regarded as his inheritance that he removed a headstone from his mother's grave and returned it to the makers. Flowers and other items left on the grave were removed and flung into the garden of his sister's house. 'That grave is my property, I paid for it,' he insisted after he was bound to the peace for two years for his behaviour.

It is traumatic for those involved in the family feud. Most will tell you that in the end the personal anguish just isn't worth it, but once it starts it's almost impossible to stop. People become bitter and entrenched. The longer a feud goes on the more 'dirt' gets dug up and the deeper the dispute becomes. What may have started out as a small tiff suddenly brings up all the pent-up emotion and anger that may go right back to childhood when a new baby is born and brought into the household, unsettling the security of the family that is already there.

Once a row starts, it is all too easy for it to spiral out of control with other family members and in-laws being dragged inexorably into the infighting and intrigue.

In Limerick city feuding families have been at the centre of several murders. The trouble is supposed to stem from a schoolyard dispute between two children of families that had once been friends and allies. The dispute was brought home and escalated into a very public war that at its height saw members of the Emergency Response Unit patrolling housing estates to prevent further bloodshed.

Nobody wants things to go that far, but there is something wonderful about the sight of powerful people feuding in public. The Irish love a good row and it seems there are many families out there ready to trade their private problems for public humiliation.

When its just a bunch of ordinary people it's pathetic, but wealth and privilege give a whole new meaning to the term 'family feud'.

It makes the rest of us feel good because it just goes to prove the old adage: 'The rich are just like us, except they have more money.'

Chapter 2

The French Diplomat's Daughter

It's a warm sunny May afternoon and the 'beautiful people' from the advertising agencies are already sitting at tables in the bright and buzzing Diep le Shaker restaurant in a Georgian laneway off Fitzwilliam Square on Dublin's leafy Southside.

Waiters scurry among the tables taking orders for meals. Bottles of wine and champagne are uncorked with a joyous pop, and upstairs along the balcony some boisterous diners are slipping seamlessly from a long lunch into early evening drinks.

But behind the lively scenes of merriment in the award-winning restaurant, which draws its clientele from Dublin's wealthy smart set, lies a long saga of bitterness and rancour that has descended to the level of an insoluble family tragedy.

As the revellers in Diep le Shaker are enjoying themselves in Pembroke Lane, the woman who once owned the converted mews building where it is sited, the elderly but still gracious Renee ffrench O'Carroll, is on the other side of town, sitting in the witness box in the High Court locked in a bitter and unseemly dispute with her youngest son Arthur.

Neither the old lady nor her balding, dapperly dressed son can bear to look at each other as they pass in and out of Court No 12 in the Four Courts, with their teams of highly paid lawyers. After eight years of feuding over her son's 'inheritance' neither their advisers nor the tetchy Judge Thomas Smyth can get the warring ffrench O'Carrolls to step back and settle their family feud.

In halting, heavily accented English, the French-born Renee ffrench O'Carroll insists that she never intended to sign the lease which gives the youngest of her five children title to the mews, on which site Diep le Shaker is now built. She claims that she only gave him a lease in his own name and that by demolishing the ramshackle old mews at the back of her house and erecting a large new building which is sublet to the owners of Diep le Shaker restaurant, her son acted contrary to her wishes and effectively took part of the inheritance of her other children.

Arthur ffrench O'Carroll once 'managed' his mother's quite considerable property portfolio. He 'popped in' to see her almost daily. She plied him with good French coffee and he brought her the newspaper. It was a type of mother and son relationship identified by the great Irish writer Percy French in one of his verses: 'The one that gives the most trouble the mother loves double.'

But then Renee ffrench O'Carroll believed her son Arthur went a step too far. She claims that the building which now houses the restaurant was erected without her permission; that she had signed a lease in his name without being properly aware that she was signing it away for good; that she had signed a lease in his favour, but he had no right to assign it to anyone else.

As the trouble over the mews escalated, relations between mother and son deteriorated. It reached the stage where the elderly lady was even refused access to her little granddaughter, Elizabeth Renee ffrench O'Carroll, the once delicate daughter of Arthur and his wife Christina whose premature birth was something of a catalyst for the events that were now unfolding in court in all their painful detail.

Sitting in a soft chair in the courtroom Renee ffrench O'Carroll is a picture of elegance. Dressed immaculately, her grey hair pulled back in a bun, expensive jewellery hanging from her thin wrists, she answers like a feisty businesswoman who knows her own mind and is determined to have her own way.

Arthur, now fifty-three years old, is also well dressed in a dark suit though his appearance is somewhat offset by the bulldog look on his tanned unsmiling face during the trying court proceedings.

It can't have been easy for him, a successful businessman and 'man about town', to have his mother speak of him in public in such disparaging terms as she did.

'Arthur was the one who had made nothing of his life,' she said matter-of-factly. 'I gave him the mews to help him advance in life. That was after the club in my basement where he made a lot of money, but he spent it. He wanted to do something similar in the Hotel Holyrood. But I was not prepared to give him the mews. I was going to let him use it. On my death it would be divided and he could fight it out with his brothers and sisters,' said Renee ffrench O'Carroll, looking at the judge with twinkling eyes and no longer even acknowledging her youngest child.

'I gave him the mews because I wanted to give him a chance. I knew it [the business] would not last – a mother does know her son, when he has had the life that he has had.'

When she was asked if she expected him to fail when he established his own business in the mews in Pembroke Lane she answered, 'Not so much fail as change to something else – because he was always looking for something better.'

In many ways it was a very sad comment for a mother to make about her son. They had both done so well out of life and it was unseemly that a family with so much should descend into such a bitter, personal and pointless feud.

For seven days they stayed locked in conflict, even though the judge and their lawyers tried to find some way to accommodate both sides. But years of conflict had hardened their hearts and neither was prepared to compromise. It was a fight to the finish and no one, not even the judge, knew what the outcome would be as the evidence dragged on, day after day.

'I am past infuriation at this stage,' remarked Judge Smyth as another obscure point of law was argued out among the barristers who attacked each other over legal niceties with almost the same ferocity as their clients.

The ffrench O'Carrolls seemed intent on having their say in public, even if nobody else wanted to hear it. Handcarts were necessary to bring in the boxes of evidence. They were determined to let the world know of their pain and separation and at times the exasperated judge had to tell them he didn't want to hear the personal minutiae of their private lives.

'Nine tenths of this is irrelevant,' he snapped at the lawyers as the personal history of the animosity that developed in the ffrench O'Carroll family was laid bare before him.

Yet they couldn't settle it. Their lawyers talked for a full day to try to reach some accommodation but none was forthcoming.

So each day the old lady, accompanied by her eldest daughter Suzanne, sat on one side of the courtroom while her son Arthur and his wife Christina sat on the other.

It all started so long ago, back in the turbulent days at the beginning of the Second World War when a teenage girl named Renee Marie de Laforcade arrived in neutral Ireland in 1940. Born on January 20, 1923, the daughter of a French diplomat, the seventeen-year-old Renee was no ordinary refugee fleeing to Ireland from the ruins of Europe as the German army advanced through her country with Panzer tanks and marching columns of Swastika-clad soldiers. She was coming to Dublin to join her father, Xavier de Laforcade, the French Minister in Dublin, the representative of the Vichy government in neutral Ireland.

Renee's parents were very much part of the French political establishment and the teenage girl joined her family, living in some style in the elegant French Embassy residence at No 53 Ailesbury Road in Dublin 4, one of the grandest addresses in the drab ration-pinched city of Dublin.

Although Ireland must have seemed strange to this cosmopolitan child of wealthy diplomatic parents, it was also a safe haven from the holocaust and destruction that had left Europe in ruins.

Renee's parents were obviously well connected. Not only did they manage to stay in Ireland with diplomatic immunity, but they also managed to bring their considerable fortune with them, no mean feat in an era where international wealth was plundered, looted and dispersed by the armies rampaging across central Europe.

Vivacious and outgoing, the young Renee soon met up with Michael William ffrench O'Carroll, a medical student and the son of Arthur S ffrench O'Carroll, Medical Officer for the Donnybrook District who lived in a rather grand house at No 77 Eglinton Road, Dublin. They fell in love.

After he had finished his final medical exams, the war in

Europe was drawing to a close. The future seemed more secure for everybody and the young couple married. The wedding of the debonair twenty-four-year-old Irish doctor and the exotic twenty-one-year-old Frenchwoman in Donnybrook Church on December 7, 1944, brought some style and elegance to the bleak social scene of wartime Dublin.

Both sets of parents were well-to-do and the young couple got an excellent start to their married life when Renee's parents gave them a wedding present of a four-storey over basement house in Fitzwilliam Square, Dublin. The house, No 55, is an elegant Georgian townhouse just off Baggot Street. It was ideally suited to the young couple: it provided them with a nice address in the centre of Dublin and a handsome income when they chose to rent parts of the basement and the mews at the back which had once been a coach house in the more leisurely Victorian era of the horse and carriage. More importantly it provided Michael William ffrench O'Carroll with an ideal place to launch a medical career.

In 1946 almost every Georgian house on the square was occupied by the best-known surgeons, gynaecologists, pathologists and medical doctors in the country. Some lived there, close to the city with a private park in the centre of the square as their garden, a place where they could stroll and talk of medical matters on a summer's evening. Tucked away among all this medical knowledge, in No 18, was an exception, the home of the painter Jack B Yeats, then the lesser known brother of W.B. There was also a sprinkling of small 'private hotels' around the square where 'gentlemen' and 'ladies' kept digs.

The ambitious young Dr Michael ffrench O'Carroll had his eye on matters outside the world of medicine. He had more than a passing interest in social politics through his friendship with another young medical doctor, Noel Browne, who would go on to become one of the best-known politicians in the country in the years that followed.

In 1947 Browne persuaded the young Michael ffrench O'Carroll to join him and the former IRA Chief of Staff Sean McBride, who also had close connections with France where he was born, to join their new left-wing Republican political party Clann na Poblachta.

However, after playing a very active part in the formation of the party and seeing it established in power as part of the first inter-party government, Michael ffrench O'Carroll became disenchanted with the leadership of McBride and the constant infighting that characterised his party.

He left to pursue an independent political career. He was elected to the Dáil in 1951 as an independent TD for South-West Dublin. Along with his friend Browne, who was also elected as an independent, he voted for de Valera as Taoiseach.

Finding that they didn't have much influence as independents, ffrench O'Carroll and Browne joined Fianna Fáil. But then de Valera called a 'snap election' in 1954, catching almost everybody unawares, and Michael ffrench O'Carroll lost his seat. He put himself forward again in 1957 but with even less success.

In the meantime Browne, who had fallen out with almost everybody over the infamous Mother and Child Scheme which he had tried to introduce against the wishes of the powerful Catholic church, went on to pursue his lone, vindictive career in Irish politics for the next thirty years.

However, as a loyal Fianna Fáil party man, ffrench O'Carroll was rewarded with a seat in the Seanad where he took an active part in politics and the social life of the city. The leisurely life of a senator also allowed him time to resume his medical career.

By now Michael and Renee ffrench O'Carroll had five children, Donal, Paul, Suzanne, Marie-Clare and the youngest, Arthur, born in 1953, the day before his mother's thirtieth birthday.

Unfortunately for the ffrench O'Carrolls the marriage didn't last. At the time, such things were not talked about outside the family, so Michael ffrench O'Carroll did the gentlemanly thing and quietly left Ireland to pursue postgraduate studies in the University of Michigan in 1968. He didn't return home.

In the protracted court case in 2006 when marriage break-up is now commonplace, it was said that he had 'abandoned' his wife and youngest son, who was the only one of the family now living at home. According to Mrs ffrench O'Carroll's lawyer the marriage break-up was particularly difficult as she was 'a lady in a certain position of society – we have forgotten some of these sensitivities.'

Portraying the tough old Frenchwoman as something of a victim, he said that she was 'left in this tall, prestigious house with no husband and a precarious income stream from letting her property.'

That does not appear to give a full picture of Renee ffrench O'Carroll, however. She had money and property and knew how to manage both. But from a family point of view she did have a difficulty with her youngest son; Arthur seems to have been badly affected by the departure of his father.

'He was always the weak one, because he was so young when his father left,' said Renee about her son, who was fifteen and dyslexic at the time of the marriage break-up.

'Arthur needs to be backed up,' she added.

Although smart and intelligent he didn't get on in school and so his mother felt more protective of him than her other children.

Michael ffrench O'Carroll worked in Britain in the early 1970s and when he returned it wasn't to Dublin, but to Cork where he was appointed Medical Officer. He started a new life and became Director of Alcohol and Drug Addiction for Cork from 1980 to 1992 when he retired. He is the author of a well-known book about addiction called *The Irish Drug Epidemic* which drew attention to the drug problem long before many politicians had woken up to it.

Meanwhile, the man portrayed by his mother as 'the wayward son' had no qualms about alcohol as he looked at the money that cheap wine and late nights was generating just around the corner in Dublin's thriving Leeson Street.

It is hard to imagine what 'The Street', as it was known, was like in the 1970s. Pubs closed at 11.30, restaurants could only serve wine and they couldn't serve that after the pubs closed. So from the moment a young man named Maurice Boland opened a basement club called Elizabeth's in Leeson Street in the early 1970s the street was alive from the time the pubs closed until the dawn broke.

Gangs of people seeking drink and merriment arrived in Leeson Street after midnight. Taxis lined up as people paraded from one club to another where prospective customers were treated with a healthy disrespect by tough bouncers and doormen – many of them off-duty policemen.

Inside, the clubs were dark and cavernous as rich old men chatted up sexy young women among the swirling throng and the beat of the disco music. For those who don't remember the era, the best way of describing it is to say that the swinging sixties arrived in Ireland in the seventies. There were a lot of liberated young people about, and Leeson Street was where they found their pleasure. And the whole heady mix was run on a river of foul over-priced wine.

It was here that Arthur ffrench O'Carroll learned his trade, ending up as manager of one of the prominent clubs along 'The Strip'. He then moved down to Baggot Street to manage a 'joint' called Vamps, just a short distance from his home in Fitzwilliam Square. (The club still exists today as a well-known late night hangout called Joys, which ironically caters for many of the customers leaving Diep le Shaker.)

But as his mother pointed out, Arthur was always on the move looking for something bigger and better. Seeing the money that could be made from nightclubs and now experienced in the business himself, he got the idea that he would open up a club of his own. What better place than in the basement of his mother's house, the very respectable No 55 Fitzwilliam Square. The basement was empty anyway; all it needed was a lick of paint, a bar and a copious supply of wine.

There had always been an illicit trade in alcohol in Fitzwilliam Square anyway. In the 1950s Anthony Cronin and his literary friends like JP Donleavy, Gainor Crist, Brendan Behan and others spilled out of McDaids or The Bailey and with six-packs under their arms made for the warren of rented basements in the square which were known as the Catacombs after the Roman tunnels where early Christians hid themselves to avoid their pagan tormentors.

Arthur ffrench O'Carroll was really only reviving an old tradition. And he made quite a lot of money doing it in The 55 Club, as it was called.

'It was very successful,' he says of that time in the late 1970s. 'We were in operation for four-and-a-half years and then we ran into trouble with the residents.'

The influence of the respectable doctors and surgeons might have waned but the residents of the street were less than happy with the bustle and noise brought to their leafy Georgian existence by the nightclub.

Fitzwilliam Square had also become a hang-out for prostitutes and when the planners finally cracked-down, The 55 Club went out of business and Arthur had to start looking elsewhere to continue his successful career in the entertainment industry.

With the cash he had made, Arthur ffrench O'Carroll bought the Holyrood Hotel in Harcourt Street, Dublin. It was a thriving old hotel and in no time at all Arthur had established an even more lucrative business with a nightclub in the basement which was patronised by members of the gardaí whose city headquarters was just up the street. Once more the money came flooding in.

But all businesses need new investment and at one stage Renee ffrench O'Carroll was made a director of the company which ran the hotel. She had to mortgage the deeds of the mews at the back of her house in Fitzwilliam Square as security for a loan to be used to upgrade the nightclub.

Misfortune followed when the hotel was gutted by fire. The Bank of Ireland, who had a mortgage on the business, was less than pleased when the insurance settlement was passed directly to Arthur. The bank refused to release the title deeds to the mews and Mrs ffrench O'Carroll eventually had to pay the bank £60,000 to get them back.

So began the saga of the mews that would eventually divide the family.

After the club and the hotel Arthur had a taste for the good life. He knew there was a lot of money to be made out there and he wanted a slice of the action. He began looking after his mother's extensive property portfolio. It consisted of No 55

Fitzwilliam Square and the two-storey mews, a large house in Blackrock called Ardenza, a valuable mews in Leeson Lane and other bits of property around the city which she had acquired through shrewd investments over the years.

Soon he decided to renovate the mews. It had been let out in flats for years and had fallen into disrepair.

Arthur got to know a variety of tradesmen and builders. He knew when to pay 'cash on the nail' to get a job done. He was even a bit of a handyman himself. He also knew how to protect her investments when other people tried to build high-rise office blocks beside them, but he had ambitions beyond running his mother's property business for her.

By now Arthur ffrench O'Carroll had met Christina Steele, a separated mother with one daughter who lived in close-by Wellington Lane. On a trip to Florida in 1986 they got engaged and they began talking about what they would do for the future.

'I had always been involved in restaurants and we got into a bit of a discussion about going into business and setting up a restaurant in the mews at the back of Arthur's house,' explained Christina, emphasising that she and Arthur were involved in the planning and establishment of the restaurant from the very start.

Everywhere they looked there seemed to be obstacles. Arthur made several attempts to get planning permission, his sister-in-law even acting as a consultant to make an application on his behalf. Several times he was thwarted when his plans were turned down. His sister-in-law said she and her husband Paul ffrench O'Carroll had never been paid.

Arthur said this wasn't quite true.

'She took a fireplace out of one of the rooms [in Fitzwilliam Square] and put it in her own house,' he claimed, explaining how she was rewarded.

With the help of a planner called Aidan Powell a new company called Property Alert Association Ltd was established and he and Christina successfully got planning permission for 'a sculpture court and gallery restaurant'.

Christina had £100,000 in an account in the Lombard & Ulster bank and she invested £58,000 in the new venture, with Arthur investing £60,000. But with further investment required, the Ulster Bank insisted that the couple have a lease for the building in their own name, which they could pledge as security. There was also a difficulty with the liquor licence.

So Arthur went to his mother and explained that if he was to get the business off the ground he needed her to sign a long-term lease on the mews over to him.

'I was only loaning the mews,' his mother insisted. 'I was foolish. I did not want to give him the ninety-nine year lease but I was told he would not get planning permission without it.'

Mrs ffrench O'Carroll said that she was only giving it to him for the duration of the restaurant's existence. It was only his as long as her son was involved directly in the running of the business, she insisted.

'I told her my fiancée was going to invest some money in the place and I was going to need security so I got a ninety-nine year building lease from my mother,' countered Arthur.

But according to his mother the lease did not even cover the upstairs part of the mews and was only granted in his name and was not transferable to another party.

But it was not all bad news. Arthur and his mother had a windfall that year when the insurance company Scottish Provident decided to build an office block behind the house in Fitzwilliam Square. Mrs ffrench O'Carroll reminded her son that when the building company CRH did a big extension to a property the other side of them they successfully sued in a 'right to light' action. Arthur began proceedings against the Scottish Provident and reached a successful settlement of £200,000, of which £60,000 went as an investment in his new business venture.

The Lane Gallery restaurant opened in 1989 and initially the business did well. Arthur and Christina prospered and old Mrs ffrench O'Carroll called most days for a coffee and to read a newspaper and have a chat with her son and her daughter-in-law – except on Tuesdays of course when she played golf in Rathfarnham.

Among the patrons of The Lane Gallery were the Haughey boys, Conor and Ciaran, and their entourage. They had been friends of Arthur since his time in the club in Harcourt Street and they even persuaded their father Charles J Haughey, then Taoiseach, to visit the new restaurant.

It was also used for political benefit dinners for their other brother Sean, the up and coming councillor who was later to become a TD and Lord Mayor of Dublin.

Although the restaurant was doing well, one businessman who patronised it remembers Arthur as an astute businessman but someone who was 'a great welcome for himself'.

He would often pull up a chair and join customers in a bottle of wine and a chat. While it was a novelty in the early days and such informality went down well with some customers, others were put off by his over-friendly manner and began to dine there less and less.

Arthur and Christina got married in 1993 and two years later they had a daughter christened Elizabeth Renee in honour of her two grandmothers. But the little girl was born premature at just twenty-four-and-a-half weeks and had to remain in hospital for three months. When she came home she needed constant nursing care and Christina and Arthur shared the task between them.

'One person couldn't do it,' said Christina. 'Arthur and myself took so much time away from the restaurant that we couldn't give it our full attention . . . our daughter was more important at the time. She had to be fed every two-and-a-half hours.'

Due to them looking after the child the business began to suffer and fall away as customers found some new restaurant where they could eat and drink into the early morning.

It was a constant struggle between the baby and the business, and the business was coming off second best. The couple thought long and hard about what to do as the business got into difficulties and decided to sublet the building and live on the valuable income it would provide.

But Renee ffrench O'Carroll was against that and she pointed out to her son that subletting the property was not part of the lease.

'She asked us not to sublet and to try to change the image,' said Christina.

'I expected it [the mews] to come back to me when it was finished and the restaurant was not a success,' said the mother.

Arthur ffrench O'Carroll and his wife had moved to a grand house in Wellington Place. Christina sold her own house and they took out a mortgage to buy the property. According to Christina she invested a further £50,000 from the mortgage in a revamp of The Lane Gallery.

By 1996 Renee ffrench O'Carroll advised them to close it altogether and open a take-away. Arthur wanted something better than that, however.

'When he told me he needed to invest more to put carpet on the marble floor to move upmarket I told him, "Don't chance it, it won't help at all." Making the curtains green instead of pink is a waste of money,' said Renee ffrench O'Carroll.

It was shrewd advice, but it wasn't taken. The expensive revamp went ahead and basically things got worse for Arthur and Christina as The Lane Gallery continued to lose money, despite the improvements to the premises.

In addition to the downstairs restaurant Arthur started using the upstairs rooms, which had once been in flats, as a private dining room and an office. He said the rooms were frequented by judges and other important people who wanted to have a private celebration of their appointment or the conclusion of some successful business deal.

But the upstairs wasn't covered by the lease. As differences grew between mother and son, Renee sent Arthur a letter demanding rent for the upstairs part of the property. He had to pay up.

In 1996 there was a discussion about a new lease to replace the one Arthur already had with his mother.

'I said I needed to protect my investment . . . My mother told me, "You are going to have to pay something if you don't look after my flats and that will be your inheritance." If I didn't do the work for her I had to pay the market rate for the upstairs portion.'

But according to his mother there was never any question that Arthur was getting his inheritance while she was alive.

'I knew that he had lost £200,000, that was his choice, and some of the money was mine,' said Renee.

'You gave him £60,000?' she was asked.

'I didn't give it to him, he took it,' she answered.

Their dream restaurant, The Lane Gallery, finally closed. 'It got a bad review in the press, as you do, and that was it,' explained Christina ffrench O'Carroll.

Although she had another job and worked part time in the restaurant, she was also responsible for keeping the books of accounts for the business. In court Christina ffrench O'Carroll was asked about company accounts and how the company that ran the restaurant had been dissolved for failing to provide company returns.

'I don't have paperwork for all that.'

'There was no profit or loss account for this company?' inquired the barrister, Michael Dempsey SC acting for Renee ffrench O'Carroll.

'I can't remember,' she answered. 'It was a long time ago.'

There were various visits to solicitors and toing and froing with leases but in the end Mrs Renee ffrench O'Carroll signed another lease. To complicate matters the original lease was lost, but in an existing copy Renee ffrench O'Carroll assigned the mews to her son Arthur for a term of ninety-nine years.

However the mother remained adamant that this was not her intention and that the day before she was due to go on holidays her son fussed her into signing papers which she didn't read on the basis that if she didn't sign them and died while on holidays her personal affairs would be in a dreadful mess and he would lose everything.

What happened a few months later drove her over the edge. She looked out one morning to find the mews had disappeared and had been replaced with a building site.

'At that stage the whole place had been taken down. I just saw JCBs when I opened the back door. They had taken off everything, cleared the site completely.'

As she watched with mounting horror, a new building was erected on the site. 'It was built into my back yard,' said Renee ffrench O'Carroll. The old ramshackle coach house was gone and the new building erected in her yard was so big there was no longer even a place for her to park her car. She said she barely had room to get her rubbish bins from the house to the laneway where they were collected.

'He had to knock it down to make sure his mother didn't have a claim,' Michael Dempsey alleged. He said that Arthur told his brother Paul that the collapse of the old building had been a 'happy accident'. According to Mr Dempsey the demolition of the old mews was no accident.

'The collapse of the old building was the final nail,' he said. 'She went out and was utterly aghast that the premises she had relied on for so long had disappeared.'

The new premises, vast in size compared with the mews that had existed on the site, is now the home of the restaurant Diep le Shaker. Diep le Shaker is owned by a company called Killardport which is controlled by a Longford-born businessman called Matthew Farrell. Killardport is in turn owned by a New Zealand-based discretionary trust called Sokel, which is controlled by Mr Farrell and which is not obliged because of its legal status in New Zealand to pay taxes in Ireland.

The restaurant Diep le Shaker has been a resounding success with its Thai food, its ambience and its location in a laneway just a stone's throw from the busy night-time hub of Baggot Street.

The singer and performer Adele Anderson of the group Fascinating Aida, who were in Dublin for their show *Stick Your Head Between Your Legs,* gives a flavour of the atmosphere when she visited just before the introduction of the smoking ban.

'We all piled into two taxis to go to a Thai restaurant rejoicing in the name of Diep le Shaker. Unfortunately, neither of the drivers knew where the restaurant was, had never heard of the street and didn't have a map. We only got there at all because Dillie [Keane] finally called the restaurant and we were directed there by the owner . . . Dillie's young friend Charlie Slevin knows the restaurant owner's daughter, so the establishment stayed open for us and they let us smoke in the non-smoking section.'

With celebrities and advertising agency types spending their cash liberally in the restaurant Renee ffrench O'Carroll was left seething that all this was going on in what had once been her back yard and she wasn't getting a penny. Worse still, as far as she was concerned, her four other children had lost part of their inheritance because of Arthur's actions.

When she issued a civil bill against her son in November 1998 it was the start of a long drawn out and extremely bitter legal dispute. Renee ffrench O'Carroll won the ensuing legal action in the Circuit Court and the judge found that she had indeed been 'done out' of her property. The court found that the ninety-nine year lease signed in 1995 was procured by undue influence and that this lease was 'null and void'.

Arthur then appealed the decision to the High Court and the old lady had to sell her Blackrock house, Ardenza, to fund the legal costs associated with the ongoing litigation.

As it descended into bitterness Renee ffrench O'Carroll was denied access to her granddaughter.

The infighting continued and the case Renee ffrench O'Carroll V Arthur ffrench O'Carroll and Killardport was finally heard in the High Court in May 2006, eight years after the first civil bill was issued and the beginning of the war of mother and son. Matthew Farrell accompanied Arthur and Christina to the High Court most days.

Renee made it clear in the legal proceedings that she was

willing to become the landlord of Diep le Shaker and take back the valuable lease for herself. 'If I have to buy back the mews that I have lent him [Arthur] I could do it, if the judge decides that is the way,' she said.

'And cut Arthur out?' asked Judge Thomas Smyth.

'Yes,' she said, emphasising that she wanted to get her hands on the lease and the 'enormous rent' that had been flowing to her son since the mews was rebuilt and the new restaurant opened on the site.

She claims that her son Arthur and Matthew Farrell are partners in the business, although her son is not mentioned in any company documents.

The question of all the money that had been spent on the mews came up. If Mrs Renee ffrench O'Carroll got it back she might have to pay for the improvements.

'I never heard of that,' said the old lady.

'Well you're hearing it now,' snapped the judge. 'New lamps for old!'

Mrs ffrench O'Carroll was told it might mean that she would have to pay a considerable sum to become landlord of the premises which is now worth at least €2 million and probably much more with Dublin spiralling property prices.

'I could borrow money,' said the old lady.

But the following day she had to admit, rather sadly, that she wouldn't have the resources to pay such a sum to buy back ownership of the mews that had once lain almost derelict and forgotten at the back of her grand house on Fitzwilliam Square.

So after seven full days in court and a case that dragged on and probably cost hundreds of thousands of euro over eight years, it was down to Judge Thomas Smyth to adjudicate. In truth he needed the wisdom of Solomon.

In the end the judge decided to reject the theory that Arthur ffrench O'Carroll had 'the ability to impose his will on his mother'. He held that it was the other way around and it was only after 1998 when the mother and her youngest son fell out so badly and they no longer spoke that Arthur had 'become completely free of her'.

Renee ffrench O'Carroll was 'a highly intelligent and astute businesswoman' and 'wily, adroit and adamant' in her views, said Judge Smyth. He said she was a strong-willed woman who 'wanted her way and she got it' and he held that when she signed various disputed leases to do with the coach house at the back of her home she knew exactly what she was doing. In a judgement that took two hours to deliver the judge found that by signing over the lease for the coach house Renee ffrench O'Carroll was giving her son Arthur his inheritance – a one-fifth share of her estate – while she was still alive.

Judge Smyth, who at all times had tried to remain aloof from the family feud that had burst like a lanced boil in his courtroom, couldn't resist giving his own views on the dispute. Renee ffrench O'Carroll had dismissed her son in 'the most imperious tones' he said, while, in contrast, Arthur's affection for his mother 'was not contrived'.

After finding in favour of Arthur ffrench O'Caroll and allowing him to retain ownership of the building which houses Diep le Shaker the judge split the costs of the High Court case, estimated at about €200,000, in half. Mother and son were ordered to pay a huge sum of money for the privilege of wrangling with each other in public.

One sunny morning I called to Renee ffrench O'Carroll's house. Elegant as ever she opened the green door of No 55 Fitzwilliam

Square. We talked pleasantly for a while and before she closed the big Georgian door she conceded that she has led a most interesting life.

'You could write a book about it,' she said with her charming smile.

Indeed you could.

Chapter 3

Better Value Beats Them All

A startled look crossed the face of Margaret Heffernan when the door of the room opened and her brother Ben Dunne walked in and stood looking at the group of people seated around the boardroom table in 'HQ', as the head office of the Dunnes Stores retailing empire in Dublin was known.

Margaret Heffernan, who was locked in a bitter boardroom battle with her younger brother Ben, was conducting an important meeting with executives of Waterford Foods, a dairy conglomerate and a major supplier of products to the supermarket chain.

'I am a twenty percent shareholder; I am here to see what is going on,' said Ben Dunne sitting down in a vacant chair near his sister.

'This meeting is cancelled,' said Margaret Heffernan.

The men around the table began to gather their papers and snap their briefcases shut. They were stunned at what was going on before their eyes. Two of the best-known people in Irish business, brother and sister, and here they were virtually spitting venom at each other in front of strangers.

As the businessmen stood up and began to file out of the boardroom Ben Dunne leaned across the table and dropped his lighting cigarette into his sister's glass of Perrier water.

He turned to his sister and hissed, 'I am here and I am going to do more than this and you'd better get fucking used to it.'

To outsiders it was shocking but to members of the family it was just another skirmish in a long drawn out war of attrition.

In the world of money, privilege and power the Dunne family were a living contradiction. They were the most powerful, the most private and most secretive business family in Ireland. They were hugely generous to charity, but never let anybody know it. They had all the trappings of wealth themselves but they were tough and uncompromising employers. The firm built up suppliers who, when they could no longer keep up or deliver at the right price, were discarded. This even happened to their cousins, the Nevilles, who once provided bread for Dunnes Stores.

They bought big houses and stud farms but they lived quite modestly. In truth, Dunnes Stores the conglomerate was run along the same lines as the father's first shop in Patrick Street in Cork.

The story of Dunnes Stores is a remarkable fable of modern Ireland. It is one of fabulous wealth, power and political patronage on a grand scale. But it is also the story of alcoholism, loneliness, drugs and hookers. It is the stuff of great drama, with a family torn apart and great reputations ruined.

At the centre of it is the genius and misdeeds of Ben Dunne Jr, the man who would eventually bring the whole house of cards tumbling down. Yet oddly enough, Ben Dunne also emerges as probably the most likeable and normal member of a dysfunctional family. He came to supplant his father in the public imagination and members of his own family could not accept that. The whole family idolised Ben Dunne Sr and eventually they came to believe that his devil-may-care son of the same name had sullied his memory beyond forgiveness.

Here was a great and wealthy empire and it had come to be identified with a man whose exploits with cocaine in a Florida Hotel made front page news in Ireland for weeks. Members of his family were determined to get rid of him lest his public ignominy should in some way tarnish their much protected veneer of respectability.

But in the end it was even worse than that. When he came back from Florida Ben Dunne went to HQ in Stephen Street Upper and went from office to office apologising to staff for his behaviour. There was a groundswell of support for a man who had a serious drug addiction but was no longer afraid of the secret.

Just the previous November his sister Margaret had praised him at a board meeting, saying what a good job he was doing. But now the festering resentment began to surface: she wanted him out.

It all went back, as things do, to the genes. They may give you genius but there is always a counterbalance and in the case of the Dunne family the price of all the wealth and privilege that was bestowed on them was that several members of the family had highly addictive personalities.

Bernard Dunne Sr was born in 1908 near the village of Rostrevor, Co Down. The son of a colourful local character who was over-fond of the drink, he left home at the age of fourteen to seek his fortune. He was about to emigrate to America but his mother asked a friend, the mother of the economist T.K Whitaker, if she could get him a job. She used her influence to get him a job as an apprentice 'shop boy' in Anderson's of Drogheda. From there he moved to Cameron's of Longford, where he was a staunch union man.

After a dispute with his own union members, he left and opened a bicycle shop. It was a great success, but he never got paid and the business went broke. It was a lesson he would never forget and it left a hard, almost mean, streak in his character that would last for the rest of his life.

He moved to Cork, becoming a buyer for Roches Stores, an old established business owned by one of the city's 'merchant princes'. There he met and married Norah Malone. In 1944 as the rest of the world was wallowing in the ruins of the Second World War, Ben Dunne Sr opened his first shop, a drapery business in Patrick Street, right in the heart of Cork city, along with an equal partner Des Darragh. In time the partners fell out and the litigation that followed lasted for years. But Ben Dunne Sr was already on the way to building his empire, Dunnes Stores.

If Ben Dunne Sr learned one thing early in life it was the benefits of publicity and its dangers. While he spent heavily on publicising and advertising his business ventures for the rest of his life, he kept far away from the limelight himself, with one notable exception, an interview in *The Irish Times*. Old Ben Dunne stuck to his mantra of 'Better Value Beats Them All', a slogan still used by the company to this day. It was his answer to everything, his fortune and success and his personal philosophy.

As his empire expanded with shops opening all over Munster, so too did his family. His first child, Margaret, was born in March 1942, Frank in May 1943, Anne in July 1944, Elizabeth in January 1947, Bernard in March 1949 and Therese in October 1950.

Apart from Anne, who suffered an illness when she was

twelve years of age, the rest of the family would eventually become players in the great drama that was Dunnes Stores as it unfolded over the next fifty years.

Ben Dunne Sr's success depended on selling vast amounts of his goods and to do that he had to sell cheaper than anybody else. He demanded ninety days credit from his suppliers so that he had the use of their money for almost three months before he had to pay it back. 'Stack 'em high, sell 'em cheap and fast' was his philosophy. His margins might have been tight but it meant he had considerable amounts of other people's money in the bank at exceptional credit terms. In that way he kept moving on, cutting costs and plotting the opening of the next new store.

With his new-found wealth Ben Dunne Sr bought Ringmahon House outside Cork city. It was the only family home his children would ever know.

Old Ben was rarely at home, however. When he wasn't in Dublin he was scouring the country for new locations. It was left to his wife Norah to raise the family. It wasn't easy on her, or any of them.

When Margaret was fourteen she was already sweeping the floors in their Patrick Street store. With the exception of Ben, the youngest, who couldn't wait to get out of school, the rest of the family did their Leaving Certificate, and Frank the eldest son went to college for a few years to become a veterinary surgeon, but he never finished the course and in time was dragged into the business.

Ben Dunne Sr first came to Dublin in 1958 and took a suite of rooms in Jury's Hotel, which was then on the corner of College Green. For the rest of his life he would live in hotel rooms, some believed the worst hotel rooms in the city because he never allowed them to be redecorated while he was installed there.

When Jury's was demolished, he moved to The Moira and a succession of other city-centre hotels until he finally settled in the Shelbourne Hotel on St Stephen's Green. He was joined here by Norah in 1967 when Ringmahon House was bought by the council for a road-widening scheme.

In 1966 Ben Dunne Sr and his eldest son Frank found Cornelscourt near Cabinteely, then a village in South County Dublin. It was the site of two disused factories and Dunne seized on it to revolutionise Irish retailing. Until then he had opened modest enough stores, following the traditional pattern of supermarkets that were sprouting up around the country whether they were run by him or rivals like Feargal Quinn of Superquinn or Pat Quinn of Quinnsworth. But Cornelscourt was an entirely new concept in size and scope and many people thought it would fail. But Dunne's dour Northern drive would not allow that to happen.

Soon the Dublin store would be the flagship of the business. It was changing the face of how Irish people did their shopping. And it was changing the face of the Dunne family. Gradually the links with Cork were cut and the children joined their parents in Dublin. They were, according to one old porter, 'hotel room brats' but for all that they weren't bad and the night porter used to assist them in sneaking in and out when they wanted to go to dances in the city.

But back then nobody knew who they were. 'If there is one thing I hate it is publicity,' said old Ben. 'No one is allowed to write about Ben Dunne. Anyone could have done what I did, but they didn't do it and that's the only difference. The two kinds of people I don't like are the people who talk about what they've done and the people who talk about what they are going to do.'

Dunne worked constantly. If he wasn't supervising his own empire he was visiting his competitors to see if they were doing it any better, or he was travelling the world to look at new developments that he could introduce in his Irish stores.

His one recreation was horse racing. With his new-found wealth he bought a fine stud farm in Co Meath, Mitchelstown Stud. This was used for entertaining and for family weekends when there was racing in Fairyhouse or Navan. But it also appealed to old Ben because there were tax shelters to be availed of, and if there was one thing Dunne hated it was paying tax.

Ben and Norah's normal routine in the latter part of their life was to spend the day viewing their stores or looking at the competition and wind up at the new Berkeley Court Hotel in Ballsbridge for a bottle of champagne and dinner and then back to their suite in the Shelbourne.

Ben Dunne Sr was immensely proud of his St Bernard range of goods. The story goes that when the Irish Export Board took a stand at a trade fair in New York, Ben Dunne went with the delegation and proudly put his Taiwan-made nylon shirts on display. A passing Irish minister called to the Irish Pavilion and when he saw the goods on display remarked, 'What do you think this is, the fucking Iveagh market?' and walked off in disgust.

The minister in question was said to be Charles Haughey, who favoured Charvet shirts from Paris and who would one day come to rue the ghost of old Ben Dunne.

Another time their paths crossed was when the two men were travelling across the Atlantic. Haughey was in first class 'with his pals' when Ben Dunne came up from 'steering' to join them for champagne. Although he was one of the richest men in Ireland he was told by a hostess to return to his seat as 'this is for first-class passengers only'.

In 1964 Ben Dunne Sr created the Dunnes Stores Trust. Although not yet sixty years of age, he was already looking to the future and the tax planning that it entailed for one of Ireland's wealthiest citizens. The trust, which was established for twenty-one years, basically divided the company among his six children but a voting majority went to his two sons, Frank and Ben.

Justifying his decision to create the trust – the source in many ways of much of the family woes in later years – Ben Dunne Sr put it as bluntly as only he could. 'I want to make the Dunne family work. In other words, the Dunnes will have to work for twenty-one years or go bankrupt. They're my family. I think the only hobby I have is work. You can make a hobby out of work just the same as people make a habit out of work.'

After he finished his Intermediate Certificate at the Presentation Brothers in Cork, the sixteen-year-old Ben Dunne Jr had enough of school. Like other members of the family he'd spent his summers and much of his spare time doing everything from packing shelves to pricing garments and now he wanted to start climbing the ladder in the family firm.

His sister Margaret was already married to Andrew Heffernan, a leading Dublin medical consultant, while Frank had been 'coaxed' into the business after leaving veterinary college and appeared to be the son and heir. But Frank had two problems, the first was alcohol and the second was that although he was a Dunne he was more interested in horse racing than retailing.

Ben filled the vacuum like a whirlwind. He, like the rest of his family, idolised his father and mother. Only much later would he learn that while it was important to take on board the good traits of parents, it was all too easy to adopt their faults and then magnify them. Nobody had read him Philip Larkin's famous poem *This Be The Verse* which opens:

They fuck you up, your mum and dad.
They may not mean to, but they do.
They fill you with the faults they had,
And add some extra just for you.

At the age of twenty-three when Ben married air hostess Mary Godwin, tension had already crept into the family circle and neither his parents nor his sister Margaret attended his wedding.

Until his marriage he and his younger sister Therese had been very close, going out on the town on a Saturday night and holidaying together in Barbados and other destinations. But now the rich young businessman had a family and the close social ties with his sister were broken. In later life he often reflected on the effect the break had on his younger sister.

Ben Dunne eventually became a director of Dunnes Stores along with his brothers and sisters. In 1981 he was involved in a kidnapping when he was snatched by the IRA as he crossed the border to visit one of their stores in Newry. He was released unharmed after what many people believe was the payment of a large ransom by his father.

If it hadn't been so serious it would have been almost comical at times. Various people were trying to negotiate to have him released and large sums of money were being driven towards the border, hotly pursued by detectives acting for the government which was adamant that no ransom would be paid to terrorists. When a 'well-connected' business associate of the Dunnes arrived at the company headquarters and told a member of the family he was 'owed a big favour' by the IRA and could have Ben released for IR£50,000, he was asked for a receipt before the money was handed over.

The kidnapping experience was deeply traumatic for the young businessman but within days of the ordeal ending, Ben Dunne was back at work. Like his father he was fiercely ambitious. He really did want to get to the top and there was only one job that he wanted: his father's.

'The days of having men on board that won't be taking a personal interest and be there twenty-four hours a day is gone. To be on the main board of Dunnes Stores you've got to be on call twenty-four hours a day and seven days a week. I think the worst thing in this country is that top personnel are not working,' Ben Dunne Sr told Andrew Whittaker in *The Irish Times* in what is believed to be his only real interview.

When Ben Dunne died in the private wing of St Vincent's Hospital in Dublin in April 1983, it really was the end of an era. Among those who stood along the railings of the Pro Cathedral in Dublin and shook the hands of 'Junior', as the younger Ben Dunne was known, and other members of the family, was Charles J Haughey, then leader of Fianna Fáil and Taoiseach-in-waiting.

Frank and Ben Dunne now became joint managing directors while their sisters Margaret Heffernan, Anne Dunne, Elizabeth McMahon, Therese Dunne and their mother Norah made up the rest of the board. But according to Dunnes Stores insiders, the family went into mourning for over a year after the company founder's death and couldn't make the urgent decisions that needed to be made. Competition was coming in from Britain and in the ever changing business they kept asking themselves, 'What would Daddy think?' It was left to Ben, the youngest son, to drive the business forward.

Because of their own commitments the rest of the family couldn't make his 8 a.m. meetings where decisions were taken on budgets, price cutting and how to handle the competition in the cut-throat world of retailing. Gradually Ben Dunne assumed control of the business, but no matter what he did he couldn't satisfy every member of the family.

It came down to a simple dynamic between two factions. Ben Dunne and his elder sister Margaret had never really got on. When he took off the business suit, Ben was impulsive and gregarious. He broke the family 'rules' by going out socially with staff, suppliers and competitors. He was a man about town who liked to mix business with pleasure. Margaret was intensely private; she idolised her parents and their insistence on privacy and tried to emulate it. Margaret had married young and she began to move in the circles of the 'professional' classes. With her father's death she wanted to play a more active role in the family firm but Ben didn't like anyone encroaching on what he regarded as his own territory.

Ben Dunne had the total support of two of his sisters, Elizabeth and Therese. Margaret had one ally on the board, Frank, but he was more interested in training horses, such as the Ascot winner Stannera, and didn't play an active role in the business. It was three to two in Ben's favour and he made sure that counted.

Although they were very different, there was a bond between Frank and Ben and it was only when the battle for control of Dunnes Stores intensified into outright war in the early 1990s that it was broken.

When old Ben Dunne died in 1983 the company had a turnover of IR£300 million and had sixty-seven stores scattered around Ireland, north and south, and one in Spain. Ten years later under the dynamic control of Ben Jr, the company had ninety-seven stores and a turnover of around IR£1 billion.

It was an awesome achievement. He was like a man possessed. He worked long and hard and drove others long and hard. Suppliers got injections of cash to make their businesses better, but if they couldn't compete in the changing international market place they found that Dunne could be unforgiving. Some of them made their fortunes, others went to the wall regretting the day they'd ever 'supped with the devil'.

Long before ordinary people had heard of 'globalisation' or low-cost economies, Dunne had trawled the world seeking cheaper products that he could sell to the willing Irish public. There was no room for sentiment in retailing: if you couldn't make the price you didn't get the business.

Ben Dunne had quickly asserted himself as joint managing director and by sheer energy and enthusiasm had soon outranked his troubled brother, taking on the role of executive chairman for himself.

There could be only one boss, Ben maintained, and like his father before him, he took the job.

Although the rewards were huge Ben Dunne appeared to live a modest lifestyle for a man of such vast wealth. He still lived in the same home in Castleknock in west Dublin that he had purchased when he got married. But there was always something lurking behind the calm businesslike exterior. One of his great resentments in life is that when the old family home in Cork, Ringmahon House, was sold he only got one piece of furniture. It wasn't even an antique. Yet he treasured it above all the trappings of wealth. Such inconsequential things can fester for years.

Like his father he avoided publicity. He didn't talk directly to journalists although there were one or two in his circle. They were never allowed to write about him directly and anything they did write that might concern him he had to see first.

He shunned what became known as the 'charity circuit' where the new wealthy made themselves feel a bit better by joining committees to organise charity balls and celebrity auctions.

All the energy and drive that he put into the business had to have some release. Ben Dunne had two vices: one public and the other very private. They were golf and cocaine.

He spent so much time working that he needed to escape from the business and at first he did this on the golf course. He brought his own particular brash style to the game and he was soon legendary on the golf club circuit, playing for outrageous sums of money, up to £30,000 on one occasion, with people like the businessman Dermot Desmond, wealthy stud-farm owner John Magnier, and the legendary gambler JP McManus. A day's winning purse would have attracted a professional player on the Ryder Cup team of the time, but for Ben and 'the boys' the gambling was 'just to make things interesting'.

Then he discovered cocaine. The drug fitted his spontaneous personality perfectly. If Dunne saw a car or something else he wanted it right away – not tomorrow or next week. Cocaine gave him an instantaneous hit, something he never got from alcohol. After his first taste he was hooked.

It was to be his undoing and yet in another way he would later see it as his saviour.

Margaret's home in South Dublin was almost a mirror image of Ben's on the west side of the city. Her husband Andy had become a wealthy consultant and at one time it appeared that she might be going to make the move from new to old money by buying Stackallen House, a rather famous stately pile in the Boyne Valley that had fallen into disrepair and came with an estate of hundreds of acres of land.

But just when it was about to get interesting after she paid what now seems a paltry sum of IR£1.95 million, Margaret Heffernan had second thoughts. When she realised she would have to fund the huge restoration project she sold the house to the industrialist Martin Naughton of Glen Dimplex.

While Ben Dunne had been building up the business, Margaret had raised her family and seen her daughter Anne, a doctor, marry into another great Irish dynasty, the O'Briens. Both families had huge interest in bloodstock and racing, but as the son of Vincent O'Brien the Master of Ballydoyle, Charles O'Brien was almost royalty in the exalted circles in which they moved.

With her family grown up and with more time on her hands, Margaret tried to exert more of her influence within Dunnes Stores. She had a different philosophy to her young brother's old family mantra of 'Better Value Beats Them All'. With a shrewd instinct she saw the Irish economy improving every year. Maybe her friends told her that the days of the cheap St Bernard brand were dead. Maybe with her social pretensions she listened to the advice of snooty southsiders who looked down on the Dunnes Stores cheap and cheerful attitude to life. Whether it was instinct or ambition she wanted to take Dunnes upmarket. She eventually ran the Cassidy chain which was part of the Dunnes Stores Group. She was given free rein but she knew and her brother Ben knew, that it was not the core business.

The other two Dunne sisters seemed to live quiet, almost obscure lives. But if the addictive personality of their grandfather had skipped a generation it certainly cut a swathe through the sons and daughters of Ben Dunne Sr: both Elizabeth and Therese suffered from chronic alcoholism, a disease so severe that it would kill both of them in their forties. Meantime, as long as Ben had his sisters Elizabeth and Therese on his side he could do as he pleased.

And that is exactly what he did. Dunnes Stores was run as his own fiefdom and although there were accountants and lawyers trying to keep him in check, Ben Dunne was like a young feudal lord. There was a myriad of companies, bank accounts, false names and off-shore investments. He could and did move money at will, thinking that no one would ever be able to trace it back to the source. He was wrong.

Apart from their natural enmity there was one other factor which fuelled the worsening relations between Margaret Heffernan and Ben Dunne. This factor was a well-known Dublin solicitor turned property developer, Noel Smyth. As one client said of him, you went to him for legal advice and you came away with a business partner. He had phenomenal natural ability and he used it to get on the inside of many of the deals he was negotiating for others.

Smyth, the son of a professional golfer, is a daily mass-goer and his opulent home in Stepaside, Co Dublin is called Lisieux due to his devotion to St Thérèse. He even brought her bones over to Ireland for a remarkable nationwide tour and was an avid supporter of the disgraced Bishop of Ferns, Dr Brendan Comiskey. But as another business acquaintance remarked, 'He might pray for you in the morning but he'll screw you for the rest of the day.'

There was something about the two of them that appalled Margaret Heffernan. They appeared to be ready to take on the world together. She particularly disliked Smyth because he was never afraid of the power of the Dunne family. She also resented what she believed was his bad influence over her brother Ben and his deep involvement in what she considered to be the private details of the family business.

When the Dunnes Stores Trust had run the twenty-one years for which old Ben had established it there was a move to break it up and reconstitute it as a normal company which would be divided up among the family members along the same lines, only now they would be shareholders who could trade on their assets instead of being bound together with the rest of the family in an unbreakable trust. But the tax implications of breaking up the trust were so huge by 1986 that it was decided by the family and their advisors to continue it indefinitely. It seemed like a good idea at the time, but in a few short years it was to become the millstone around the family neck.

In February 1992 Ben Dunne set out on a golfing trip to Florida with a group of friends, business acquaintances, a professional golfer and even a taxi driver he had literally picked up on a business trip to the tax haven of Jersey and brought along for the ride. When he arrived in Orlando, home of Disneyland, Ben Dunne went on a ferocious cocaine binge.

Disappointed with the hotel his party was staying in, he booked them all into the biggest and plushest hotel in the city, the Grand Cypress Hotel where he took a suite on the seventeenth floor at a cost of $1,200 a night.

On the night of Wednesday February 18 at around midnight, Ben was alone in his suite and on a serious cocaine session. A serial telephone addict when he was drinking or on drugs, he got out the local Yellow Pages and rang Escorts in a Flash, ordering a girl to come to suite No 1708.

Denise Wojcik arrived at about 1.30 a.m. where she was greeted by her host with a bottle of Dom Perignon champagne and a $400 tip. The bedroom was up a stairway in the suite and almost immediately the two of them started to snort lines of cocaine which Ben Dunne chopped up with his membership card to the exclusive K-Club golf and country club outside Dublin.

At about 6 a.m. in the morning after they'd been up all night,

Wojcik rang her roommate Cherie Rudulski and told her that if she got over to the hotel she would get $300 for two hours work.

But then Ben Dunne's mind began to go haywire. He couldn't open the safe in the room where he had over IR£4,000 and $9,000. He began to pace and panic and when Denise tried to calm him down he began to shriek at her, 'Leave me alone!'

She called hotel security and Ben talked to them on the phone and explained his problem. He then told Denise to leave and when she went into the bedroom to get dressed he began to wave a piece of broken furniture around.

'He was like some crazed King Kong jumping up and down and swinging this object over his head,' she said later.

Ben Dunne then opened the door of the suite and was confronted by a security man clad in black. He had some terrible flashback to his kidnapping by the IRA eleven years before and suddenly freaked, moving towards the balcony of the mezzanine which towered seventeen storeys above the hotel lobby. The security man backed off and called for help.

Dunne started shouting down to the businessmen having their breakfast below, hoping that some of the Irish golfing party who were with him would hear his cries and come to his aid.

'Then I saw them clearing the floors below me and I thought they were going to do me in. The Rodney King episode where a black guy had been beaten up by the LA police had been on the TV recently and I thought the same thing was going to happen to me. I thought they were clearing the place to make sure that nobody would get a video of it,' he would explain later.

'I was on the balcony and the police said that Major Marcus wanted to speak to me. I said there were no majors in the police. I was calling for my friends, wondering where they were. They never came. I wanted to stay out in the public view where they couldn't touch me. I didn't trust the police and I wanted to bring my pals along. I wasn't suicidal. I was fighting to stay alive,' Ben said later.

Three police cars were dispatched to the upmarket Orlando hotel and the multimillionaire Irish businessman was arrested and charged with a series of serious drug offences, including trafficking which carried a mandatory jail sentence.

The first person he called was Charlie Haughey, ringing him at his private number in Abbeville. Haughey, ousted as Taoiseach just the month before, said he would do what he could. He contacted a member of the influential Kennedy clan to see if they could help. But by then it was too late – the events in the Grand Hyatt Hotel were taking on a momentum of their own.

When the story broke on the front page of the *Sunday Tribune* in Dublin it was what the *National Enquirer* calls a 'hey Martha' moment, meaning the guy reading the paper can't contain himself and calls his wife to tell her about it.

Dunne arrived back in Dublin in full confessional mode. Unaided by any high-priced public relations advisers he adopted a simple strategy of 'hands-up', confessing his sins in lurid detail to business associates, friends and several journalists who gained access to the inner sanctum that week.

Trevor Danker who wrote a social column for the *Sunday Independent* and knew Ben Dunne, set me up with a long telephone conversation with Dunne in which he described what had happened in Florida and how sorry he was. There was only one condition: that he could read the finished version before it was published.

The conversation was so good that I merely transcribed the story the way he told it. The following day his Mercedes pulled up outside the *Independent* offices in Abbey Street and Trevor

Danker brought my typescript down to Dunne who was waiting in the car. He came back a few minutes later and said Ben had asked him if I had taped the conversation. I said I hadn't, I just had good shorthand.

He requested one sentence to be added: 'Ben Dunne hopes his family and his brother Frank would show him the same tolerance that he had shown to their failings.'

It was simple, but it was also loaded. It was a coded message to his brother and two sisters that they should understand his addictive personality they way he understood theirs.

But Margaret Heffernan, who never drank in her life, and had a puritanical streak, was unforgiving. If there was one thing she hated, it was the way Ben bared his soul when he fell from grace. She was particularly displeased when the serious charges were dropped and her brother only faced a case of possessing a small amount of cocaine. She was truly horrified when he was released on condition that Noel Smyth, his solicitor, should be his 'guardian', and his only punishment would be twenty-eight days in a luxury London rehab unit called the Charter Clinic.

'I'm sorry the little bastard didn't go to jail,' she told Noel Smyth in an angry telephone call on her mobile phone. The message was intercepted and passed on to journalist Rory Godson who published it in the *Sunday Times*, adding to Margaret's torment.

But if he wasn't going to jail Margaret Heffernan was determined that he was going to pay for the disgrace he had heaped on the family name.

After leaving the clinic Ben Dunne collected his wife Mary and his family and took them on a prolonged holiday to Spain. While he was away the remaining members of the Dunnes Stores board met in Dublin on July 16, 1992, and after an absence of a year from direct involvement in the running of the company Frank Dunne proposed that a new set of rules be drawn. Margaret Heffernan, Elizabeth McMahon and Therese Dunne agreed.

Frank, who at one stage hadn't visited the company in over two years, had now conquered his own personal problems and agreed to resume the active role of joint managing director, which had been largely dormant during Ben's reign.

For the remainder of that year Ben and Margaret worked together in Dunnes Stores, but the tension was palpable at the company headquarters in Stephen Street. Executives were forced to take sides as the Dunnes battled for control, moving and counter-moving against each other.

Ben had also got involved in a row with his sister Therese who was caught for drink-driving near her home at Merrion Gates. After she was charged, he ordered that her car be taken from her and she be provided with a driver. Therese, who had once been his closest friend in the family, was filled with resentment about this and was going to have her own revenge.

Ben then went off to Singapore and, sitting in a hotel room, spent £20 million on cheap clothing without, Margaret maintained, even negotiating normal credit terms for the company. When he came back Margaret Heffernan was furious and ordered him to cancel the orders. Dunne failed to turn up at a meeting and she had to do her best to salvage the situation by calling in favours from long-time suppliers who agreed to cancel without prohibitive penalties. The company was split with dissension.

One day Ben Dunne burst into the office of Patrick O'Donoghue, an accountant with Oliver Freaney & Co who was carrying out an examination of the company books.

'You fucking bollocks!' Ben shouted at the accountant,

threatening to hit him. 'I'm a street fighter and you won't get me out of this company as easy as you think.'

The accountant said he had never encountered 'such vile and offensive personal abuse' as he had to put up with that day.

The company eventually got a court order against Ben, preventing him from coming to the office. He has since told friends that he was deliberately trying to provoke a crisis and 'that is one of the reasons I am alive to day.'

On February 15, 1993, the first board meeting of the year was called. Top of the agenda was a proposal to sack Ben Dunne as executive chairman. When it was put to a vote his closest ally, Therese, switched sides. Frank, Margaret and Therese voted against Ben, leaving him with only the support of his sister Elizabeth.

Frank was now installed as executive chairman of the company, outranking Ben in the hierarchy for the first time.

It was devastating in the light of what he had done, transforming the family business into the first billion-pound retailing company in the country.

If he couldn't run it he wanted to get out. Ben quickly moved to sell his stake to his brother but a deal could not be agreed because of the complicated nature of the Dunnes Stores Trust and the tax liability that would occur if it was broken up.

Then Ben Dunne purchased a shell property company called Dunloe with which he intended to go into retailing and rival the family business. He made his wife Mary and his sister Elizabeth directors. The rest of the Dunne family moved against him again and this time all his executive responsibility was removed at a board meeting on April 18. Instead of getting better it got worse.

Ben was taunting Margaret Heffernan, telling her that he had given more than IR£1 million to the former Taoiseach, Charles

Haughey, the man who had humiliated her father all those years ago at the trade fair in New York.

He laughed as he told her, 'But no matter how hard you look, you'll never find it.'

By now the festering resentment was so deep that she was determined to find it. She employed the Dublin accountancy firm of Price Waterhouse Cooper with the sole aim of finding the Haughey million, and anything else Ben may have handed out in breach of company rules when he ran Dunnes Stores as his personal empire.

Ben Dunne, who was close to the Haughey clan, had given IR£100,000 to one election campaign according to political sources. Ben was well known in the Haughey home, where he had attended the various weddings of the Haughey boys on the lawn of the mansion, mixing with Dermot Desmond, James Stafford, PJ Mara and other important figures in the Haughey financial and political web.

One guest remembers him calling Sam, the family waiter, and ordering bottles of champagne for his table. When Sam was finished popping the corks Ben, who rarely carried cash, wrote a cheque for IR£5,000 and palmed it to the waiter as a tip.

Despite her protestations, Margaret Heffernan also had her connections to the Haughey clan. She personally signed three cheques, two for IR£1,000 each and a third for IR£1,500, as contributions to the election fund of the Taoiseach's son, Sean Haughey, for his election campaign in 1991.

Now she was determined to find out just exactly how much her brother had given to CJ Haughey and whether his taunts were idle boasts or grim reality.

Never one to shirk an encounter or a battle Margaret Heffernan ordered her Mercedes one morning in early July and told the driver to take her to Abbeville, the splendid Gandon mansion of Charles J Haughey, who had retired as Taoiseach in January 1992 amid a plethora of good wishes and a final statement in the Dáil that he had 'done the state some service'.

Haughey was probably the most able politician the state had ever seen. Autocratic and arrogant he lived way beyond his means, flaunting the trappings of his office like some ancient chieftain. There was Abbeville itself, a huge house with more than fifty acres in North County Dublin, Inishvickillaune, his lavish island holiday home off the Kerry coast, his mistress the journalist Terry Keane, his horses, his Charvet shirts imported from Paris.

But Haughey was also one of the most hard-working, intelligent and progressive politicians who had ever come to power. He was a small man with big ideas. His one great problem was that his lifestyle did not fit with the modest salary of an Irish prime minister. By the time he finally came to power in 1979 he had an overdraft of IR£1.14 million with Allied Irish Bank.

How he paid it off and the part played by Ben Dunne would only emerge much later, but when it did it would ruin Haughey's dignified retirement and but for the revelations of his mistress Terry Keane it would become probably the greatest embarrassment of his life.

As Margaret Heffernan drove up the long avenue to the house that summer's morning the stands of oak and beech were in full flower and racehorses rested in the sunshine in front of the mansion. The Mercedes was waved through by the security man and the driver turned left and circled onto a sweep of gravel in front of Abbeville.

Margaret was met at the steps that morning by Charles Haughey himself and the two of them walked into the fine hallway and then turned sharply into a small study crammed with the trophies of a long and glorious career as an elder statesman.

Haughey sat behind his desk and Margaret Heffernan took a seat facing him. They exchanged small talk of a desultory nature until Margaret Heffernan came straight to the point of her visit.

'My brother Bernard says that he has given you over a million pounds. Can you confirm that this is true?'

Charles Haughey had been in politics too long to fall into the trap of answering such an awkward question.

'I can't be responsible for what your brother is saying,' he said.

He then proceeded to tell her that her brother was 'unstable' and was possibly in need of medical help. Hard as Margaret tried she couldn't get anything further out of him.

Returning from Abbeville that day Margaret Heffernan, originally sceptical about Ben's claim that he had given a million pounds in company money to Haughey, was now convinced of its truth.

She then called to Des Traynor, the Dublin financier who was chairman of CRH, the building conglomerate, and operated from either their offices in Merrion Square or the foyer of the Berkeley Court Hotel, where he met an endless stream of rich businessmen who wanted to hide their money 'offshore' or away from the prying eyes of the Irish taxman.

Traynor, a small man and a convincing liar who handled Haughey's personal finance, said he knew absolutely nothing about Ben Dunne giving Charles Haughey a million pounds. He told Margaret the story just wasn't true.

Then something happened to take both Margaret Heffernan and Ben Dunne's mind off their increasingly bitter feud.

On July 26, 1993, Elizabeth McMahon, Ben's sister and last

remaining ally in the family, died at her home in Ailesbury Road in Dublin. She was just forty-six years of age. A chronic alcoholic, she had married Brian McMahon of a well-known toffee manufacturing company in Dublin at the time, Cleeves. They had a number of children but the marriage was unhappy and they had broken up.

Elizabeth McMahon was known around Dublin as 'the nicest of the Dunnes' and she was very close to her sister Margaret, even if she had decided to side with Ben in the family power struggle. For a brief moment the family were united at her funeral in Donnybrook Parish Church.

'Our mother was a peacemaker at home with Frank, Margaret, Ben and Therese. She was also a peacemaker in Dunnes Stores. We intend to continue that legacy,' said her son Brian at the funeral mass.

She was 'the quiet one' said Margaret Heffernan. 'I have to say that she was too nice to be a Dunne.'

Her Dunnes Stores shares were split among her children who remain major shareholders in the business to this day. Her daughter, Sharon, like Anne Heffernan, is now in a senior management position in Dunnes Stores.

But the peace didn't last. Among those caught up in the crossfire was the firm's head of security at the time, Sean Cavanagh, who was fired after receiving conflicting orders from Margaret Heffernan and Ben Dunne.

'She [Margaret] was slapping the desk; she was sitting with me across the table and her face was white as a sheet with black hair streaming across her face,' he said later, describing the tense meeting at which he was sacked.

By October two financial controllers at Dunnes Stores, Michael Irwin and Niall Walsh, were removed from their positions and four other executives resigned as the company descended into full-scale civil war. Ben Dunne began High Court proceedings to stop Margaret Heffernan or the board sacking anyone who earned over £30,000 at Dunnes Stores.

She said she had not challenged him over his 'regrettable behaviour' in Florida, but added stingingly, 'The personal trauma was not limited to himself, but reflected adversely on the rest of his family and on the company.' She said it had never been the wish of the Dunne family, other than her brother Ben, 'to engage in publicity seeking'.

Her brother, the man who had built Dunnes Stores into one of the most profitable retail outfits in Europe, was now responsible for 'irreparable loss and damage to the company', and his behaviour was 'intolerable'. She said he went on a 'buying spree' and was now involved in activities detrimental to the board.

'I regret to say, however, that far from building up its [Dunnes'] commercial strength, the actions of the plaintiff [Ben Dunne] in the last two years or so were calculated to cause extreme damage to the business,' Margaret Heffernan said in an affidavit lodged in the High Court in Dublin.

It appears Margaret and her brother Frank wanted to erase the memory of Ben Dunne Jr. In the company headquarters the large portraits of Ben Dunne Sr convinced a visiting executive to ask, 'Is he still alive?' When he was told that the old man had been dead for years he remarked that it was like 'the cult of the Ayatollah in Iran'.

But that is the way the remaining members of the family wanted it.

Basically, the Dunne family wanted Ben to go away. They didn't mind paying him a salary of about £1.5 million a year, but they didn't want him near the company. But boisterous Ben was having none of it. He wasn't the type who could ease into cosy retirement with games of golf and long holidays in Barbados.

After his binge in Florida he had one more disastrous fling with cocaine – and jumped into an empty swimming pool breaking both his ankles. At least, that was the story that was put out for public consumption. He was told in therapy, 'Cocaine and the family business will kill you.'

Ben Dunne never took cocaine after that episode. But it did produce some moments of great hilarity. While he was recovering at the Mater Private Hospital in Dublin the ever restless Dunne insisted on going for a pint to the nearest pub, Birmingham's in Dorset Street. Ben crossed the lounge on crutches and ordered a pint, spending a few hours at the bar with his cronies.

He liked it so much that he came back the following evening. Feeling he had some influence in the place he complained at the end of the night that the carpet had so much drink soaked into it that walking on it was like trying to walk on treacle.

The owner told him it was tough business and he didn't own one of those fancy Southside lounges that made millions and could afford to rip out the old furnishings every few years. The following morning a van turned up with rolls of carpet and the carpet layers told the bemused owner, 'Mr Dunne told us to do the place up, upstairs and downstairs.'

They duly did the job but by the time they were finished Ben had been discharged from hospital and never came back to see the new carpet.

He also visited Kinsealy a number of times and Charlie Haughey felt obliged to push him around the gravelled walks of the estate in a wheelchair as the two of them talked. On one such visit they viewed the new-born cygnets in the ornamental lake near the big house.

'If I'd known what he was going to do later on I'd have pushed him into the fucking lake,' said a rueful Charlie Haughey to a friend when details of the payments made to him by Ben Dunne finally came out in the wash.

After his painful recovery Ben vowed never to touch cocaine again. More importantly, for his sanity he decided he had to finally get out of Dunnes Stores for good. He concentrated his considerable energies on sorting out Dunnes Stores once and for all and came up with a plan: either the remaining Dunnes could sell him the company or they could buy him out at a price to be agreed.

The board of Dunnes Stores, Frank, Margaret and Therese, decided that because of the tax implications of breaking up the Dunnes Stores Trust they could do neither. It should remain a trust, nominally run by a group of anonymous trustees, mostly lawyers and accountants.

Ben Dunne decided to go to court to declare that the trust established by his father all those years ago was 'a sham' and that he was oppressed as a minority shareholder.

As the finest lawyers in Ireland lined up for a slice of the Dunnes action it seemed that the most vicious family squabble ever witnessed in Ireland was about to go to court, and the story in all its lurid detail would be played out in public in the Four Courts in Dublin.

'The trustees have nothing to do with it, it's a family fight,' wailed one of them to a newspaper correspondent.

Watching from the wings, like a bird of prey, Charles Haughey could smell trouble. This time he called Margaret Heffernan, and once again her classy Mercedes was driven up the long winding avenue to Abbeville. This time Mr Haughey was in a more conciliatory mood. He didn't admit to getting money from her brother, but he tried to impress on Margaret Heffernan the importance of a family settlement. The Dunnes were a great family and they should not, he said, be going into court to claw each other in public like a gang of street traders in Moore Street who had fallen out with each other.

But by January of 1994 it was too late for that. The High Court ordered each party to disclose highly confidential information to other parties involved in the dispute. Teams of high-priced lawyers were ready to represent the various parties involved in what was complicated business legislation, but in truth amounted to little more than a deep loathing between Ben Dunne and his sister Margaret Heffernan.

The Dunnes Stores trustees, accountant Noel Fox, Edward Montgomery, a well-known solicitor and Frank Bowen and Bernard Uniacke also accountants, were 'joined' in the court proceedings by Margaret Heffernan, Frank Dunne and Therese Dunne. They were represented by Niall Fennelly SC and John Cooke SC as well as teams of solicitors and junior barristers.

Ben Dunne was represented by his solicitor and friend Noel Smyth, who had employed three of the best barristers in the land to fight the case, Dermot Gleeson SC, Peter Kelly SC and Paul Gallagher SC.

The case was split into two parts to be tried at two different hearings. The first would consider Ben Dunne's claim to break up the family trust because it was 'a sham'. The second action would then consider his case that he was 'oppressed' in the family business and assess damages if he were successful.

But about midnight on Sunday night, less than forty-eight hours before the case was due to open on November 16, 1994, Niall Fennelly, Senior Council for Dunnes Stores rang his neighbour on Ailesbury Road, Dermot Gleeson who represented Ben Dunne.

They wanted to talk.

The following Tuesday the onlookers arrived early at Court No 4 in the Round Hall of the Four Courts in Dublin to get the best seats. The various parties were present for the 11 a.m. deadline before Mr Justice Murphy, but surprisingly some of the most important legal council were missing.

Judge Murphy, who had represented Frank Dunne in his previous life as a barrister, asked if anyone objected to him hearing the case. The lawyers shook their heads to say no and then requested an adjournment. They came back that afternoon to tell the judge that the litigation – a case which promised to scandalise and titillate the public for weeks on end – had been settled.

The Dunnes Stores Trust had finally been broken apart. Ben Dunne had his way and was bought out of the family firm for the princely sum of IR£125 million, to be paid over a three-year period.

A few weeks after the settlement Ben Dunne went out and celebrated his good fortune by buying a fine painting by Sir John Lavery, Requiem of a Mass for Michael Collins.

The bell had finally tolled for Ben Dunne, but the collateral damage would spread out far and wide in the years that followed. The case had left a time bomb ticking away.

In the end it wasn't Margaret Heffernan who revealed the secret of the 'Haughey million', it was Ben himself, although he did so unwittingly. The famous Price Waterhouse Cooper report which Margaret had commissioned had uncovered a trail of bogus accounts, false invoices and 'off the book' deals which was subsequently leaked to the journalist Sam Smyth and ruined the career of the up and coming Fine Gael minister, Michael Lowry.

But it did not mention the payments to Charlie Haughey. It was Ben Dunne who had included them in highly confidential affidavits which were prepared for the court case but did not come into the public domain until another journalist, Cliff Taylor, finally broke the story of the IR£1 million gift to Haughey from Dunnes Stores. It took the McCracken Tribunal to reveal the lurid details.

Less than a year after she had been a central figure in the battle for the billion pound Dunnes Stores company Therese Dunne, the youngest of the sisters, was found dead. Her long-time boyfriend Gerard McPadden called around to her luxury flat off the Merrion Road in Dublin 4 and when he could get no answer contacted her housekeeper Sally McDonald.

They got into the apartment and found the forty-five-year-old multimillionaire Therese Dunne slumped in an armchair in the sitting room. She had choked on her own vomit. Although she did not have alcohol in her system, she was a chronic alcoholic like her sister. The inquest was told that her drinking could have contributed to her death.

Therese Dunne left over IR£4 million in cash to be shared between her siblings, Margaret, Frank, Ben and Anne. She also left over a million each to the McMahon children Brian, Paul, John and Sharon.

'I lost my two sisters to alcoholism which had an impact on my life,' Ben Dunne would later declare. 'I should have tried to help them more. They didn't survive; they both died and I was in the middle of all my turmoil. They played a big role in helping me to sort myself out. I really loved the two of them. I was very close to those two girls. I don't think anybody sets out to be an addict.'

Therese Dunne left her shares in Dunnes Stores – valued at well over IR£100 million, to her sister Margaret. With Ben out of the company this gave Margaret Heffernan effective control of

Dunnes Stores. After all the years the schoolgirl who had started sweeping floors in the shop in Patrick Street as a fourteen-year-old was now in control of the family empire.

The war was over but feuding has left what remains of the Dunne family scarred forever.

Epilogue

Margaret Heffernan now runs Dunnes Stores, a billion euro company. She remains an enigmatic figure like her father, declining interviews in the media and maintaining a low profile apart from her work for the charity Children in Need. Her son Michael has become the first member of the 'third generation' to become a director of the family firm.

Frank Dunne remains chairman of the company and remains equally reclusive. He divorced his wife, gave up alcohol and unlike his brother Ben could walk down the street and nobody would know him.

Ben Dunne recovered from the turmoil of Dunnes Stores and now runs a chain of highly successful fitness centres around Dublin. His high profile advertisements feature his booming voice and the price-cutting philosophy that characterised his years running Dunnes Stores. He is clean of drugs, appears to enjoy life and is now a well-known and liked public figure, turning up on chat shows and dispensing his particular brand of wisdom. For many people his name is still associated with the family company although he has no involvement in it whatever.

He recently addressed a grocery conference and couldn't resist a dig at the directors of Dunnes Stores saying they weren't keeping a proper eye on the competition.

Noel Smyth bought out Ben Dunne's interest in Dunloe, the

vehicle by which Ben Dunne had intended to challenge the family business. He turned it into a profitable property development company. He remains intensely devoted to business and religion.

Charles Haughey's efforts to keep the lid on Ben Dunne's financial generosity failed. When details of Ben Dunne's affidavits were leaked to the media, the McCracken Tribunal was set up to investigate payments to Charles Haughey and Michael Lowry. It discovered that Ben Dunne was telling the truth when he taunted his sister about giving the former Taoiseach more than IR£1 million during his time running Dunnes Stores.

In April 1997 Ben Dunne told Judge McCracken that in late 1987 the businessman Des Traynor had approached Noel Fox, Dunnes Stores accountant, seeking to get Mr Haughey out of his financial difficulties and pay off his IR£1 million overdraft with Allied Irish Banks. Traynor said he was looking to put together six prominent businessmen to contribute IR£150,000 each to pay off Haughey's bills. When Ben Dunne was asked to become one of them he told Traynor, 'I think Haughey is making a huge mistake trying to get six or seven people together . . . Christ picked twelve apostles and one of them crucified him.'

So he put up the entire amount IR£750,000 which went to clearing Haughey's massive bank debt.

Haughey continued to deny that these payments were ever made. However, he held a series of meetings with Ben Dunne's solicitor Noel Smyth, the last of which was held in the home of Gerry McGuinness, a neighbour of the Haugheys in Kinsealy. At these meetings Mr Haughey made a number of admissions and after each Mr Smyth, like a character from a detective novel, wrote down what had happened, put it in a sealed envelope and posted it to his office.

He then offered the Moriarty Tribunal the sealed envelopes. Haughey had no option but to tell his legal advisors and later the tribunal that he had told lies and misled them, and had to endure the humiliation of changing his story.

Although these revelations were devastating for Charles Haughey, the evidence of Ben Dunne also revealed the existence of the Ansbacher Deposits, a web of financial accounts managed by Des Traynor and his associate John Furze for almost every wealthy family in Ireland at the time.

But probably the most colourful episode of Ben Dunne's testimony was his revelation that he had called to Abbeville one Sunday evening in November 1991 while returning from a golf game in Baltray. It was the week that 'The Boss' had finally been deposed by his former political confidant Albert Reynolds. The two men had a brief chat and Ben felt that Haughey, who was allowed to stay on as Taoiseach until the end of the year, was 'looking a bit depressed'.

The retail tycoon took three bank drafts from his pocket totalling in value IR£210,000. They were made out in fictitious names of T Scott, G Montgomery and M Blaire.

'Look, that is something for yourself,' he said, handing them to Mr Haughey as they stood near the fountain in front of Abbeville.

'Thank you, big fellah,' replied the Irish prime minister.

Chapter 4

The Volkswagen King

As he sat in his cold office in Howard McGarvey & Sons in Townsend Street, Dublin scanning the daily newspaper reports from the battlefields of World War II Stephen O'Flaherty wasn't absorbing the great speeches of Winston Churchill or the historic battles that were unfolding in the various theatres of war around the globe. His interest was focused in a narrow, almost obsessional, way on the vehicles that were transforming the fortunes of war from 1939 to 1945.

From neutral Ireland one detail caught his eye. It was a logo then almost unknown to Irish eyes, but a symbol that would one day become synonymous with the man and the country he would help to transform. It was the VW insignia of the Volkswagen, the brainchild of the German dictator Adolf Hitler: the vehicle he christened 'the people's car'.

In time this potent symbol would lead to fame and fortune for Stephen O'Flaherty, but it would also lead to heartbreak and tear his family apart.

O'Flaherty had one great weakness: women. After his death he would leave behind a bitter legacy that lives on today in the form of his 'forgotten' son, Ian.

Tall and good-looking, he was a passionate man who lived life on the principle that if you wanted something you had to go out and grab it.

'If there was a woman in the room and she had any kind of looks he would jump on her – he didn't really mind as long as they were big and blonde,' says a former business associate.

His tangled love life cost him a multimillion pound fortune. But O'Flaherty, 'a legend' in the motor business, went on to make and lose several fortunes as he lived the high life of a European playboy.

But that was much later.

In the early days, before he became a wild rover, he had other things on his mind: a dream to bring the people's car to the winding roads of Ireland.

'I was convinced that what the Irish market needed was a small economical car. I thought of the Volkswagen, which I had never seen but which was very well reported on for performance during the war in the deserts and in the Russian snows,' said Stephen O'Flaherty thirty years later.

It was an astute observation. One day it would make him a multimillionaire and a celebrity, when such people were thin on the ground in neutral Ireland.

O'Flaherty's quest for the ideal car to suit the rough gravelled tracks that passed for roads in isolated Ireland would also help to end the years of isolationism and industrial stagnation that had plagued Ireland. Almost single-handedly, he put wheels under the working man and the small farmers who were then the backbone of the Irish economy.

Stephen Andrew O'Flaherty was born in Passage East, Co

Waterford on September 15, 1902, the youngest of five children, three boys and two girls. His father Michael, originally from the Aran Islands, was a first cousin of the IRA activist, communist agitator, author of *The Informer* and philanderer, Liam O'Flaherty. His mother was a Tipperary woman, Mary Maher, from the small village of Clogheen.

When Michael O'Flaherty, the son of a poor farmer, left the Aran Islands at the age of nineteen he signed up to join the Royal Irish Constabulary (RIC) in Rossaveal in the heart of Connemara. He served in Tipperary until 1882, Cork until 1886 and then was promoted to acting sergeant and dispatched to Passage East in Waterford. He married Mary in November 1888.

In 1916 he retired from the Irish police force on a sum of £64.2.8p a year. It was a good time to go, especially for a policeman living in the south of Ireland. Momentous events were about to unfold in this part of the country: the Irish War of Independence would be unleashed by the murder of two innocent policeman by Dan Breen and his commandos, who were inventing what came to be known as guerrilla warfare.

As a young man Stephen O'Flaherty, who lived with the family at Woodstown, would see the old order changing with the guerrilla war in Munster, the rise of Sinn Féin and the IRA, and the eventual overthrow of the British regime and the police force in which his father had served for most of his lifetime.

Educated at the local national school in Woodstown and at Youghal Christian Brothers School, Stephen O'Flaherty did the university entrance exam, the Matric, but he decided against going.

'I didn't fancy five years in a non-earning capacity,' he said. But the family were probably too poor, and with the stigma, 'son of an RIC man', he was more likely than most to want to emigrate from a country that had just been torn apart by the War of Independence and was about to embark on the bitter strife of the Civil War. So he did what so many young men did in those days: he took the boat to England.

With his interest in mechanical things he got a job in an engineering firm in Manchester and at night he studied accountancy. He spent six years in England where he married his first wife, Dorothy. When he returned to Ireland in 1928 he was the proud father of two young boys, Michael and Nigel.

At the age of twenty-six Stephen O'Flaherty joined the accounts department of Ford in Cork. He was promoted to the position of traffic manager and spotted by Ford executives as a man with potential. But he declined a transfer to the company's British headquarters in Dagenham.

By 1933 he was restless and ambitious and, as he said himself, decided to take 'a one-way ticket to Dublin'. In the capital he got a job in McCairns Motors, the General Motors distributors for Ireland where he soon rose from the accounts department to become secretary of the company and general manager. But in 1939 O'Flaherty was laid off by McCairns as the company tried to adjust to the slump in the motor trade following the outbreak of the Second World War.

'I learned that a small engineering business in Townsend Street was for sale and went to see the two kind old ladies who controlled it and did a deal,' he remembered. The company he acquired was called Howard McGarvey & Sons which was engaged in general engineering but specialised in servicing steam engines.

During the war years he turned his attention to munitions and built a large gun for the Irish army, or so he would later claim. He said it was test fired but was never heard of again.

O'Flaherty also acquired a small firm called Wardle & Co, a carrier and storage business which operated out of an old tram shed at No 162, Shelbourne Road, Ballsbridge, Dublin 4. He soon moved his business in Townsend Street out to Ballsbridge.

As the war continued O'Flaherty watching from neutral Ireland soon realised that steam was dead, and his company would follow it if he didn't move with the times. He got a lucky break when he discovered a consignment of Adler cars which had been held up at customs in Dublin because of the war.

He bought the consignment and had them assembled at his makeshift plant at Ballsbridge. Not only was he learning the motor business, but when he sold the Adlers he made a handsome profit. O'Flaherty began to transform the steam engine company into a car importing and assembling business.

But not everything he touched was a success. He also imported a consignment of Willies Overland Jeeps, but a sudden devaluation of sterling left him stranded with the assembled vehicles and not for the first time he had to offload the consignment at a loss.

In 1946, with the war over, he renamed his company with the grand title of Motor Distributors Ltd (MDL) and acquired a number of small, niche motor cars, brands like Nash, Singer and Lagonda. He also obtained the franchise for Aston Martin; the cars came to Dublin fully assembled and were sold through his sales outlet.

Even though the war was over there wasn't much of a market for expensive motor cars in Ireland, a country in terminal depression after the Economic War and afflicted with de Valera's policy of isolationism.

Stephen O'Flaherty was looking for something that was cheap, reliable and affordable for the small farmers and shopkeepers who were still suffering from the rationing and shortages of the recently ended war.

'I knew that the only hope of making a real success in the automobile industry in Ireland was to get a small competitive car – something to compete with the Ford, Morris and Austin. There was only one available – the German people's car, the Volkswagen,' he said.

Apart from his passion for cars Stephen O'Flaherty had one other great advantage over his international competitors. Because of the war the Allies had an in-built hostility to all things German and the British and the French had a trade moratorium against their recently defeated enemy. When O'Flaherty set off for the Paris Motor show in 1949 he was coming from neutral Ireland which had already established trade links with German industrialists, hungry to do business and find new markets to revive their ruined economy.

Volkswagen itself had almost been broken up at the end of the war. By a quirk of fate a British Army officer, Major Ivan Hurst, who needed vehicles in a hurry to move his troops around war-ravaged Germany at the end of hostilities, had revived the Bavarian car company for his own needs – and earned his place in motoring history.

At the Paris motor show Stephen O'Flaherty found a couple of Volkswagen executives skulking in a corridor, largely ostracised by the big French, Italian and British dealers. Among them was the Volkswagen general manager Dr Heinz Nordhoff.

O'Flaherty impressed on him his admiration for the Volkswagen and he pored over the design blueprints, considering the possibility of assembling it in Ireland. Although desperately seeking markets abroad, the Germans were reluctant to commit to such a project. Even four years after the war they had great pride in the German craftsmanship that went into the VW and they didn't want it compromised by an Irishman they knew nothing about – a man who came from the fringes of Europe with little or no track record in the motor business.

But O'Flaherty played them at their own game. He was a consummate businessman and he eventually convinced the Germans that they needed him more than he needed them.

'I wasn't too impressed at first,' he said later. 'I thought it was too basic a car but after lengthy negotiations and four visits to the Wolfsburg headquarters, I secured the first consignment of unassembled Volkswagens to be brought into Ireland.'

His passion finally triumphed. The Germans decided to give the Irishman a try.

Later that year the consignment of six unassembled Volkswagen cars packed into wooden crates and described on the ship's manifest as 'completely knocked down', were landed at the Dublin docks.

O'Flaherty had the first of many battles with his bank managers to get the premises ready and fitted out for its new purpose. Ironically, it was next door to The Swastika Laundry, a company which had a fleet of little red vans with the black Swastika logo used by the Nazis painted onto the side. To see them driving around Dublin in the 1950s was such a bizarre sight that the German writer Heinrich Böll was stunned when he first landed in Dublin. For one appalling moment he had the surreal notion that he was back in war-torn Germany.

The six kits were assembled in Ballsbridge and then driven back to Germany to be examined by the Volkswagen engineers. After studying them with due care and diligence the Volkswagen engineers pronounced in favour of the Irishman and the first Volkswagen car ever assembled outside Germany was driven into the back of the works and still survives in its original condition in the Volkswagen Museum in Wolfsburg.

In 1950 Motor Distributors Ltd assembled forty-six cars and sold them all. Two years later 2,155 cars were assembled and sold. One of O'Flaherty's great strengths was his organisational abilities. Not only was he assembling the new cars but he was travelling the country and using his network of contacts to open up Volkswagen dealerships all over Ireland.

The only problem was that the Royal Automobile Club classified the car at fifteen horsepower, which meant extremely high tax compared with rivals in Ford and Austin. O'Flaherty got working on his political contacts and friends in government, particularly the upcoming young men in Fianna Fáil, and had it knocked down to ten horsepower for taxation purposes, bringing tax and insurance into line with other family cars of the time.

By now Stephen O'Flaherty had established a strong relationship with the Volkswagen headquarters in Wolfsburg. With trade beginning to open up again and the restrictions ended on Germany, executives at Volkswagen began to look at the vast British car market. They decided to award the franchise to a man they knew and were doing business with and in 1952 Stephen O'Flaherty acquired the rights to assemble and sell the VW in the British market. O'Flaherty set about the task of selling the cars with his customary zeal.

Another factor in spreading the popularity of the Volkswagen 'Beetle' as it was now christened, was car racing. O'Flaherty had been an enthusiastic racer himself, taking part in the Monte Carlo twenty-four-hour race. His son Michael, who was now studying agriculture in Trinity College Dublin, was into car rallying in a big way.

Michael's co-driver was another talented agricultural student called Paddy Hopkirk from Belfast. To finance his own rallying hobby, Hopkirk got a job as a salesman in the Ballsbridge works – nicknamed 'Testicle Viaduct' because the assembly plant was so tightly fitted into the old tram shed that it was dangerous to the anatomy of the men working there.

Not only did Hopkirk race with Michael but he got his own Volkswagen and had it serviced 'at the right price', because of his connection to the firm.

'Stephen was very good to me and loaned me a Beetle on occasions,' he said.

In the 1954 Circuit of Ireland he led the first stage in his Beetle and remembers that rallying in Ireland in those pre-TV days was a national obsession and he was its first motoring superstar.

Hopkirk's success in the Volkswagen helped sales no end, and the canny Stephen O'Flaherty knew it. He loaned Hopkirk his top specialist, Larry Mooney, to tune his car and win races on the international circuit.

Soon the converted tram shed could no longer cope with the volume of business. O'Flaherty spotted a brand new factory out on the Naas Road outside Dublin, which had been commissioned by the tailoring firm of Montague Burton as a warehouse but was never used. After a series of further battles with his bank manager the assembly plant was moved from Shelbourne Road in 1955.

O'Flaherty, never one to waste an opportunity, soon reopened the old tram shed as a Volkswagen dealership. Selling a complete Beetle, with no extras, at £499, he simply couldn't make enough cars to supply the Irish market.

However, still not satisfied, he went back to Germany and acquired the Mercedes concession for both Britain and Ireland.

In 1957, when the British ban on trading with Germany was lifted, O'Flaherty knew that he wouldn't be able to compete with other distributors without a huge injection of investment – and he wasn't a man who liked to have partners. So he sold the British franchise for Volkswagen to the London company, Thomas Tilling Group, for over £300,000 in cash, a vast fortune at the time. He stayed on as deputy chairman of the group under Lord Brabazon of Tara. In 1960 he sold the Mercedes concession to the same company for £1,316,000, making him the richest man in Ireland at the time.

'I thought it was the appropriate thing to do as it entailed a lot of work going back and forth between Ireland and England to look after my interests on both sides. I had now no interests in England, but I had plans to start a major basic industry at Shannon which had nothing to do with cars,' he said later.

Stephen O'Flaherty was now a rare thing in Ireland at the time, a cash millionaire. He and his wife Dorothy (Dot) and their two sons Michael and Nigel had earlier moved to Straffan House, a huge estate of 500 acres with at least one mile fronting the River Liffey in Co Kildare.

The estate had originally belonged to the French wine-producing family the Bartons, who built the mansion on a bend in the Liffey after fleeing the French Revolution and returning to the home of their ancestors. It was subsequently the home of the film producer Kevin McClory and later again Matt Gallagher, the building magnate before it was bought by Michael Smurfit and turned into what is now the K-Club.

With his sons Michael and Nigel finished university, they were increasingly looking after the business, and Stephen O'Flaherty began to enjoy other areas, although motor cars were never far from his thoughts.

O'Flaherty took an interest in horse breeding and acquired a horse called Atherstone Wood which did quite well, although it ran in the Sweeps Derby without much success. He said his main interests were 'gardening and golfing' although in truth he didn't bother much with either. He was captain of Old Kilcroney Golf Club outside Dublin, but this was more of a social club than a golf club, it seems. He also acquired a large green motor yacht which was the talk of Dun Laoghaire harbour where he became a member of the National Yacht Club.

In 1961 Stephen O'Flaherty was gambling in a London Casino when in walked horse breeder Maxwell 'Maxie' Cosgrove and his wife Murial (or Tina as she would later become). Even today she remembers that night vividly. The tall, well-spoken O'Flaherty was in a high-stakes game at the green tables gambling against wealthy Greeks and fearlessly holding his own.

The Cosgroves were coming from the Newmarket sales with their horse-racing friends, Lord Derby and the trainer Henry Wragg. The two Irishmen, O'Flaherty and Cosgrove, exchanged pleasantries and a couple of bottles of champagne were popped to celebrate the occasion.

It was love at first sight for Tina Cosgrove and Stephen O'Flaherty. Although he had a roving eye for the women he was, paradoxically, a staunch Irish Catholic who knelt down every night before he went to bed and said his prayers. But nothing could stop the momentum that began that night in the London club. Back in Ireland the businessman and the racing socialite began a clandestine affair.

'Tina' came originally from Clontarf in Dublin but her family had farming interests in Limerick. Although she was a glamorous figure on the social scene she was also the mother of five young children. She continued to live with her husband Maxi in the family home, Riversdale House outside Dublin, long after the affair began.

In 1967, however, Tina Cosgrove became pregnant by Stephen O'Flaherty. By now the restless O'Flaherty had handed over the running of his business, Motor Distributors Ltd to Michael and Nigel. He still went into the office and plagued them with bright ideas for developing new innovations in the car trade, but he was largely a figurehead. He had given his wife Dorothy and the two boys twenty-five per cent of the company each, while he held on to the remaining twenty-five per cent.

With his mistress about to give birth to his child, Stephen O'Flaherty finally had to come clean and tell his wife the truth.

Of course she had known about his flings with other women. She had put up with years of philandering from her wayward husband because she knew he was such a driven man. But a mistress and a child was a step too far, especially in those more straitlaced times.

The break-up of Stephen and Dot O'Flaherty's marriage was bitter and divisive. And it was all done in secret. At the time Catholic Ireland was not a place where pillars of society such as Stephen O'Flaherty could publicly flaunt a second relationship.

In a rare interview with *The Irish Times* in July 1967, when his youngest son, born to his mistress Tina, was just seven months old, he painted a picture of himself as a happily married tycoon with great thoughts and ideas on his mind.

'One of Ireland's most successful businessmen, he looks every bit of that as he sits quietly and chats happily in a soft, native accent which a lifetime of travel has not altered. A modest, genial man, it is doubtful if he ever thinks much about himself and he appears uneasy for a moment at the prospect of answering a couple of personal questions,' said the reporter for the newspaper.

'Tolerant, I like to think I am,' said Stephen O'Flaherty. 'But I'm afraid I'm a bit impatient at times – although I was worse a few years ago, when I expected things to be done 'yesterday' all too often.'

The Volkswagen King as he had been christened by journalists had ideas about how to run a company and a country.

'Quick decisions are best. You can make many mistakes that way, but the person who never made a mistake never made very much,' he said. 'I'd like to be a dictator in Ireland for about three years. My first decision would be to halve the present Dáil and double the salaries of the members. Big governments, like big boards of directors, invariably prove the least efficient. A one-man-in-charge form of administration is the ideal way to get things done.'

He was full of ideas. He even had a solution to the smell from the River Liffey as it flowed through the centre of the city and gave it the name Dirty Dublin. It entailed building a weir at Butt Bridge to keep the river high behind it and therefore stop it running out with the tide and leaving the muddy slime that stank to high heaven in the summertime and was the bane to all Dubliners who had to walk by it.

By now Michael O'Flaherty was running MDL while Nigel was over in England learning accountancy and the motor trade.

Stephen O'Flaherty insisted that despite his wealth, his big homes and his material possessions like paintings and jewellery, he was still something of a philistine, and proud of it.

'I buy a picture because I like it and I don't care if it was painted by John Jones or Picasso,' he said. His favourite painting was a large, ugly and rather badly painted 'reclining nude' which

81

he hung in pride of place in one of his many houses. He boasted that it was by an unknown artist and depending on who he was talking to he'd bought it in Beirut or on the railings of Hyde Park in London.

'He had absolutely no taste; there wasn't a decent picture or piece of furniture in the house. He had all this money and yet he was quite superficial,' said one who moved in the O'Flaherty social circles at the time.

Stephen O'Flaherty moved with the moneyed classes and he had a brilliant mechanical mind, but at heart he was still a tough car dealer trying to extract the last couple of bob from a deal.

Although he claimed to be in semi-retirement, as he described it, he nevertheless confessed that his recreation was business. And he was always on the look-out for a bargain, a deal or a percentage.

'One gets tired of most things after a time. Even a holiday gets boring after a couple of weeks, but business provides interesting developments all the time. You're either worried, or cheerful or scheming, but it's never dull.'

That also applied to his personal life. The birth of their son Ian, christened Ian Cosgrove to avoid a scandal, led to Tina Cosgrove finally moving out of Riversdale House and leaving her husband and their five children behind.

Not giving his own name to his youngest son served to protect Stephen O'Flaherty, a devout Catholic who was racked by good old-fashioned Irish Catholic guilt over the break-up of his marriage.

Then, in January 1969, O'Flaherty had a major heart attack and was taken to St Vincent's Hospital where he was treated by the country's eminent heart surgeon at the time, Risteard Mulcahy.

Lying seriously ill in the private wing of the hospital, his mistress Tina was by his side when his wife Dot arrived into the hospital, filled with concern that the man who was still her husband was at death's door. There was a terrible row between the two women. The matron spoke to the two of them afterwards and told them to sort it out between themselves, but they would certainly kill him if they continued this carry-on.

It is reported that the matron told O'Flaherty, 'Your wife or your mistress has to go – both of them will kill you.' He had no recollection of making a decision but in the end Tina won the battle to stay by his side.

Dot O'Flaherty was determined to have her revenge on the man who had deserted her, however. As Stephen O'Flaherty lay critically ill in his hospital bed Dot came into the hospital one last time in a rage and demanded that Stephen O'Flaherty give her Sherlockstown House near Sallins, Co Kildare, the smaller but no less stately home to which they had moved after finding Straffan House just two big after their sons had left home and bought places of their own. More importantly she demanded that he hand over the remaining twenty-five per cent share in Motor Distributors Ltd, his last remaining share in his Irish empire. This he did in a moment of weakness that he would regret for the rest of his life.

He was paid a nominal £1 for his stake in the multimillion pound business he had established in 1950 and single-handedly built into probably the most profitable and successful company in the country.

On September 9, 1969, it was announced in the newspapers that 'Stephen O'Flaherty is relinquishing all his directorships within the O'Flaherty Group in order to lessen the pressure of business commitments'. Reports said he would continue to act as a consultant to the companies and would remain as chairman of Monsell Mitchell & Co, a Dublin importing firm.

His eldest son Michael became the new chairman of the company and his younger son Nigel, who had returned from England, was appointed managing director.

When he finally left St Vincent's Private Hospital in Dublin, Stephen O'Flaherty, Tina, Ian, his doctor, their driver and their nanny, Daphne Ewing, moved into the Dorchester Hotel in London. After a few expensive months the entourage moved to Portugal where they lived in the Pennina Hotel and on Sir Chester Beatty's estate where they took a 'cottage'. O'Flaherty then built a palatial home in Portugal for himself, Tina and Ian at Caberro. All his bills were paid for by Motor Manufacturers Ltd, one of the companies within the Volkswagen group.

Towards the end of 1969 Maxi and Tina Cosgrove were officially separated.

In the deal with his wife and sons it was agreed that Stephen O'Flaherty would be paid £10,000 a year for the rest of his life, a considerable sum but nothing compared with the wealth that the VW franchise was earning for the extending O'Flaherty family. He also got the use of an apartment in London.

'How could they do this to me?' he asked.

But Stephen O'Flaherty was never one to rest. He had already embarked on a cleaning business buying a small company, Bells Dyers and Cleaners Ltd, which operated from Pembroke Road in Dublin and he was thinking about starting a nationwide chain of cleaning shops.

Always on the move, Stephen O'Flaherty was back in Dublin in 1970, living at Apartment 19, Elm Court on the Merrion Road and trying to figure out just what had happened while he was lying seriously ill in the nearby St Vincent's Hospital and had handed over his share of Motor Distributors for just £1.

He wrote the following letter to his consultant, Risteard Mulcahy, at his office in Clyde Road, dated April 15, 1970.

Dear Mr Mulcahy,

It has been on my mind to write to you for the past year since I left St Vincent's Nursing Home, but during that entire period I have been living virtually out of a suitcase and I have not found it possible to do so.

I did visit you on one occasion since I left the nursing home with the object of having a chat with you, but this was not possible at that particular time.

What I am anxious to know is what you said to Mrs O'Flaherty when you brought her to a private room in the nursing home some time about February of last year. Whatever you did say to her at that time resulted in the fact that I have not heard anything from her to the present day, and of course I had not given anybody permission to say anything to Mrs O'Flaherty which might have upset her in any way, but it is clearly obvious from the end result that something very serious transpired without my knowledge or consent.

If the action taken was to lessen the tensions for me, it certainly had the opposite effect and the end result of the conversation was that I was requested, and agreed, to hand over Sherlockstown with all its furniture, equipment and cattle and resign from all the family companies which I had built up over a period of fifty years.

When I left the nursing home, therefore, I had to move to an hotel – The Dorchester – and to recuperate eventually in an hotel in Portugal and as I said at the outset, have lived since that time out of a suitcase.

Before I left the nursing home the Reverend Mother called to see me and enquired why I had banned visits from Mrs O'Flaherty and I told her that that certainly had not been of my doing and of course pointed out that I was unable to make contact with the outside world, being confined to bed twenty-four hours a day and had no telephone.

I asked the Reverend Mother where she had got her information and she told me that Mrs Cunningham [the matron] had told her and I can only assume, therefore, that Mrs O'Flaherty might have told Mrs Cunningham. Obviously it seemed that the instruction originated from me, which is incorrect.

For the record therefore I would be obliged to learn, even at this late stage, what you said to Mrs O'Flaherty when you spoke to her in St Vincent's Nursing Home, and whether anybody had influenced you in whatever was said, because I certainly did not, and in fact had no knowledge of any discussion which might have taken place between you.

At your entire convenience I will look forward to hearing from you.

Yours,

Stephen O'Flaherty

There is no record of any reply to this letter.

On December 11, 1970, Maxi Cosgrove died suddenly. He died without a will but in the Ireland of the times his wife Tina decided it was best for her to renounce any entitlement to his estate.

She also gave up her rights to her five children. Stan Cosgrove, Maxi's younger brother who would later find himself in the unwanted glare of world publicity as 'Shergar's vet' (the Aga Khan's horse which was kidnapped and killed by the IRA), was made guardian of the five children, in addition to the ten he already had by his own marriage.

Stephen O'Flaherty quickly found that he was an 'unwanted presence' in the Leeson Park headquarters of Motor Distributors Ltd, the company which controlled what was once his empire. There was no office for him and it was made quite clear that he was no longer needed in the business.

Frozen out of Volkswagen Stephen O'Flaherty threw his considerable energies into a new project. He decided to return to Waterford where he was born and become something of a local squire. He bought a beautiful house, Weston, on the river Nore and he and Tina set about having it remodelled to suit the needs of the wealthy new owners.

Flying between Portugal, London and Waterford the furnishings were ordered from the top London store of Aspreys. 'It was all done so beautifully,' remembered Tina as she sat on the lawn in front of Mount Juliet in Co Kilkenny where she was holidaying in 2005.

But O'Flaherty was a restless and autocratic man. Tina stayed in Portugal one time while he went to Ireland to do business and when he came back he announced that he'd sold the house, without even consulting her and without them ever having spent a night in the place.

In indifferent health and with the changing climate in Ireland, Stephen O'Flaherty began to worry about the future of Ian, his youngest son, born out of wedlock.

In 1971 he consulted the eminent barrister Anthony J Hederman SC, later to become Attorney-General of the Irish Republic. Hederman recommended a young up-and-coming solicitor and horse owner Finbar Cahill as the man who would protect young Ian and have him recognised as the son of Stephen O'Flaherty and Tina Cosgrove, and not as Ian Cosgrove as he had been originally named.

Making Ian Cosgrove a ward of court, Tina Cosgrove set out the intimate details of her relationship with Stephen O'Flaherty.

She described how she married James Maxie Cosgrove of 'Riversdale', Palmerstown, Co Dublin at University Church in Stephen's Green on March 28, 1951. They had five children, Helen, Peter, Shona, Abby and Christopher. She said that in 1961 she became estranged from Maxi Cosgrove after meeting Stephen O'Flaherty. She said she had 'frequent sexual relations' with him from 1963 and became pregnant in April 1966. Their son Ian was born on January 14, 1967.

'I say that the reason the child was registered as apparently the issue of my marriage with the said James Maxie Cosgrove was that we were still husband and wife at that stage and no deed of separation had been entered into and that I thought it the most prudent thing, at that time, from the point of view of the child to so register his birth. But I say and I believe that it was the desire of the said Stephen O'Flaherty to have a child.'

In 1974 a battery of high-powered lawyers, Hugh O'Flaherty, Anthony J Hederman SC, John O'Connor SC and Ernest Woods SC were employed to sort out the family affairs. The president of the High Court, his Honour Aindrias Ó Caoimh, declared that Ian O'Flaherty was the natural son of Stephen O'Flaherty and Tina Cosgrove. Although he remained a ward of court his parents were appointed his guardians. Stephen O'Flaherty lodged £50,000 in court, a huge sum at the time, which was to be invested for his education and upbringing.

The child's name was changed from Ian Cosgrove to Ian O'Flaherty – the Volkswagen King now had a third son, who as he grew up to be a man would become the 'forgotten' son of Stephen O'Flaherty.

Another friend of O'Flaherty's was a well-known Dublin solicitor Alexis Fitzgerald, a partner in the old Fine Gael firm of McCann Fitzgerald. When Stephen O'Flaherty, restless as ever, consulted him about regaining his share of the Volkswagen fortune which he had handed over that fateful day in hospital, the solicitor realised that any litigation would be highly risky and it would bring the whole sorry mess of O'Flaherty's tangled sex life into the public domain.

He sensibly advised against it, but he came up with another idea. He told O'Flaherty to forget the past and use his considerable energy and ingenuity into building himself a new empire.

What better place to start than in the car business. O'Flaherty was now seventy years of age, but he was still bristling with ideas and burning with a desire to get back into the business which he knew so well.

Leo Campbell, his accountant, told him about the new Japanese 'miracle' cars that were beginning to trickle into Europe. They were cheaper and more reliable than the British, German and Italian cars which dominated the market. O'Flaherty read up on Datsun and Toyota and decided to go to Japan to see if he could get the agency for himself.

But he had no real money. So he turned to another well-known Irish businessman, James Stafford, who had made his fortune in shipping and property in Wexford. Stafford now lived in Dublin and was an influential businessman with links to the Fianna Fáil party and particularly to the up-and-coming Minister for Finance, Mr Charles J Haughey. He knew O'Flaherty through the small social circle of wealthy businessmen and politicians in Dublin at the time and he agreed to invest £150,000 of his own money in a new firm which would import and manufacture the new Japanese cars.

Stephen O'Flaherty, Tina and James Stafford went out to Japan. O'Flaherty was such a legend in the car business that the doors of the most influential Japanese businessmen were opened to him. After a few meetings he got the franchise.

'To celebrate, we all went out to a wonderful party in one of the great geisha houses. Tina was blonde and all the girls were fascinated by her. It was a wonderful dinner, we were so well looked after,' recalled Stafford.

They came back to Ireland not only bringing the Toyota franchise but also the rights to use the name Toyota Ireland Ltd – an honour specially given to O'Flaherty by the Japanese in recognition of his contribution to the car business. They had plans to manufacture the cars at a new assembly plant on the Naas Road near Dublin and just down the road from the Volkswagen plant which was still churning out cars for his sons.

On his way back to Ireland Stephen divorced his first wife Dorothy Gladys O'Flaherty in Haiti and on October 20, 1972, at Alexandria, Virginia in the United States Tina and Stephen O'Flaherty were married.

Under the terms of his agreement Stephen O'Flaherty was to own fifty-one per cent of Toyota Ireland but James Stafford would be chairman and hold the remaining forty-nine per cent. It was also agreed that on O'Flaherty's death Stafford would become the fifty-one per cent owner of the business.

Stephen O'Flaherty might have been legendary in the car trade but he also had a bad reputation in business. While his sons were regarded as honourable, people were wary around the 'old man' because he was such a buccaneering figure.

'He had considerable ability, but he got things by sheer determination and greed, and if you were in business with him he was always trying to take advantage of you. That was just the way he was,' said one associate at the time.

'Stephen started misbehaving almost immediately,' remembered Stafford of his time in Toyota Ireland. They had dinner in O'Flaherty's house to try to sort out the deal. He remembers being irritated that the very good wine was left on a radiator and was lukewarm by the time it was served.

'He put a cheque on the table to try and buy me out – and I was sorry I didn't take it that night, because he never offered me as much again,' says Stafford.

Again Stephen O'Flaherty was finding it difficult to raise the cash to set up a manufacturing and distribution network to make and sell Toyota cars. In the meantime he was importing the car assembled and putting the Toyota Corolla on display in the Ballsbridge showrooms of Volkswagen and Mercedes.

It was there that two motor dealer brothers Tim and Denis Mahony, famous Dublin footballers in their day and now running a car showroom in North Dublin, first saw the yellow Japanese car. They realised the potential of the new Japanese imports and seeing that this asset was completely underused they began to stalk Toyota Ireland.

Between January and April 1973 just seventy-nine Toyota

cars were sold in Ireland. Stephen O'Flaherty and James Stafford had fallen out over the future of the business. Neither of them was giving it the time, energy and investment it deserved they were so busy fighting with each other.

Tiring of the constant battles with O'Flaherty, James Stafford sold his forty-nine per cent of Toyota Ireland to the Mahony brothers. Stafford did rather well out of the deal, but never imagined the success it would bring to its new owners.

O'Flaherty held on for about a year before realising that he was fighting a losing battle. He too sold his stake to Tim and Denis Mahony. The sale led to a falling out between the Mahony brothers, with Tim buying out his brother Denis's share in the early days.

Tim Mahony then went back to the Japanese and negotiated more favourable terms to begin manufacturing their cars in Ireland. In time the Toyota franchise made Tim Mahony among the wealthiest men in Ireland. Like Stephen O'Flaherty he bought himself a stately home called Mount Juliet in Co Kilkenny, an estate which he has turned into a world class hotel and golf resort. Ironically Tina O'Flaherty holidays there once a year.

'Stephen O'Flaherty was the pioneer of the industry in this country,' said Bill Cullen, who also ended up with another motor franchise that O'Flaherty brought to Ireland, Renault. 'He brought VW to this country, he brought Renault and later sold it on to Con Smith. He brought Toyota to this country and sold the franchise to Tim Mahony. The man was a business legend.'

Constantly on the move, no sooner had Stephen O'Flaherty finished with Toyota than he decided to move into oil exploration, founding a company called Aran Energy which also went on to become legendary in the annals of Irish business.

'You couldn't trust him as far as you could throw him,' remembers one of the young businessmen with ambitions to become an oil tycoon. 'He was an absolute robber baron.'

The exploration business at the time was a bit like the dot.com mania that would happen in more recent times – fortunes were made and lost in hours as share prices surged up and down on rumour. Whatever a company actually discovered was immaterial, what mattered was what people believed and gambled on. But as well as being a 'robber baron' there was also something likeable about the roguish O'Flaherty.

'He always wanted to do you out of a per cent, or put one over on you, but if you knew him well enough that was just part of the way he operated,' said an associate.

Another remembers how an international businessman duped O'Flaherty out of tens of thousands of pounds and wouldn't pay it back. Determined to get his money, O'Flaherty booked into the corner suite in Claridges Hotel in London, the most expensive rooms in the hotel. He invited the foreign associate to dinner. As they were eating in the suite, friends whom O'Flaherty had organised walked in and out of the rooms dressed menacingly in trench coats and wide-brimmed hats.

'They're the IRA. It's their money and if they don't get it back they're going to kill me,' he told the startled businessman in a scene worthy of the film *The Long Good Friday*. 'And,' he added, 'after they're finished with me they going to go after you.'

It worked. The next day he got his money back.

At this stage Stephen O'Flaherty, Tina and Ian, now a seven-year-old-boy being brought to St Gerard's school in Bray by limousine each morning, were living at Stepaside House near the small village of Stepaside in the foothills of the Dublin mountains. His parents led a nomadic life when Ian was growing up, however, living in Sir Chester Beatty's estate in Portugal and in the Villa Veduz in Marbella, Spain. They were constantly on the move, partying with the international jet set which included wealthy businessmen, minor European royalty, and even the handsome Sean Connery, the most famous actor of his generation because of his role as the playboy spy James Bond.

But of course there was a downside to the high living: Ian was living a very unsettled life, changing homes and schools with alarming regularity.

'The villa was a rather nice house in the centre of Marbella, it wasn't palatial or anything. It was rather over-decorated and they had this thing about champagne and caviar, it had to be champagne and caviar every day,' said one guest. 'They really didn't have that much taste, it was all kind of superficial.'

Stephen O'Flaherty, now an old man, dyed his hair and it bleached out a straw colour in the strong Spanish sun. 'He looked ridiculous,' said an acquaintance.

But he also added colour to the jet-setters who colonised the resort before cheap air travel turned it into a mass destination for golfers and thrill-seekers. O'Flaherty courted the Dublin businessman Gerry McGuinness who had started the *Sunday World* newspaper and wrote the 'Chairman's' column which dealt with the social and business set. The parties and goings-on of Tina and Stephen 'Wheels' O'Flaherty, as he was called in the column, and the activities of the 'Marbella set' became something of a fixture in the newspaper.

One of the Irish crowd remembers having a meal in a fancy restaurant and when he went to settle the bill Stephen O'Flaherty asked how much of a tip they were giving. When he was told, O'Flaherty replied, 'Don't bother with a tip, we won't be coming back here again.' The businessman reflected for a minute, 'That summed him up for me.'

The family lived in a succession of addresses in the fashionable suburbs of South Dublin, finally settling in a sprawling seafront estate at Monkstown, Co Dublin called The Albany.

Stephen O'Flaherty could never sit still, he was always bubbling with ideas for new ventures. This is illustrated by a letter he wrote to *The Irish Times* and published on Wednesday June 30, 1976.

Some years ago it occurred to me that Ireland might make some capital out of its very strategic position in the Atlantic. This has occurred to me again because of the improvement I have seen in Spain since I first visited it nearly twenty years ago.

I think Spain has gained enormously from her association with the United States in leasing some harbours and airfields on a five-year basis to the United States Navy and Airforce.

I think Ireland could do likewise because of her strong relationship with the United States over the past century or two and my idea would be to lease one or two southern, western or maybe northern ports to the United States Navy and some space for airfields to the United States Airforce, subject to certain conditions.

The conditions which occur to me would be:

a. Rent of about £500 million per annum.

b. United States personnel to be, as far as possible, of Irish origin.

c. All food, clothing and supplies to be provided by Irish industry.

d. Motorways to be constructed from ports to Dublin.

e. The border should go and possibly a United States peacekeeping force should assist.

In Ireland's present economic slump the idea such as the foregoing, is a businessman's approach and possibly there are many political problems which might have to be considered.

Yours,

Stephen O'Flaherty,

Marbella, Spain

Of course it was a notion verging on the lunatic, but at the same time it was, as he described it, 'a businessman's approach'. As such it could have provided much needed capital to the Irish economy decades before the so-called Celtic Tiger actually took off.

The O'Flahertys' home in Monkstown was broken into. After he was cruelly tied up by the thieves an estimated £250,000 worth of jewellery and valuables were stolen.

The robbery and trauma, the heart problems and ill-health he had suffered over the previous decade, combined with the jet-set lifestyle finally took its toll and Stephen O'Flaherty died on April 23, 1982, at St Vincent's Hospital in Dublin aged eighty.

His death notice in *The Irish Times* was spartan for a man who had made such a huge impact on post-war Ireland and the world of motoring.

Stephen O'Flaherty died peacefully in his eightieth year.

Deeply regretted by his family, relatives and friends.

House private. No letters.

That was it. Neither of his wives, Dot or Tina, or his three children, Michael, Nigel or Ian, were mentioned in the death notice. The family 'sensitivity' over his affair with Tina and his forgotten son Ian remained.

He was buried in Deansgrange cemetery in Dublin the following day under a headstone that, rather typically, he had designed himself.

His old friend, Taoiseach Charles Haughey, was represented at the funeral. Others in attendance included Brian Dennis, President of the Society of the Irish Motor Industry, Denis Mahony, and Dr Michael Smurfit who would later acquire Straffan House, where Stephen O'Flaherty had once lived so happily.

Reports of the funeral in Monkstown church made no mention of Dot, Tina or any of his three sons. Even in Ireland of 1982 there was a code of *omerta* about such things.

'After he died his first wife Dorothy came to see me in Monkstown,' recalled Tina many years later. 'She said, "I would never have done what you did for him".'

But the bitterness of the break-up of Stephen O'Flaherty's marriage remained. There could be no mention of Ian O'Flaherty in the presence of Dorothy. The two 'boys' Michael and Nigel who now controlled the O'Flaherty empire made it quite clear that Ian could never have a part of the family business while Dot was alive. It was strictly her and her two sons who ran and owned the business and nobody else was getting a share.

Over the years when the 'boys' were in their father's house, Michael and Nigel had often told Stephen that they would find a place for Ian in the business – but they stressed this could only be done 'at the right time'.

Michael, in particular, showed a concern for Ian and tried to be a steadying influence on the young man who was more than thirty years his junior. But as the only son of wandering parents Ian's was a difficult life and he was probably closer to his nanny, Daphne Ewing than he was to his parents.

After he was moved from two of Dublin's top schools, St Gerard's in Bray and St Michael's in Ailesbury Road, Ian was sent away to boarding school at Glenstal Abbey near the village of Murroe, Co Limerick. It was there, a year after his father's death, that he learned that his mother had married once more. Tina's third husband, John Garcia, was a wealthy American and the newly wedded couple moved to the United States.

In his sixth year in school Ian O'Flaherty was expelled after throwing a snowball at a monk, and he joined his mother at her new home in Guilford, Connnecticut where he went to college and studied computer science.

He was, said his mother, 'a slightly angry young man'. He wanted to make his own way in the world, and like his father he was hugely interested in cars and car racing. From 1988 until 1991 he raced seriously on the circuit in the US and when he came back to Ireland to live in the Albany Mews he raced in the Irish Formula Opel Lotus championship.

When eventually Dot died the O'Flahertys, now one of the richest dynasties in Ireland, were about to celebrate fifty years of the Volkswagen in Ireland. Ian attended the glittering gala dinner in Dublin, but after that, silence. When he went to seek his share, he was quietly rebuffed. Eventually Michael and Nigel stopped taking his calls.

Michael lives with his partner Bryan Smullen in Guernsey in the Channel Islands. Nigel's first wife, Esme, is deceased. He then married Monica O'Flaherty, and his present wife is Geraldine. Between his three wives, he has seven children. He also has three grandchildren.

Nigel's eldest son Stephen now runs the O'Flaherty empire and his other son Michael also holds a senior position in the firm.

Ian, now living in Coral Gables, a million-dollar suburb of

Florida where he runs his own legal services business and is doing quite well for himself, approached a firm of solicitors in Dublin to take a legal action to recover or get some claim on what he believes is the 'lost' fourth share in the business from his half-brothers, now both in their seventies.

'I don't see why he shouldn't be in the business with them and be part of it,' says Tina. 'At one time there were four shares in the business and his father had one of them and I feel that he is entitled to something. It is not as if he is a distant cousin or anything.'

There is a multimillion fortune at stake but for Ian O'Flaherty it isn't about the money. It's about his children, Kayla, Luke and Brendan O'Flaherty, by his ex-wife Lisa.

'It is all about being treated like the others,' he says, referring to his brother's children. But Ian has never been treated like family. He's always been the 'forgotten son'.

'They never intended to bring Ian into the business during his father's lifetime but Stephen used to say to them, "You will look after him", and they always said "yes",' says Tina. 'Ian always felt there would be a place for him in the business, after all he is Stephen O'Flaherty's third son.

'It is not himself, it is his children that he is worried about. There is a discrepancy between how they are being treated. Nigel had three wives and all three families have been provided for. There has been a lot of soul-searching on Ian's part. He only decided to go down the legal route because they would not meet him. He was brushed aside.'

That is why Ian has become isolated from his brothers and bitter that he and his family have not shared even part of their father's legacy. He was left some property in Waterford when his father died worth about £500,000, a considerable sum at the time, but Ian was young and wild and it went on fast cars and high living. In any event it was still very small in comparison to what his two brothers earn every year from the family business.

Nigel O'Flaherty remains chairman of Motor Distributors Ltd, which is among the wealthiest private companies in Ireland. From a virtually anonymous office in Leeson Park bought by his father more than half a century before, they control the Volkswagen, Mercedes, Audi, Skoda and Mazda franchises in Ireland. They also have a manufacturing plant in Waco, Texas which makes commercial cherrypickers.

The hugely lucrative O'Flaherty companies make profits of about €40 million a year and has a nest-egg of €262 million in shareholders' funds that is growing all the time. Mercedes has made several attempts to buy back the franchise from its Irish distributor but talks have never progressed. Should it ever be sold it would be worth a king's ransom.

The O'Flaherty family have vast investments, luxury homes in Ireland, Spain and the United States, yachts, fast cars and all the trappings of the glitzy world which they inhabit. Their privacy was protected by a coterie of motoring journalists who knew the O'Flaherty story but were not willing to risk the perks of their own jobs by revealing it to the general public.

While the tangled private lives and loves of other prominent business people became public knowledge in the media, the secret world of the O'Flahertys remained a closed book. The family were almost unknown to the general public and never mentioned in the gossip columns or the celebrity magazines. That's the way they wanted it.

The silence of the O'Flaherty clan was legendary. Until Ian O'Flaherty came back to Ireland, that is, to consult with legal advisors to begin the quest for a share of the family silver.

'Hundreds of millions are passing down the line to the sons

and grandsons of Stephen O'Flaherty. There is no difference between my children and my brother's children, but there is a huge disparity in their situation,' says Ian.

'I always thought Michael and Nigel would take me under their wing and bring me into the business, but that never happened. I wrote to them three or four years ago and said this, but they didn't do anything about it. It's my children's future I'm thinking about. Yes, I am looking for a share of the family wealth.'

Several years after consulting the prestigious legal firm, however, Ian's case was quietly dropped after getting no further than the research stage. Ian O'Flaherty suspects powerful business interests are working against him, but there are those in the business world who don't believe that he has a strong enough legal case to try to reclaim the share in the Irish Volkswagen business that his father handed over from his sick bed in St Vincent's Hospital.

He resorted to putting the spotlight of publicity on his older half-brothers, blowing the family secret wide open but this has been equally unsuccessful. Michael and Nigel O'Flaherty and their families have ignored any public interest in their 'lost brother' believing that it will all just blow over and go away.

But Ian O'Flaherty is determined that the family feud should be out in the open. If nothing else, he wants to cause maximum embarrassment to his half-brothers by telling the world that he's out there and he is the 'lost son' of the legendary Irish car manufacturer who made and lost a king's ransom in the space of his eighty years on earth.

Chapter 5

The Little Sister

As he stood on the steps of the Westbury Hotel in central Dublin looking down on the flower sellers on the corner of Grafton Street and anticipating the arrival of his friend, Taoiseach Charles J Haughey, PV Doyle cut an imposing figure. Tall and slim with a narrow 'bog brush' moustache and slicked back hair, he had the caddish appearance of a B-movie star from the 1950s.

In a few short hours Mr Haughey would officially open Doyle's latest hotel and the occasion would attract what would only much later be recognised as a rogue's gallery of Irish life. But at the time those who would gather in the gilded salon in central Dublin that evening were considered the pillars of society.

With just hours to go to the grand opening there was the smell of fresh paint and the carpet layers were still tacking down a colourful hand-woven Voske Joyce rug that would be the centrepiece of the foyer of the city's newest and grandest hotel. But Pascal Vincent Doyle seemed aloof and unconcerned about the chaos around him as he stood gazing into the middle distance, a habitual cigarette hanging nonchalantly from his thin lips.

Perhaps as he stood surveying the teeming street, thick with the cries of the flower sellers and the sounds of the passing parade, he was reflecting on his own good fortune. Perhaps with such an auspicious occasion looming he may even have been thinking of his mortality and the fate of his fine inheritance when he passed on and left it to be divided among his five children.

Little did Pascal Vincent Doyle know that within a few years he would be dead and the empire of hotels, construction and investments he had built from scratch would be tearing his family apart; that his younger son and heir apparent, David, would be forced out of the business as ugly rumours circulated about him in the lofty places and low joints where money, media and politics met.

Where did the rumours start? David Doyle would never find the answer to that question for certain. But he had his own ideas and certainly it coloured the path his life would take. The treatment he received at the hands of his family, and particularly his beautiful younger sister Bernie, would sour his relationship with most of his family for more than a decade. There was hardly much consolation for him in the fact that Bernadette Doyle, or Bernie Gallagher as she would become, proved that she was well capable of following in her father's footsteps. To reclaim the business her father built hers was a 'white knuckle ride' that included running a huge hotel chain, merging with an even more powerful competitor and finally, fighting off predators who came stalking the family empire.

Like all family wars there were casualties and collateral damage. Among them was to be the once close relationship between the beautiful young heiress Bernadette and her baby-faced brother David.

How different it had been in the early years when the Doyle

empire seemed invincible, its various hotels symbols of the new Ireland that was emerging from depressing years of Catholic repression and state control. The Burlington was big and brash, The Berkeley Court oozed new money and power, while The Westbury possessed the grandeur suited to a city such as Dublin, a city of writers and talkers that had for too long languished as a backwater and was now about to open up as a world destination.

Pascal Vincent Doyle was born in Dundrum, Co Dublin in 1923, then part of the open country of South Dublin, now part of the urban sprawl that extends to the foothills of the mountains. He was one of seven children of a well-to-do local farmer and small-time builder. He was educated at the Christian Brothers School in Westland Row and really wanted to be a veterinary surgeon but he failed Gaelic in his Leaving Certificate. If you failed Irish, you failed the whole exam and as a result Doyle could not go on to university, a huge blow to the young man. He dabbled a bit in business but at the age of twenty-two he decided where his future lay and joined his father in the family building firm.

When he died in 1988 at the age of sixty-four, he was the multimillionaire owner of thirty-three hotels in Ireland, Britain and the United States. He was also the owner of a large construction and development company. His wife Margaret still lives in their fine period residence Thornhill House, set in over three acres of splendidly manicured gardens almost unseen in the heart of the well-off South Dublin suburb of Mount Merrion.

There wasn't anything like the money in construction that there is today, but PV Doyle was a careful businessman, building in safe upmarket areas of South Dublin where the new middle classes and well-heeled civil servants wanted to live.

He had a taste for the entertainment industry, developing a cabaret venue called The Country Club in Rathfarnham. Although he learned a bit about management, he decided that he couldn't devote enough time to this business so he sold it and got on with building another housing estate.

After building the Montrose Hotel on the Stillorgan Road near RTÉ in 1964, PV Doyle decided that he liked the hotel business and instead of selling it on as he had originally intended he retained it and used the cash flow to fund the construction of a series of hotels that would eventually stretch across Ireland through London to Washington DC.

'Dublin hotels are still catering for the ascendancy,' he said in one interview, referring to the grand hotels like The Russell, The Shelbourne and The Hibernian, all within a stone's throw of each other around St Stephen's Green. They were places for the well-to-do and the political establishment, but few ordinary people ever set foot inside their doors.

PV Doyle was determined to open his doors to the masses and give them a taste of what had up to then been reserved for the privileged and the wealthy. It was a vision in which he succeeded admirably.

Over the years his business acumen and his political connections ensured that his hotels flourished. He spotted the Assistant City Manager for Dublin, George Redmond, in The Burlington one day and he made it his business to sit down with him for a cup of afternoon tea and a chat. When the conversation was over, he passed the city official with responsibility for planning an unmarked brown envelope with 'a few hundred pounds for yourself'.

That's how business was done in those days. PV Doyle did not ask for a favour, nor did the Assistant City Manager offer one, but there was an understanding with which both men were comfortable. Doyle knew that if he was stuck and wanted something, the most senior city official was just a phone call away and well disposed to oblige with any request he might make. The same procedure would have taken place in those days if a priest called to the house, but instead of looking after his immortal soul, PV was looking after his very mortal business.

It was the era of the 'almighty dollar' and the government was pumping money into marketing Ireland as a safe, friendly and cheap destination for wealthy Americans to visit. PV Doyle knew there wasn't enough local business to keep his hotel beds occupied, so he made sure most of the visiting tourists stayed in his hotels by paying a commission to a major American travel firm for every 'Yank' that slept in his hotel.

It was obvious to close observers of the political scene at the time that PV Doyle was in the inner circle of the country's largest political party, Fianna Fáil. A cursory glance would tell you that at the time of a general election, a crucial time in political life, suites of rooms were made available to party fundraisers, first in the Westbury Hotel and later in the more opulent Berkeley Court. Streams of wealthy individuals would call with large sums of money to donate to the election campaigns, and in return favours would be granted if the party were successful and went into government.

PV Doyle was more than just a businessman who supported a particular agenda because it suited his financial interests. He was also one of a small group of wealthy individuals who bankrolled the lavish lifestyle of the leader of Fianna Fáil, his good friend Mr Charles Haughey. Along with Ben Dunne, the stockbroker Dermot Desmond, and a tightly knit group of select individuals, he contributed the funds necessary to ease the financial burdens of Mr Haughey, who enjoyed a lifestyle which included a Gandon mansion in Kinsealy and its adjoining stud farm, Charvet shirts bought in Paris and an expensive mistress who enjoyed every minute of the good things in life.

When Mr Haughey first became Taoiseach he had an overdraft of almost £1 million with Allied Irish Bank and no way of paying it back. It was then that this group were called upon to come to his assistance, 'in the national interest' as the genius who sorted out Mr Haughey's tangled financial affairs put it.

It is believed PV Doyle's contribution to Mr Haughey's extravagant lifestyle was about £300,000 over a period of years. This was a very considerable sum at the time. He was also an investor in Celtic Helicopters, a company founded by the Taoiseach's son, Ciarán Haughey.

In return, PV Doyle had access to the very top. He was appointed chairman of the Irish Tourist Board at a crucial time in the development of the hotel industry. He was also appointed to Mr Haughey's 'pet project', the Customs House Development Authority, which oversaw the introduction of the huge financial services centre into the Dublin docklands. It is believed that he carried out both tasks with the same diligence with which he ran his own business affairs.

Another obvious manifestation of his closeness to political power could be observed most days in the foyer of his hotel, The Burlington. There the legendary banker Des Traynor, a man who seemed to have no staff and no permanent office, plied his trade. Over cups of coffee he handled millions of pounds for wealthy individuals, moving their 'hot' money and other funds illegally to the Caymen Islands. For thirty years he was the organiser of the 'Ansbacher deposits'. These mysterious funds were held by wealthy Irish people who wished to set up trust funds that could be accessed by their families after they died or to hold large amounts of money 'offshore' and away from the prying eyes of the taxman or other curious parties. Some funds were legitimate but much were put offshore to evade the penal rates of tax applying in Ireland at the time.

Through a small private bank in Dublin called Guinness & Mahon, Des Traynor could move people's money offshore and untaxed, if necessary, to the Cayman Islands. But the beauty of the scheme was that the money never left Ireland. It could be reclaimed at any moment it was required from Guinness & Mahon in Dublin. There might be £50 million in these 'deposits' at any one time and only Traynor knew the secret codes which identified the individuals and the amounts which they held in the 'Ansbacher deposits'.

Only those on the inside track were ever invited to become part of the Ansbacher scheme. PV Doyle and his son David were among the lucky elite. It wasn't all that surprising, not only was the mysterious Mr Traynor a daily visitor to the hotel, he was also financial advisor to the Doyle family.

PV Doyle and his wife Margaret Briody had five children, Michael, Eileen, Anne, David and Bernadette. There was a certain patriarchal approach in PV Doyle's old-style attitude to life. He intended for his sons to take on his business interests and his girls to look beautiful and marry well. He wasn't disappointed, but by the time he died social attitudes had changed and his youngest daughter had a very different idea about her role in life and in her father's business.

Early on, the eldest son Michael was destined to take over the building arm of PV Doyle's empire. He would also inherit a stake in the hotels, but in time he would develop an intense dislike for the tensions unfolding in his family. He stayed well clear of the limelight that seemed to shine on the rest of them and although he worked in the Burlington Hotel as a young man he never took a direct interest in the running of the hotel chain.

The eldest daughter Eileen became a solicitor and married Raymond Monahan, a Co Sligo solicitor and property developer. While she has remained an influential shareholder and director of the business she never played an active role in the day-to-day running of the company.

PV and Margaret Doyle's second daughter, Anne, married Thomas James Roche, the son of Tom Roche, another close associate of Des Traynor, an ardent Fianna Fáil supporter and the man who welded a number of companies into Cement Roadstone Holdings (CRH), now a billion euro conglomerate and the country's second biggest business after Allied Irish Bank.

Anne has never played an active role in the business and when the company eventually went out of the Doyle family control and became a public company she handed over her seat on the board to her husband.

David Doyle, the second youngest in the family was born on April 21, 1958, and his sister Bernadette was born on November 17, 1959. Both of them had a comfortable upbringing in South Dublin. Although they both went to private schools they didn't go on to university. Instead they followed their father into the family business.

PV Doyle was, in many respects, a rigorous and distant man. He didn't drink alcohol though he smoked like a trooper. He was to be found most days in the foyer of one of his hotels, watching what was happening around him like a heron stalking the seashore in search of prey, constantly trying to make his hotels better and planning new ventures. He was always visible on important occasions greeting favoured guests and making sure that the business was running as smoothly as a well-oiled machine.

He was a self-made man and although he set up the PV Doyle Discretionary Trust for his family in 1965 he expected his children to work for their money.

Despite his wealth he lived an almost frugal existence. A Dublin journalist, who was granted a rare luncheon interview on the eve of the opening of his plushest new hotel, The Berkeley Court, told the story of the two of them sitting down in the empty dining room to taste the new cuisine. PV Doyle handed the young reporter an impressive menu and wine list. He selected a bottle of Chateau Margaux Grand Cru and then, slightly flustered by the opulence of the menu, requested nettle soup and lobster thermidor.

PV Doyle watched with quiet amusement. When the waiter turned to him he ordered a mixed grill and a bottle of Coke – neither of which was on the menu. The reporter came back to the office feeling extremely foolish for trying to appear sophisticated when he was merely out of his depth.

The two youngest Doyles, David and Bernadette, may have been born with a silver spoon in their mouths, but the old man was determined that they would learn the business from the ground up.

David Doyle had been working in the bars and kitchens of the family hotels since he was twelve years of age, serving a tough apprenticeship in the school holidays. After Blackrock College and a stint at the catering college in Cathal Brugha Street in Dublin, he went to America to work in hotels like the Beverly Wilshire in Los Angeles. When he returned to Dublin it was as an assistant manager in his father's flagship hotel, The Berkeley Court.

'I can't honestly say that there was a time when I didn't want to go into the hotel business,' he would later declare.

Bernadette Doyle also worked in The Burlington on school holidays. After she left the Holy Child convent school in Killiney she worked in various positions in the hotel group until she was appointed to the second most important task in any international hotel chain, marketing director of Doyle Hotels.

By now all of his children were comfortably off and in January 1975 their prospects improved dramatically when their father gave each of them a gift of £201,047, which would be in excess of a million euro in today's money.

David had moved up the executive ladder and was now involved in running an international business. He and Bernadette Doyle had adjoining offices in The Burlington Hotel in central Dublin and as the two youngest members of a long-tailed family they were said, by friends, to be very close to each other both professionally and socially.

'David and Bernie complemented each other and they were exceptionally close at the time. He was running the business and she was marketing manager and they had offices next door to each other in the Burlington. It seemed like the ideal way to run the business.'

It appeared at the time that their futures were assured and the pecking order had been set.

They were certainly thrown in at the deep end when PV Doyle died suddenly in Blackrock Clinic in Dublin on February 6, 1988, at the relatively young age of sixty-four. In his will he left everything he possessed to his wife, Margaret.

David was appointed his successor, becoming chief executive of the company. It was an exciting time in the business and the young boss had great plans to expand and improve. He wanted to open a chic hotel on a derelict site the family had secured on St Stephen's Green in the centre of Dublin. He also wanted to acquire further hotels in America, particularly in Washington DC and New York.

But if David Doyle thought he had inherited his father's mantle and would hold it unchallenged he was to be proved wrong.

David's best friend at the time was another ambitious young Dublin hotel executive John Fitzpatrick whose father Paddy Fitzpatrick like David Doyle's father was legendary in the hotel business in Ireland. The two old men had been rivals, in the best possible sense.

Their sons became best friends, hanging out in Dublin with a 'rat pack' of well-off bachelor friends. They included Gerry Purcell, the wayward son of a millionaire cattle dealer who once lost £7 million gambling on the international money markets, Michael Smurfit Jr the son of the cardboard manufacturing tycoon of the same name, and the young O'Reillys, sons of Dr AJF O'Reilly.

To further cement their closeness, David Doyle's best friend was also going out with his sister Bernie at the time. It seemed like a perfect match.

'The three of them were the best of friends,' according to one insider at the time.

Then John Fitzpatrick was dispatched by his father to Manhattan to open and run his father's new New York Hotel. Meanwhile David Doyle married his sweetheart, a former air hostess Christina Kelly. John Fitzpatrick was best man at his lavish wedding. It was innocent at the time but as if to emphasise the 'nouveau riche' side of the festivities his friends hired a small aeroplane to fly over the church in Foxrock trailing a banner saying, 'Your goose is cooked'.

It wasn't the only goose to be cooked. So was the romance between John Fitzpatrick and Bernadette Doyle. Ambitious young John Gallagher owned an alarm company that did work for the

Doyle Hotels. He was also a bit of a fixture on the social scene and after a whirlwind romance he stole Bernadette's heart and he married her at an extravagant society wedding in Dublin.

The young Mr Gallagher and his wife Bernadette then formed a powerful alliance with her sister Anne and her husband, the wealthy Tom Roche Jr.

For a while everything continued as normal, but then tensions began to surface in the family for the first time.

'It was generally felt in the industry that David and the family had a falling out over his policy of heavy investment in the existing hotel properties,' reported *The Irish Times*.

He spent about £1.5 million on a new conference centre for The Berkeley Court, another £1.2 million to give The Montrose Hotel a new façade and £1 million for a new bar in The Burlington Hotel.

These may seem small sums by today's business outlays but in pre-Celtic Tiger Ireland it was a massive investment programme at a time when troubles in Northern Ireland and other global difficulties were affecting the tourism business. It meant that the other family members were not getting the dividend they felt they deserved from the profitable hotel business.

'Defenders of Doyle say that the steady rise in group profits in the wake of the investment which he had recommended were all the justification that Doyle needed,' reported the *Sunday Business Post*.

Adding to the tension was David Doyle's confidence in his own ability.

'PV was frequently described paradoxically as a benevolent autocrat. Unfortunately, David appeared to have inherited his father's iron will and tendency to take decisions without bothering too much about extensive consultations with fellow directors,' said a profile writer as the family rows and tensions became public knowledge.

David Doyle also believed that he could import exciting new concepts for the family hotel business from America, where he had learned much of his trade. Among them was teaming up with the worldwide Marriott chain to put the brand name on some of the hotels in the Doyle Group.

This was not a plan that found much favour with his mother who had inherited her husband's shares and still held a controlling stake in the business. Margaret believed that 'Doyle' meant more in Ireland than 'Marriott' or some other fancy imported concept. At the time she was probably right. Indeed she was so proud of her husband's legacy that following his death she commissioned a series of portraits which were placed in a prominent position in the foyers of all the hotels in the family chain.

But not even the memory of their father could keep the family together. Loyalties were divided and a serious split emerged.

Between them, the Gallaghers and the Roches decided that David Doyle wasn't doing such a good job of running the Doyle Hotels after all, and maybe his little sister Bernadette could do it better. The bare bones of a business coup was organised.

David Doyle, according to those in the business, was an hotelier. He lived and slept the business. He wanted to continue the major investment in the Doyle Hotel properties which after years of expansion now badly needed to be upgraded. Bernadette, on the other hand, believed that they could have it both ways. She argued that the investment plan should be scaled back and that the group could become more 'cheap and cheerful' rather than maintaining the rigorous standards demanded by her brother. In this way the hotels could remain successful and the other family shareholders would still earn the healthy return which they had come to expect from the business.

After a series of boardroom clashes David Doyle called the senior hotel staff together on the evening of Wednesday June 15, 1994, and with tears in his eyes told them he was leaving the family business. It was a huge shock within the industry and in the upper echelons of Irish society where the Doyle family were so well known.

In the press release issued through a city public relations firm, the family feud was glossed over by saying David Doyle had left to 'concentrate on his own business interests'.

'No sooner had he departed the meeting at The Burlington Hotel than his sister Bernadette rose to tell personnel gathered in the room: I am your boss now,' reported several newspapers. There was no sentiment involved, it was back to business.

The World Cup, with Ireland led by Jack Charlton, kicked off in the United States a few days later. The country got on with the business of football hysteria and the Doyles' spat was quickly forgotten.

Bernadette Gallagher took over as chief executive of the Doyle Hotel Group.

'It is no secret in the financial world that PV's widow Margaret and her five children and their respective wives and husbands are deeply divided,' wrote the *Sunday Independent* social diarist Trevor Danker later that year.

Like her late husband, Margaret Doyle craved family unity, but all her efforts to bring about a family reconciliation failed. The bitterness was further compounded by rumours floating around Dublin.

'After Doyle left the company the atmosphere of recrimination was further poisoned by damaging and unjustified rumours surrounding Doyle's personal life,' said the *Sunday Business Post.*

Although David was happily married the 'chattering classes' were only too willing to circulate an untrue rumour about him. The well-connected TD who was also the subject of this malicious story would later publicly deny that he was gay. Today it might raise a wry laugh, but in the mid-1990s such tales could do untold damage.

The pernicious rumour swept around Dublin, it was discussed in bars and restaurants and became the stuff of common currency. The fact that there was no truth in it didn't matter. It was obviously designed to damage him and his credibility in the business world.

In February 1995 Danker, who was close to some of the main players in the Doyle drama reported on 'behind the scenes' moves to try to resolve the family feud.

'There were remarkable scenes in the Burlington Hotel last Wednesday night (27/2/1995) as half the Bar Library assembled in the lobby floating between members of the Doyle family,' he wrote in his column in the *Sunday Independent.* 'The family, riven by internal divisions since David Doyle resigned as managing director, is on the point of patching up its differences.'

Each of the family members had arrived in the hotel at lunchtime and at 2 a.m. they were still in 'deep discussion' with their legal advisors in different parts of the cavernous lobby.

But the discussions didn't resolve anything. Bernadette Doyle was determined to hang on to her new-found power and David Doyle could not agree a price to sell his stake back to the other members of the family.

The stand-off lasted for another year. Then, just as suddenly as he had left to 'pursue his other interests' the Doyle Hotel Group announced that David Doyle had been reappointed as managing director.

Under the new arrangement Margaret Doyle divided up a certain amount of her shares, giving up her controlling interest in the Doyle Hotels. Each of her five children now had an equal share.

David Doyle would become MD, Bernadette was made deputy chairman, and a non-family member, Paddy Galvin, a respected academic businessman who had previously been chairman of Waterford Glass, was brought in as chairman of the family company. Peace, it seemed, had broken out among the warring factions.

Almost prophetically, David Doyle had been asked years earlier about how he got on with other members of his family, and particularly about his relationship with his father.

'Every day we have hundreds of disagreements – that's what business is about,' he had answered.

But after a short honeymoon it was apparent that the disagreements between the various members of the board of Doyle Hotels were so fundamental that there was no going back. According to reports there was a direct clash between David Doyle and his sisters and brothers-in-law about the direction of the business. Almost as soon as he was back in the hot seat there was another family crisis.

'The similarity between his business style and that of his father has contributed significantly to his problems and particularly the strains between himself and his brothers-in-law, Tom Roche and John Gallagher,' went a report of the tensions in the *Sunday Business Post*.

David Doyle might have had some chance if he had support in the family for his grandiose plans for the business. But that was not the case.

His elder brother Michael, who had concentrated on the construction side of the family business but also had a share in the hotels, eventually tired of all the internal squabbling.

'He just took off; he didn't want any part of the family struggle,' according to sources. Michael Doyle made it clear as soon as the infighting started again that he wanted to be bought out. He had plans to turn an ancient Martello Tower at Sandymount, on the seafront in Dublin 4 into a posh restaurant. He actually developed the historic tower spending well over a million pounds, but he hadn't got the proper planning authorisation and after a brief opening the building was boarded up and has stood for years as a monument to the folly of trying to get anything done quickly around Dublin.

Said by outsiders to be one of the nicest of the family he may have realised earlier than his young brother David that the three sisters and their husbands were a formidable alliance and there wasn't much point in taking them on. He just wanted to get on with his own life and be bought out of the family business as soon as possible.

It is estimated that Michael Doyle got between £20 million and £25 million and his share of the company was divided among the four remaining children of PV Doyle.

But with Michael out of the way David was now even more isolated on the board. When David's mother sided with his sisters about the direction of the business there was no place left for him to go.

As the family feud came to a head and their differences about the future of the business escalated, David offered to buy out his sisters for £100 million. They turned him down.

On July 4, 1997, it was announced in a terse statement that the board of the company had voted him out of office as managing director and that his sister Bernadette would resume the position. It was a humiliation from which he would never really recover and even years later the bitterness that divided the family would remain.

There was now a tense stand-off between the two sides.

'David Doyle was ousted as chief executive last July. Since then he has not replied to letters from the group about buying his shares. These are in the process of being redeemed by the company,' reported *Business & Finance* in September 1997. 'Although still a director, his refusal to communicate with the board stems from the problems he has with the restrictive covenants which the board is trying to enforce, according to one source.'

There was a genuine fear among the family that David Doyle would launch a rival hotel chain and with his experience of the industry he might do serious damage to the family business.

But it wasn't to be. He didn't have the resources in the first place, but he also realised that once he had run the biggest hotel chain in the country he was hardly going to get much satisfaction from running a business that would always be compared unfavourably with the empire established by his father.

Two years later the family reached a settlement and David Doyle sold all but a small percentage of his holding in the family business for £40 million. He and his family lived between Spain and Dublin and he cut the connections with the business, appearing to have settled for a quiet life far from the family feud and away from the glare of publicity and the rumours that had once upset him so much.

David Doyle was gone from the family hotel group and wouldn't return, but he would figure briefly in another corporate battle because the saga of the Doyles was far from over, although the part he would play in the dramas to follow was marginal.

With Bernadette Gallagher now at the helm of the family, tough decisions needed to be taken. After buying out their brother for what turned out to be a very good price the three daughters of PV Doyle, Eileen, Anne and Bernadette, and their husbands were now in complete control of the family firm.

The feud might now have been settled but the financial affairs were such that the family were faced with a number of choices to plug the gap left from paying off their two brothers with more than £60 million from the family war chest.

Advisors looked at the possibility of the Doyle Hotels going public which is what David Doyle had wanted in order to break the family hold on the business. By floating the company on the stock market the three sisters would be able to sell some of their shares and secure their positions financially. They could also structure a deal in such a way as to retain a major stake in the company, although institutions such as banks and other investors would determine that a new layer of professional management would be brought in to run the hotel chain.

The other option was to sell the business altogether. David Doyle had already tried to buy them out for £100 million, but his offer was rejected out of hand. They knew the business was worth more than that, but more importantly it was still a 'family' business and there was fierce loyalty to their father's legacy, especially from Bernadette Doyle who had been involved in the business for so long.

There were other factors. The business was still doing well and generating huge amounts of cash and earnings for the family. On top of that they would each be faced with a very large tax liability if they suddenly disposed of the 'family silver'.

With Michael Doyle out of the company and David Doyle

holding a minor stake the sisters decided in the end to accept an offer to merge the Doyle Hotels with their great rivals, Jurys, which was already a public company. In late 1999 the new entity, Jurys Doyle, made its debut on the Dublin stock exchange.

Between them the Doyle women walked away with £398 million in cash and got a twenty-three per cent stake in the new company, Jurys Doyle. It was a massive profit given what they had paid their brothers for their stake just two years before. Suddenly the three sisters were among the richest women in Ireland.

The only stipulation that Margaret Doyle, PV's widow, made to the deal was that her husband's portrait should continue to hang in pride of place in the lobbies of the hotels he had founded.

Bernadette Gallagher and her sister Eileen Monahan took their seats on the board of the new company, but the retiring Anne Roche nominated her husband, Tom Roche Jr, to represent her in the new arrangement.

The next few years turned out to be relatively boring in terms of the high-profile Doyle family who probably enjoyed the respite from the limelight that had dogged them for so long. But it couldn't last.

Shrewd and all as PV Doyle had been in selecting the sites for his Dublin hotels back in the austere Ireland of the seventies and eighties nothing could have prepared him, or indeed most people, for the emerging Ireland of the new millennium.

Times changed. The old days of broken down cars, sky-high taxes, inbuilt poverty and emigration were gone. His hotels, which had once depended on the 'mighty dollar' from visiting Yanks, were now more dependent on the newly rich Irish people taking their families away for leisure weekends, or international businessmen trawling Ireland for investment opportunities.

Irish people poured back from abroad into the 'model

economy' of Europe. American dollars were flooding into chemical industries along the estuary of the River Lee and into call-centres and computer industries. The Irish Financial Services Centre, of which PV Doyle had been a founding director, changed the skyline of Dublin forever with big glass cathedrals of commerce mushrooming along the once dilapidated docklands.

Stylish new hotels purpose built to attract the expense account travellers opened up in the capital. The businessmen who had once stayed in The Berkeley Court and the big functions that kept The Burlington and Jurys going moved to more elegant venues such as The Four Seasons in Ballsbridge or Citywest out on the M4 motorway which had better facilities and was more easily accessible for people from outside Dublin.

Jurys Doyle changed direction, catering for the stag parties and flights full of low-cost passengers descending on Dublin and other Irish cities courtesy of Michael O'Leary and his airline, Ryanair. Their Jurys Inn chain, which was marketed as a cheap and cheerful place to stay, became the success story of the group.

But something else was also happening, almost unnoticed. It was a phenomenon that would soon launch the little sister Bernadette Doyle into battle once more and she would need all the experience she had gained in the previous family skirmishes to see her through.

Ireland experienced a massive property boom. Real estate prices in Dublin soared. Houses that were bought in good neighbourhoods of Dublin in the early 1980s for IR£50,000 (€65,000) were worth €1 million or more in the soaring Celtic Tiger economy of the new millennium.

PV Doyle had always been careful to locate his flagship hotels on prime sites, particularly in Dublin. The Burlington was strategically placed between Donnybrook and the city centre, and

Arthur ffrench O'Carroll got involved in years of litigation
with his mother Renee after demolishing a mews
and building which is now Diep le Shaker restaurant.

The French diplomat's daughter, Renee ffrench O'Carroll,
was given a grand house on Fitzwilliam Square
as a wedding present by her parents.

Charlie Haughey and Brendan Halligan offer their condolences to Ben Dunne Jr outside the Pro-Cathedral in Dublin before the funeral of his father, the founder of the Dunnes Stores empire.

Ben Dunne Sr, an autocratic businessman and adored father.

The laughing boy, Ben Dunne Jr who ran Dunnes Stores
until the cocaine episode in Florida led to
a boardroom battle with his sister Margaret.

Margaret Heffernan ousted her brother Ben and eventually
banished him from the family business.

Stephen O'Flaherty, the Volkswagen King, built the first VW Beetle to be manufactured outside Germany.

O'Flaherty's first wife Dot in the drawing room of their home Straffan House, now the K-Club.

Stephen O'Flaherty walks between the lines of shiny new cars assembled at his plant at the Naas Road, Dublin.

Domestic Bliss: Dot and Stephen O'Flaherty prepare for a children's pony ride at Straffan House.

Stephen O'Flaherty (right) and an associate negotiate another automobile deal.

The Volkswagen King walking in the gardens of his palace.

Michael O'Flaherty, Stephen's eldest son pictured in festive mood
with his father's second wife, Tina.

The Volkswagen Princes: Stephen O'Flaherty, grandson of the founder with his uncles Michael and Ian, his father Nigel and family friend Brian Smullen at a gathering in 1997 to celebrate fifty years of Volkswagen in Ireland.

Nigel O'Flaherty and his wife Geraldine.

The legendary hotelier PV Doyle outside the Berkeley Court Hotel in Dublin, his proudest business achievement.

David Doyle, eventually forced out of the family business in a bitter feud with his sisters.

Buccaneering property developer Sean Dunne pictured at the races with his glamorous wife Gayle. Dunne took on the Doyle hotel empire and ended up with the two best-known hotels in Ballsbridge.

Happy families: Bernadette Doyle, who eventually took over the family hotel empire, with her brother David and their mother Margaret.

I did it my way – the publican patriarch Pat Coman leaves a Dublin court after the torturous battle with five of his six sons.

Denis Coman eventually wrested control of the family firm from his father after the original deal fell through.

Patrick Coman leaving court with two of the six daughters who stood by him in the family feud with his sons.

Queen of the Castle: Enya, the most successful female recording artist in the world.

Máire (Moya) Brennan was upset when her sister Eithne (Enya) left the family band, Clannad.

Charles Gallagher Sr eventually took control of Abbey after a prolonged and bitter family feud with his older brothers.

Charles Gallagher Jr who succeeded his father and currently runs the famous building company.

The Progressive Democrat TD for Longford, Mae Sexton, who ended up in a bitter feud with her sisters after their father gave her a piece of property in Longford known as The Shed to give her a leg up on the political ladder.

Businesswoman Freda Hayes who succeeded her father as the boss of Blarney Woollen Mills but later founded Meadows & Byrne after she was ousted from the family business.

Those were the days: the Taoiseach Bertie Ahern with his lover and style guru, Celia Larkin.

Businessman and Fianna Fáil fundraiser, Des Richardson, who played a crucial role in the formation of Bertie Ahern's power base, St Luke's.

Tim Collins, the man with the midas touch and a friend of Bertie Ahern 'from outside politics'.

Back then the Westlink toll bridge seemed like a good idea: Tom Roche Jr, the Taoiseach Bertie Ahern, and National Toll Roads chief executive Jim Barry.

Tom Roche Sr, an Irish business visionary. He was threatened with bankruptcy and millions in debt when he died.

The man who never gave up: Michael Wymes going to court during the Bula saga, the longest running litigation in the history of the Irish state.

The Westbury was off Grafton Street. The Berkeley Court, which was built on part of the old Trinity College botanic gardens in Ballsbridge, was probably the most valuable of the lot.

The value of the land on which PV Doyle had built his hotels suddenly became worth far more than some of the ageing hotels which occupied the sites. Although the company made profits of €45 million in 2004 it came mostly from its low-cost brand, Jurys Inn. The company chairman, Richard Hooper, declared that the performance of the Dublin hotels was 'disappointing'. The predators began to circle.

Jurys Hotel, adjacent to The Berkeley Court in Ballsbridge, Dublin 4 was a low-rise building and it became apparent to some smart people that if the site was bought and the hotels torn down the planners would give permission for a high-rise development which would maximise the value of the site.

By 2005 as developers searched desperately for sites around the city centre to build apartments for the new rich, a consortium headed by the shrewd developer Bryan Cullen, hotelier JJ Murphy and solicitor David Coleman spotted an opportunity that nobody else had appeared to notice.

They realised that if they took over Jurys Doyle they could then break up the group and keep some of its valuable sites. They formulated a grand plan to sell off some of the hotels as going concerns to fund the purchase and then demolish the pride of PV Doyle, The Berkeley Court and the adjoining Jurys Hotel and The Towers.

The property consortium, fronted by Bryan Cullen and called Precinct, hoped to be left with a five-acre site in Ballsbridge, one of the most valuable pieces of development land in Europe. With property prices going through the roof they knew they could put up blocks of million-pound apartments and walk away from the deal with a huge profit.

Cullen and his associates had a track record; they had cut a similar deal with the Gresham Group which owned The Gresham Hotel in O'Connell Street and other properties. Both sides had walked away from that deal happy with the outcome.

So Cullen approached the board of Jurys Doyle with his proposal to buy the entire company in order to advance his property interests.

The board rebuffed the approach but they were spooked. They knew that what Cullen was trying to do made sense and if they didn't take some form of action themselves someone else would come along with more money to tempt the shareholders and the next bidder was going to succeed.

As the impending changes in the company were discussed at board level Bernadette Gallagher, in particular, made it clear she was against selling any part of her father's legacy.

After a number of discussions with their financial and property advisors the board of Jurys Doyle countered the property speculators by putting the low-rise Jurys Hotel in Ballsbridge up for sale as a development opportunity.

Now a third figure emerged. Sean Dunne, a tough builder and property developer who ran a multimillion business from an office in Merrion Square, cast his eye on the Jurys site and was determined to have it. 'The Dunner' as he is known was a close friend of the former Finance Minister Charlie McCreevy and a ruthless operator who lived on Shrewsbury Road, the most sought after address in Dublin.

After a bidding war involving a who's who of Irish property magnates, Dunne emerged as the new owner of the Jurys site, paying €260 million – over €50 million an acre – for the property.

'There were thirteen bidders. All bar two exceeded the guide price. They were, most of them anyway, hard-nosed, self-made builders cut from the school of life who have taken huge risks and made millions,' wrote Maeve Sheehan in the *Sunday Independent*.

But Precinct, the company who had made the original offer to buy the entire Jurys Hotel Group didn't go away. They came back with another offer and this time they were backed by international business magnates the Rubens brothers, who were known to have a bottomless pit of cash for such profitable deals, and Anglo Irish Bank, the most adventurous lenders in the business.

After twice turning down Precinct's approaches the board of Jurys Doyle held a crucial meeting. They finally decided to recommend the offer to the shareholders, telling them they should accept the bid which valued their company at €1.1 billion.

They gave the Precinct consortium until August 19, fourteen days, to come up with a firm offer to buy the company.

The two Doyle sisters, Bernadette Gallagher and Eileen Monahan, along with their brother-in-law Tom Roche Jr are said to have disagreed and opposed the deal. Another old Dublin hotel family, the Beattys, who had been one of the main shareholders in Jurys were also against it. So while the new directors, mostly financiers and professional types, were for selling, the old hotel families formed an alliance to try to hold on to their legacy.

Meanwhile Sean Dunne was considering how he was going to protect his interests now that others were squabbling over the loot; his purchase of Jurys might or might not be ratified under the new arrangement. He knew Bryan Cullen of Precinct very well: they were two of the city's best-known builders and developers. But this was business and there was no quarter given or expected.

He looked for an assurance from Cullen that the deal for Jurys which he had agreed would stand if the company was taken over. When he couldn't get it he went to war. A long-time rugby enthusiast, he was more than familiar with the playing field strategy of 'get your retaliation in first'.

'Friends say Mr Dunne was stung by Precinct's high-handedness and lack of courtesy in failing to contact him after his €260 million bid had been accepted. He considered their actions to be particularly arrogant because Precinct owned no shares and had no power to influence the deal,' said a source close to Dunne.

The sums floating around were outrageous, even for the most voracious of the Celtic Tigers. Sean Dunne, having spent €260 million on the site of Jurys, now plunged into the stock market and spent another €205 million buying up a twenty-one per cent stake in Jurys Doyle almost overnight.

Another developer, Liam Carroll, who made his fortune lashing up cheap and cheerful apartments all over Dublin, spent €11 million in the hope of becoming a 'deal-breaker' for one of the warring factions. Controversial developer Pascal Taggart, once a financial advisor to the Doyle Group, spent over €2 million buying shares.

It was like a crazed version of the celebrity charity auction. Unless your name was in that hat you were not really considered a big player in the city.

It was also said that developer Paddy Kelly was interested, although he asserted he wasn't. Derek Quinlan, the former revenue inspector who was putting together syndicates to buy such property assets as Claridges in London and The Four Seasons in Dublin was also rumoured to be in the hunt, but never emerged as a buyer.

But really all these names were just a distraction from the real three-cornered fight involving the board of Jurys Doyle, Precinct and Sean Dunne.

Just when observers thought it couldn't get better there was another twist. August 19, the date for Precinct to come up with the money to buy out the shareholders for €1.1 billion, passed without any cash arriving at the table. It emerged on August 23 that the board of Jurys Doyle had withdrawn their backing for the deal because Precinct could not raise the cash after their main banker, Anglo Irish Bank, withdrew its support.

The problem that Bryan Cullen had identified at Jurys Doyle remained, however – several of its flagship hotels were more valuable as building sites. Tough decisions needed to be taken.

'When Bernie Gallagher walked the corridor to the boardroom of The Burlington Hotel in Dublin on Tuesday morning, she was already resigned to the fate of the hotel chain founded by her legendary father, PV Doyle,' reported Maeve Sheehan of the *Sunday Independent*.

But Ms Gallagher was not going to let it go without a fight – even though at that stage she was playing her cards close to her chest.

By the time the meeting ended three hours later, the board of the company, with the consent of Bernie Gallagher, had agreed to sell The Berkeley Court, her father's proudest achievement, and the Montrose Hotel in South Dublin which had founded the empire back in 1964.

'There is no doubt that the family shareholders' representatives would have wanted to keep the hotels, but they are very pragmatic business people. Emotionally their preference is not to sell,' continued Sheehan, who speculated that the family were now looking for a way to 'rescue the family business'.

'Throughout this whole slightly sordid episode, played like a soap opera in the media, people seem to have lost sight of the 800 jobs that will be sacrificed to satisfy speculative greed,' wailed union boss David Begg of the Irish Congress of Trade Unions.

But by now it was way past greed, this was all about family as far as the Doyle sisters were concerned.

While all this was going on the Doyle sisters, led by Bernadette, who owned twenty-three per cent of the company, could not get involved in the bidding war because the company results had just come out and it was a 'closed period' during which directors were barred from buying shares under the rules of the stock exchange.

The morning the closed period ended, the Doyle family interests struck with a vengeance. The first day that they could trade they bought €42 million worth of shares in just five hours. Within the week they had splashed out €83 million to increase their stake in the company to just under thirty per cent. When this was coupled with the shareholding of their allies the Beatty family and another 'old' shareholder, Elizabeth Nelson, they controlled forty-two per cent of the company.

They were also in secret talks with their brother David to buy his two per cent share, which could become vital if the contest with Dunne got any tighter. David may have been talking to them, but after seeing the killing they had made when they merged with Jurys he was holding out for more than they were prepared to pay.

It was at this stage that an Extraordinary General Meeting was called to approve the sale of the Jurys Hotel in Ballsbridge to Sean Dunne. Would the Doyles support it or not? In the end they did – but it was John Gallagher who voted for the family to approve the deal, rather than any of the daughters of PV Doyle. It was symbolic in that they were holding out an olive branch, but they were also letting Sean Dunne know that if he wanted a fight on his hands they would give it to him.

By then their talks with their brother David Doyle had come to nothing. He wasn't prepared to sell at the going rate and they were not prepared to pay over the odds to buy his stake.

As things stood the combined forces of Sean Dunne, Liam Carroll and David Doyle could gain control of Jurys Doyle but all three had different interests and there seemed little possibility of them uniting against the Doyle sisters.

'The girls are taking pole position in the battle for Jurys. Quite a cat fight is promised,' wrote the financial commentator Shane Ross. 'No longer are the ladies sitting demurely in the background. This weekend they seem to be a bit better at the takeover business than the men. They are deadly. It is not just the Doyle side that has benefited from the female touch. Sean Dunne has his own secret weapon in his recent bride, the capable Gayle Killilea.'

Killilea a glamorous young newspaper columnist had become Sean Dunne's second wife after a whirlwind romance. They were married on board the famous Aristotle Onassis yacht, the Christina O, with heavyweight financial, racing and political friends flown in from Ireland and other parts of the globe. The Taoiseach Bertie Ahern rang from his office and his message of goodwill to the newly married couple was broadcast over the yacht's loudspeaker system.

Gayle, a former social diarist who was training to become a barrister, was now installed in Dunne's office as a media advisor while he pitched hundreds of millions of euro into his battle with the Doyle sisters.

'These are not women scorned,' wrote Ross, referring to the Doyle sisters, 'nor are they greedy. These are noble women with higher motives. The sisters are thought to have sworn to stick together. Some sources say they have even copper-fastened family solidarity – in writing. They do not want another painful family split, like the long-running saga when their brother David

129

departed.' Money, he said, was of less value to the Doyles than the memory of their father.

What most of the commentators forgot in all the excitement of the bidding war that had gripped the country was that there was another Doyle still in the game. David Doyle's two per cent of Jurys Doyle was now valued at a staggering €40 million.

But he hadn't forgotten all the ugly rumours of bygone years, or the way he had been fired from the family company and sent into exile at the height of the feud.

'Former Doyle Hotel Group managing director David Doyle will not sell his key stake in Jurys Doyle Hotel Group to his sisters,' said a well-placed leak to financial journalist Tom Lyons in the *Irish Independent*. 'Mr Doyle, who was fired from the hotel chain twice by his sisters under acrimonious circumstances, will hang tough, and if he sells will only do so to the highest bidder outside the family.'

The timing of this 'leak' at a crucial moment as his sisters squared up to Sean Dunne was very interesting to observers of the Doyle family. It was a clear message to them that they may have won the family war but the bad blood was still there and the residue of bitterness still remained in the Doyle family over earlier events.

In the early stages of the battle Sean Dunne, who enjoys a pint in Doheny & Nesbitts pub in Baggot Street, had never met Bernadette Gallagher who would be inclined to lead a more refined social life. It wasn't that there was bad blood between them, it was simply that in the game of monopoly they were playing with the Dublin property market there had been no need for them to talk.

Now, with both sides employing teams of financial advisors, it was down to the nitty-gritty of doing a deal. The Doyle consortium, which was nominally led by John Gallagher, had the financial muscle to beat Sean Dunne. But what were they going to do with a company in which he held almost twenty-nine per cent? He was likely to become something of a nuisance and both sides knew it.

Then the developer Liam Carroll sold out to the Doyle sisters and it was down to a straight fight. There could only be one winner - either Dunne was going to take over the company or, more likely, Bernadette Doyle was going to recapture her father's legacy.

Eventually, with the Doyles face to face with Dunne they assured him he would get Jurys and he could also buy their father's flagship hotel The Berkeley Court, giving him a ten-acre development site in the heart of Dublin's most expensive residential district. Another two acres, the UCD veterinary college owned by the government, was also up for grabs; Sean Dunne needed a deal if he was to complete his portfolio.

In the end it was inevitable. He got the entire Jurys Doyle site in Ballsbridge, paying an extra €119 million for the Berkeley Court Hotel. In return Bernie Gallagher and her sisters bought his shares in Jurys Doyle and got their daddy's hotel chain back.

It was missing a few bits and pieces and they were all a little battle-scarred, but in the end Bernadette Doyle had shown the world that she was her father's daughter.

When it all started seven months earlier she was just another board member, a little more glamorous than the rest it might be said, but she wasn't by any means the biggest shareholder or the most influential member of the board. Yet with a series of carefully orchestrated strategic moves she had cut through all the financial engineering and emerged with most of her father's legacy intact.

Sean Dunne sold his shareholding and pocketed an estimated €20 million in profit. It was a rough ride but he declared himself 'happy' with the outcome.

It was a neat deal, even if both sides ended up paying far more than they could have just a few years earlier.

As for David Doyle, in the end he had no option but to sell his small stake back to his sisters. Although he had tried to insert himself as a 'player' at a vital moment when his stake was a very important asset, his sisters never even contacted him with a firm offer. The only pleasure he got from the eventual sale was that all the bidding had driven the share price sky high and he got a far higher return than he could have ever expected in more normal trading conditions.

But while his sisters Eileen, Anne and Bernadette now own their father's hotel chain once more, David Doyle no longer has any stake in the family company which was founded by his father and which he was due to inherit.

There must have been a smile on the portrait of PV Doyle the night the deal was done, however. The Doyle girls might have lost his flagship hotel, but they had won the most hotly contested corporate battle ever fought on Irish soil.

While their brothers have taken their own path the sisters restored the name of Doyle to the hotel chain their father founded and are now in charge of a business worth more than a billion euro, something their father could never have imagined even in his wildest dreams.

But of course PV Doyle was never a dreamer. He was, like his daughters, cold, calculating and most of all pragmatic when it came to the business at hand.

Chapter 6

A Woman's Heart

His ambition was to die with very little; it looks like he is going to achieve that ambition,' said Mary Coman sadly, her bright blue eyes almost brimming with tears as she looked down from the witness box on her husband Pat, the man she called 'Dad'.

For sheer drama and bitterness 'The War of the Comans' showed how far a family could fall. Here inside the imposing Four Courts in Dublin were eighty-year-old Patrick Coman, one of the city's best-known pub owners, and his wife Mary pitted against five of their six sons and supported in their family war, publicly at any rate, by three of their six daughters.

At stake was a multimillion euro fortune that old Patrick Coman had built up over nearly half a century. Yet here he was watching a huge chunk of it disappear into the pockets of high-priced lawyers as he battled through the latest in a series of legal actions against his sons for control of the pub and bottling company he had founded as a young man.

'We have lost everything we valued: we have lost our fatherhood and motherhood,' said Mary Coman in a quiet but determined voice, expressing every mother's anguish at a family torn apart by feuding and infighting. As the family had descended into recriminations, threats and even physical violence, one lawyer had described it as 'bloodshed'.

Her sons, she said, had an 'obsession with legal carry on' but it seemed, from the amount of litigation consuming the Comans, that it was a family trait.

The sons of Pat and Mary Coman, dressed in business suits, sat around the courtroom implacable as their seventy-year-old mother spoke. As the drama unfolded, one spent most of his time staring at the back of his mother's head, another fidgeted constantly, his eyes focused on the ground, while a third sat with arms folded, careful not to look straight ahead.

As the days in Court No 6 wore on, the sons never sat together, unlike the old pair and their three daughters. Without fail they sat close together with one daughter, heavily pregnant, sitting beside her mother while the other two sat to the right of their father.

Now as his wife spoke for the first time, Pat Coman wept gently at her words and one of the three daughters, her head leaning on his big square shoulder, cried her eyes out too.

How different it had all been when Pat Coman a barman in Tipperary asked Mary to be his bride.

'When Pat Coman asked me to marry him that was a gentleman's agreement; when we went into the Cathedral in Thurles and signed the register, that was a legally binding agreement,' said Mary Coman without hesitation when the judge asked her if she knew the difference between a 'gentleman's agreement' and a 'binding agreement'.

In those simple few words she put it better than any lawyer or legal textbook ever could.

Back when they married in Thurles, Co Tipperary, life had

seemed so simple. Pat Coman was a big, strong Tipperary man who had played rugby for his club and his province. He was ambitious and had his eyes set on leaving rural Ireland and moving to Dublin where he would get on in the world.

Like many young Tipperary men he wanted to make his fortune and he followed in the footsteps of the masters. Above the door of many Dublin pubs were the names Kennedy, O'Dwyer, Fitzgerald, and they all came from the villages in the hills around Thurles. Each new arrival who came to the city got a job as a barman and a helping hand when they wanted to go into the drinks business themselves. Many of them played hurling with 'Commercials' and there the team spirit ensured that when they started out on their own other club members would give surplus bits of pub furniture, mirrors and other bits and pieces to help get them set up.

Another famous Tipperary publican, Louis Fitzgerald, who runs a string of pubs and hotels around Dublin, describes what it was like living on a farm in Tipperary and moving to the big city to make his fortune.

'There wasn't much point in staying around on a farm, especially when it was barely economical. My father had cousins in the pub business way back and my mother would have said a job in a bar was a good job. We were brought up on a farm and we were well used to hard work, so it was out of the frying pan into the fire. It was hard physical work, but there was no going back – it was going forward I was.'

Pat Coman was one of the Tipperary men who had blazed that well-known trail many years before when Louis Fitzgerald was still a little boy working on his father's farm. After working for a time in various pubs Pat Coman had struck out on his own, finding a nice corner house in the fashionable Dublin suburb of Rathgar.

Back then, in 1957, Rathgar was a small market village. There weren't many cars on the roads and Eamon de Valera and his inward-looking Fianna Fáil government were in power. Ireland was in the midst of a financial and intellectual depression, isolated and church-dominated with books and films banned for the slightest infringement of Catholic moral teaching. But in the redbrick Victorian villas and the Edwardian houses around Rathgar lived the monied middle classes, the solicitors, bankers and senior civil servants. Unlike the run-down areas of the city it was a good place to start a business and Patrick Coman established himself as a man worth knowing. He was steady and trustworthy and he got to know his customers and ran an orderly house.

Pat and Mary gradually built the business into a thriving pub with a reputation for good drink and hospitality. When the pub was refurbished in the modern style, people went out of their way to spend an evening in Comans – it was a place to be seen.

But Pat Coman was not a man to stand still. Another famous Dublin publican, Dessie Hynes, used to say that running O'Donoghue's in Merrion Row was like owning a bank. With a steady trade he just had to make sure that everything was in running order and he would collect the money at the end of day.

Comans was a bit like that. Patrick Coman had to keep an eye on things but basically the business was running itself. He considered buying another pub and expanding in that direction, but then he looked around and saw that all the other publicans were buying in their drinks from the big brewers like Guinness or from other large wholesalers who didn't have 'the personal touch'.

He knew that he had good connections in the trade and that other publicans would support him if he opened his own wholesale and bottling business. It was a brave move, because he was taking on Guinness and a lot of other vested interests. But by 1966 he had a substantial business behind him, bankers to back him and he was a big, tough man who relished a challenge.

He hadn't misjudged the market. His many friends in the pub business supported his new venture and over the years he turned the wholesale drinks and bottling business into a multimillion pound business and the company became worth far more than the pub that had originally funded it.

Restless and autocratic he ran his pub and his business as his own empire. He decided things in consultation with Mary but there was nobody else to answer back.

While he was building up the new business, his wife was taking care of the Rathgar pub and managing their growing family. They had twelve children, six boys and six girls, and as the elder ones became teenagers they went into the business, working after school as lounge boys or filling the shelves and doing other chores either in the pub or the bottling plant during the holidays.

They were learning their father's trade from the ground up as well as cutting overheads. But they were also trusted aides and Patrick and Mary Coman knew that one day they would be handing on the business to the rest of the family.

By now the family had moved to a large detached house on Rathgar Road, well able to accommodate a family of six boys and six girls. A sweep of gravel leads to the immaculately kept house with stone steps leading to the front door. Inside, the rooms, with high ornate ceilings, are fitted out with antique furniture and the best of everything.

It is the residence of a very comfortable businessman. Set on more than half an acre of manicured grounds and gardens, it has a swimming pool and a tennis court in the back garden. In the Ireland of the 1970s the Comans were posh.

But the family were not the vulgar rich. They weren't part of the social circuit; they had their own friends and they stayed very much out of the limelight, concentrating on the family and the expanding business. The Comans worked hard for their money and they enjoyed it discreetly.

As each of the children married, their father dipped into the cash mountain that his two companies were generating and bought them a house, mostly in the Rathgar/Terenure suburbs as a wedding present.

It became part of the family tradition. But it also became part of the family downfall and indirectly it led to the bitterness and bad blood that would spill out into the very public family 'bloodbath' of Court No 6 in the High Court in Dublin.

As the business expanded there was one problem on Pat Coman's cloudless horizon: tax. Irish governments love raising taxes and Irish businessmen are most reluctant to pay it.

In the 1970s and 1980s there was a crippling tax regime. Businessmen saw it as a conspiracy by the state to steal their hard-earned money. The really rich and influential got involved in the Ansbacher schemes, investing money in family trust funds in the secretive Cayman Islands. Others opened 'bogus non-resident accounts' which meant they didn't pay tax on their money as allegedly they didn't live in the country any more. Others took their money in suitcases to Northern Ireland, the Isle of Man, or Jersey in the Channel Islands.

In time most of them lived to regret these manoeuvres. Huge tax investigations were launched after the Dunnes Stores payments debacle and the *Sunday Independent* investigations into bogus non-resident accounts.

Unlike many of his colleagues, Patrick Coman didn't avail of any of these offshore tax schemes, but like all good businessmen he was still anxious to pay as little tax as possible and so he got sound financial advice and opted to take a different route.

In 1988 when he was sixty-four years of age Patrick Coman began to think about mortality and what would happen when he died. 'If anything happened to Pat we would be crippled by tax,' said Mary. 'His ambition was to die with very little, it looks like he is going to achieve that ambition.'

Of course when she said he wanted to die with very little that did not mean he wanted to throw away his lifetime's work or leave it to some charitable institution. It simply meant that when he died he wanted to leave as small an estate as possible so that his business would not be settled with a huge tax bill.

The best tax advisors told him he should think about handing over a share in his business to his sons before he died. In that way it would not be liable to tax after his death.

He wasn't one to hand over his lifetime's work on a whim so he decided that he and Mary would hold on to fifty-two per cent of the two companies they jointly owned, Comans Ltd, which owned the public house in Rathgar, and Patrick Coman Ltd, the bottling plant now based in Tallaght, Co Dublin.

The rest of the company would be divided up among their six sons, Geoffrey, Thomas, Denis, John, Patrick and William, with each getting eight per cent, regardless of whether they worked in the business or not.

It was the old way of doing things – passing the business on to the sons but not the daughters. However, Patrick and Mary Coman didn't forget their daughters.

Their girls, Elizabeth, Monica, Ella and the triplets Catriona, Polina and Darina, would get a house each when they married and would inherit the rest of the Coman's considerable property and fortune when their parents died.

It seemed like a perfect solution. The business would be left in the safe hands of their sons, their daughters would be well provided for, and Patrick and Mary could sit back and enjoy a tranquil old age.

But that wasn't how it worked out.

'Every one of those boys left our home to get married and settle down . . . and here we are today, what happened to our relationship?' Mary Coman would later ask, plaintively from the witness box. 'We could be living in Spain, but our wish was to give a start in life to all our children,' she explained.

For a few years the new arrangement worked reasonably well. But old Pat Coman failed to realise that he had handed over the business to the next generation and he should leave it to them and get on with enjoying life.

He still owned fifty-two per cent of the pub and bottling plant and he still ran them like the patriarch he was. His sons, young and dynamic, wanted to do things their own way but they were stymied by their father who held on to ultimate control of the two companies.

In an attempt to head off a growing rift between the father and some of his sons, the Comans were advised to bring in outside businessmen as independent directors of the multimillion pound drinks empire. It was hoped that their experience, common sense and distance from the family as 'outsiders' would bring a more dispassionate approach to the running of the family business.

Although his health wasn't good Patrick Coman still refused to distance himself from the business, or take sound independent advice from the new directors of the company. He insisted that what he said was rule of law within the company, even when others felt very uncomfortable about his actions.

In 1995 things came to a head when Pat Coman went to buy a house for one of his six daughters. Without consultation with his sons he wrote a cheque for IR£300,000 from the business as a deposit on the house for his daughter. When it was discovered that this wasn't enough, he put the money back into the company and wrote out another cheque, this time for IR£360,000.

It displayed a father's love for his daughter, but to his sons it was no way to run a business. They had spent years trying to control him, but this huge withdrawal from the company without proper consultation was too much for them to bear. The cheque was stopped by the company, leading to a serious breakdown in the relationship between Pat Coman and his sons.

At a board meeting he was accused of 'dipping his hand in the till' and of running the business as his 'personal fiefdom'. He and his wife Mary, who was also a director, took exception to these remarks. The board meeting broke up after there was a flurry of blows and some pushing and shoving.

There were accusations and counter-accusations of assault, and at one stage the police were even called as relationships between the sons and the old man deteriorated.

The feud had a terrible effect on the family and over the following months the tension and aggravation took its toll on the health of old Pat Coman.

'At the time, Dad was seriously ill. He died five times,' said Mary Coman.

Eventually the other directors, his sons, apart from William Coman who retained his share but was not involved in the running of the business, reached a compromise. The money for the house deposit would be paid but it would be treated, to use the accountancy terms, as an advance against the freehold of the public house in Rathgar.

The old man appears to have nodded approval to this deal, but deep in his heart he wasn't for changing his ways.

Two years later Patrick Coman took out another huge cash deposit, this time to help two of his other daughters who were 'getting their foot on the property ladder'.

He and his wife then went off on a pilgrimage to the shrine of Our Lady of Lourdes. While they were away the cheque was stopped. The daughters were now extremely disappointed that their brothers objected to the family business helping to fund their house purchases. After all, it was family money and the sons had done rather well while they had to wait for their inheritance.

Relations deteriorated further. Mary Coman was so incensed by the sons' treatment of their father that she marched into the public house in Rathgar and demanded that her son Denis, who ran the pub, should return personal items of memorabilia that she had donated to the pub, including old family photographs and her husband's rugby cap.

Every board meeting was a series of disagreements with the father and mother pitted against their sons.

'All the votes were the boys against the parents, parents against the boys,' said company solicitor David Larney who, like other family advisors, found himself having to take sides in the dispute. The two independent directors, respected accountant John Donnelly and businessman Patrick Loughrey, founder of the highly successful food business Cuisine de France, resigned rather than participate any further in the continuing family conflict.

Apart from the obvious difficulty for the sons in having their father dipping into the company money there was the added problem that as the Dublin property market boomed the cheques Pat Coman was writing were getting far bigger than anyone had anticipated.

By now the relationship between the Coman parents and their sons was characterised by bitterness, hate and legal wrangling. With so many children and grandchildren, family events became a growing nightmare with family members taking sides in the feud.

A board meeting on November 6, 1997, resolved that any monies taken out of the company by Patrick Coman would be treated as an advance against the future ownership of Comans pub in Rathgar by the sons. Patrick and Mary Coman voted against this boardroom resolution but lost on a vote of the directors.

In a counter-move they went to the High Court in 1998 and, as fifty-two per cent owners of the businesses, asked the judge to remove their sons as directors of the company so that Pat Coman could regain full control of the business. They failed in this action.

By now both parties had resorted to lawyers and had stopped talking to each other altogether.

The bitter dispute, Coman v Coman, surfaced in the High Court in 2001 when Pat Coman made a second attempt to have five of his six sons, Geoffrey, John, Patrick Jr, Thomas and Denis, legally removed as directors of the two family companies.

Neither the sixth son, William, nor any of the daughters took any part in the litigation.

Patrick Coman wasn't successful and in retaliation for his legal action in December 2002 the companies stopped the salaries of Patrick and Mary Coman until outstanding loans of £1.25 million were repaid to the company. This was the money that Patrick Coman had withdrawn, mostly to put deposits on houses for some of his daughters and other 'loans' he had taken out. It was outright war.

The family went back to court. This time Pat and Mary Coman demanded that their salaries should be paid and that they should be recognised as directors. They said that at this stage they had outstanding bills that they couldn't pay, including a bill for IR£400,000 in solicitors' fees for the ongoing litigation that had split the family.

The parents said that if they used up their cash resources and some IR£250,000 in bank shares they would be virtually penniless apart from their sole property asset, their mansion on the Rathgar Road, which was now worth about IR£4 million.

'I have been told,' Mary said, 'they [the sons] are going to starve us into submission. It was in the paper that we have a IR£4 million house in Rathgar; we bought it for £6,000. We have no resources. Pat Coman could be gone in half an hour.'

She was right in one respect: despite these outward trappings of real wealth the Coman sons eventually put the squeeze on old Pat Coman to such an extent that he no longer had the resources to dip into the extensive cash pile that the company he founded was generating. He was wealthy in terms of property and assets, but he didn't have the hard cash to mount a lengthy battle with five of his six sons.

The family were 'at daggers drawn' and after much persuasion on both sides their advisors called a summit of the warring factions.

On February 5, 2003, a group of lawyers, accountants and financial advisors gathered in the offices of solicitor David Larney in Earlsfort Terrace in Dublin to try to hammer out a final settlement of the dispute. Tensions were now running so high in the family that the parents were in one room with some of their daughters, while the five sons were in another room. Other members of the family were across the road in the Conrad Hotel, and for over eight hours emissaries went from one room to the other and over and back to the hotel, trying desperately to reach a settlement that would end the family conflict once and for all.

At the end of the shuttle diplomacy, at about 11 p.m. that night, Gerard Hogan, an eminent Dublin Senior Counsel, was left clutching an A4 sheet of paper covered in squiggles of writing in red biro which constituted a peace treaty between the warring Comans.

As it turned out it was a little bit like the Treaty of Limerick, it wasn't worth the paper it was written on. When it came to be analysed there were further disputes about what exactly was written on it.

For the purposes of the deal that night the entire Comans business was valued at €13.46 million. It was proposed to strip out the €1.25 million that Patrick Coman owed the business and €250,000 to pay for the battery of costly legal and financial experts assembled in Earlsfort Terrace and the other fees involved in settling the case.

According to Gerard Hogan SC, it was agreed that the sons of Patrick Coman would pay their father and mother €7 million for their fifty-two per cent share of the business.

The sons had demanded 'a complete break in business and regrettably in personal terms' from the parents. They wanted Patrick and Mary Coman out of the business that they had founded nearly fifty years earlier and which was the foundation of the family fortune. They also wanted them out of their lives altogether.

For the old pair this was a devastating clause and Mary Coman would later come to say that the idea of a 'clean break' with the sons she had borne and nourished and given a start in life was the hardest cross she had to bear in her long life.

The money didn't mean as much as the damage the feud was doing to their family.

The settlement was, Gerard Hogan agreed, 'a back of the envelope' calculation which he later found 'embarrassing'. The 'squiggles' he made in red biro that night would later cost a lot more in legal fees as lawyers disputed whether it constituted an agreement or not.

As if to emphasise that he was still rooted in the cattle-dealing country ways of his forefathers in Tipperary, Patrick Coman also insisted on 'spit money' of €50,000, which should be handed back to him to seal the deal. This was an old custom on a Fair Day in the country when a deal was completed and the seller would hand a coin or a grubby note back to the buyer in what was known as 'luck penny' or 'spit money'.

But whether he ever intended the Earlsfort Terrace peace treaty to be the real deal or just another battle in the family war of attrition remained a moot point.

When the Coman sons went to enforce the deal and take over the business completely, their father insisted that it hadn't included the 'bricks and mortar' of Comans pub in Rathgar. He accepted that they owned the licence but he now insisted that he should be paid an additional sum of over €1.25 million for the building – cancelling out the loan for the same amount that he was expected to pay back to the company.

After all the blood, sweat and tears of that night in Earlsfort Terrace the war between the Comans was on again. So it was back to the High Court in Dublin for yet another expensive instalment of Coman v Coman.

It now emerged in court that old Patrick Coman didn't believe that his sons would be able to come up with the €7 million to buy him out of the business. What that illustrated more than anything was that he was behind the times. Given the assets at stake – a well-known pub in a much sought after location and a highly profitable bottling plant – 'the boys' had absolutely no problem in getting their bankers to finance the deal.

It was now down to a judge to decide whether the negotiations of February 5, 2003, constituted an agreement or not. The boys were insisting on implementation of the February agreement and the parents were insisting it wasn't a valid deal.

The two Senior Counsel who drew up that agreement, Brian O'Moore SC for the parents and Gerard Hogan SC for the boys, said their disagreement was 'gossamer thin'. Another sticking point for old Patrick Coman was that while his sons would be able to use company money to fund the purchase he would have to pay €800,000 in tax from the settlement proceedings.

Patrick Coman didn't like the idea of losing another huge lump of cash, even though the tax advisors on both sides clearly believed they had cut the tax liability as far as they possibly could.

'Taxes are a fact of life . . . for everyone,' said the judge when he was told about this facet of the dispute.

The latest courtroom drama was launched amid a frenzy of photographs and the glare of unwanted publicity.

'Whether subconscious or not, the daughters and mother always seemed to be colour coordinated,' wrote June Caldwell in the magazine *Business Plus*. 'Decked out in bright hopeful colours one day, Mary Coman wore a blue linen suit and her daughters dressed in bright pink, with pink bags. On another day, when the stress seemed nothing short of aching, they all wore mixes of sombre black, with the odd dash of optimistic white.'

The judge, one of the more sensible on the Irish bench, was enthralled but seemingly horrified that the family feud was being dragged into his court and the details of their private lives exposed, when it could all so easily be settled if the family members could just get their heads together.

'There is only €7 million at issue here,' said Judge Joseph Finnegan after two expensive days in the High Court which probably cost €500,000 given the numbers of lawyers and expensive witnesses filling the courtroom. 'They will get through it very quickly if they keep going like this.'

But if the legalistic disagreement was just gossamer thin, the split in the family was having horrendous consequences for the Coman family. It wasn't until Mary Coman went into the witness box that the full, awful truth of the rift that had opened up between a father and mother and their sons and daughters emerged.

'It is a terrible thing for a mother to look down and see we are now outcasts of the family. That is a very serious thing. I want it aired, you don't do that to a mother and father,' she said, picking on the phrase that her sons had included in legal documentation that 'all relationships will cease'.

'I was in hospital in 2003 and not even one of my sons made enquiries about me. It is shocking. There were other family events at which we weren't welcome. We are now outcasts of the family.'

The terms thrown around the courtroom reflected the state of the family.

'As a lawyer I was incredibly determined to stop the bloodshed,' said one.

'Trying to reach a settlement was like a battle, the first deal was wrong, the second deal was flawed, it just went on and on,' said another. Solicitor David Larney characterised the situation as 'madness' and Brian O'Moore SC admitted that the relationship between the father and sons was 'atrocious'.

It wasn't just a case of washing their dirty linen in public, it was a question of baring their souls and exposing all the private grief and disagreements that touch many families in all their raw ugliness.

'I want to tell my sons and the world: we have been characterised as a greedy old pair, but I want to tell my sons they have the best father, they should be proud of him and they should not be dragging him through the courts like this,' said Mary Coman, bringing the case to an emotional pitch rarely seen in the staid environment of a commercial dispute.

But her sons sat stony-faced through her emotional plea from the witness box.

'There is always time to sort it out,' the judge told the high-powered lawyers, John O'Donnell SC and Patrick Hanratty SC for Patrick and Mary Coman and Michael Cush SC and Brian Sperrin SC for the sons, after hearing five days of evidence.

As if to put a sting in the tail he also had a warning for both sides. 'I could make a decision that nobody can live with, a solution that neither side would be overjoyed with,' said Judge Finnegan, a wise and compassionate man.

He was clearly intimating that as the divisions were too deep he could decide that the whole company would have to be sold off to outsiders and the proceeds divided up among the warring factions.

Hours later the litigation ended. Patrick and Mary Coman signed over their interest in the Comans businesses to their five sons and retreated to the silence of their big double-fronted home.

Although he appeared gruff, Patrick Coman was obviously an emotional man just as his wife Mary was an emotional woman. In the last picture taken of him as he left the court and the business behind he walked up the Liffey quays flanked by two of his daughters. In a defining gesture he turned to the photographers, pursed his lips and raised his hand in the air as if waving part of his life goodbye.

Today Comans pub is a thriving business. One of the warring sons, Denis, went on to become President of the Licensed Vintners Association and took over the running of the pub completely. The others are running the drinks wholesale business.

But for the extended Coman clan, family life has been destroyed. After the bitter and cantankerous public feud no amount of money could salvage that precious gift of a happy family for Pat Coman and his wife Mary who should have spent their declining years in the bosom of their twelve children.

Chapter 7

Queen of the Castle

The great castle lurks over Killiney Bay, its turrets, towers and battlements dominating the shoreline that stretches through South Dublin and on into Wicklow. Along its numerous passageways pads the beautiful, dark and mysterious woman who is the sole occupant of this lonely, romantic folly. She alone knows its secret 'safe' rooms and hiding places.

She needs to keep alert for intruders. Stalkers have come clambering over these stone defences, frightening her in the dead of night. These are not thieves or robbers but misguided, even slightly insane, souls drawn to the mysteries of this place by the ethereal creations of its owner, the mysterious and reclusive Enya.

Ayesha Castle is home to one of the most successful musical artists in the world today. The forty-five-year-old Donegal woman, who was born Eithne Ní Bhraonáin on May 17, 1961, and who has never performed her strange haunting rhythms live on stage, has sold more than seventy million records worldwide and is a multimillion euro industry all to herself.

Well not quite. There are two other people who play a central part in her life, Nicholas (Nicky) Ryan and his wife, Roma. Nicky is a former sound engineer who now manages her career, while Roma writes the lyrics to many of the songs that have made them all rich beyond their dreams. It was the Ryans' faith in the waif-like Enya that has given her the comforts of a castle in Killiney and fame that reaches to the far corners of the world.

But it was also their friendship, the friendship between the musician and her mentors, that led to a bitter and long-term falling out with other members of her family that has only healed with the passage of time.

Ayesha Castle was built in the early 1850s by a Dublin businessman, Robert Warren. He named it Victoria Castle after the British Queen who visited Dublin in 1853 to open the Great Exhibition. It was later owned by the Provost of Trinity College, Rev Humphrey Lloyd and passed on to members of his family. The castle was gutted by fire around the turn of the century and then passed on to Colonel RM Aylmer in 1947. It was his daughter who sold it to Eithne Brennan, or Enya as she had become in the mid-1990s after a string of hits made her a multimillionaire.

Enya has music in her blood, but she was reared in cottages rather than castles as one of the nine children of an engaging musician and singer, Leo Brennan.

Leo's parents travelled the length of Ireland with the Connacht Concert Company, a music-hall outfit where everybody did their bit to keep the show on the road.

'I'm still singing the songs my dad taught me all those years ago. I tell the stories of those songs, songs about food like 'The Cucumber Song', or one of my favourite titles, 'You Can Muck

About With Brussels Sprouts But You Can't Muck About With Love,' said Leo.

He later led the Slieve Foy Showband and in 1968 with a growing family decided to settle down by buying a public house in the small Donegal village of Crolly (where the dolls came from) which he renamed Leo's Tavern. He's been running it since and spending much of his time talking to visitors about his internationally successful children.

His wife Baba was also musical, although her taste was more towards 'serious' music, church music and choirs. Between them they ensured that their children learned to play instruments and were given singing lessons by professional teachers which meant most of the family had a classical as well as a folk music education.

In 1970 three of Leo's children, Máire (Moya), Ciarán and Pól started the folk group Clannad with their uncles Noel and Pádraig Duggan. Their rich blend of instruments, Gaelic language lyrics, traditional and new, and harmonies imported from the West Coast of America ensured that they were noticed and they won first prize that first year at the Letterkenny Folk Festival.

But it took more than five years before the band went professional. A chance encounter with a restless young Dublin journalist called Fachtna O'Kelly led to him becoming their first manager. He had written a rave review for the *Evening Press* of a concert they played with Horslips in the National Stadium in Dublin and after it was published Máire contacted him to say thanks and they arranged to meet.

'When Fachtna turned up he also had a friend with him, Nicky Ryan, who was something of a sound engineer,' said Máire. 'We had a great evening together and became excited by Fachtna's and Nicky's enthusiasm for what we were doing.'

After arranging and completing a highly successful tour of Europe, O'Kelly turned them around again fairly quickly and sent them off to folk festivals in France. But then there was silence; they found it hard to contact him.

Dublin was a changing city and nothing exemplified it more in the late seventies than Bob Geldof and the Boomtown Rats. O'Kelly, who knew Geldof from the tight Dublin music network, had taken over the Rats after getting Clannad on the road. As the Rats burst on the scene in Moran's Hotel and other venues he was devoting most of his time to the up-and-coming band.

'Meanwhile we stumbled through the French tour and decided that Nicky Ryan – already travelling with us as our sound engineer – should take over more of Fachtna's role, becoming the spokesman for the band,' said Máire Brennan in her book *The Other Side of the Rainbow*.

So came the involvement of Nicky and Roma Ryan. But the Ryans were more than just managers. They were also actively involved in producing and arranging the music. Together the band produced a string of acclaimed albums through the late 1970s, winning awards and attending folk festivals.

Almost a decade after the band was formed, Nicky Ryan suggested that another of the Brennan sisters, eighteen-year-old Eithne, should join Clannad.

'It was music that Enya was into and I had a band that, as far as I was concerned, were kind of stale at this stage. I knew Enya could sing and that she had a broader range than Máire, so I brought her into the group. It was my suggestion, not Clannad's. Reluctantly she said she'd join us. From that moment on I felt responsible for her future,' Nicky Ryan told Dublin journalist Tony Clayton-Lea.

'It was right in at the deep end,' recalls the woman who would become Enya. 'On the way to the first gig we picked up a ·

keyboard for me. I hadn't even played it. It was: okay, we're on stage, I know this song, what's the key?'

But the arrival of Enya stirred tensions in the band. She never really felt part of the group or that she was getting the recognition she deserved from her sister, brothers and uncles because she was 'the new girl' and they had 'paid their dues', in musicians' parlance, with their long and tiring trips around Ireland, England and the continent.

'It was fun,' Enya says of her days with Clannad, 'but I had no musical input. My brothers were doing the writing and arranging, so it felt temporary.'

There was also growing tension between the band and the Ryans. Nicky Ryan and his Belfast born wife, Roma, had literally taken over the running of the entire operation from organising tours and gigs to writing and arranging material for the band.

But the Ryans had seen something in Enya that the others had missed. As tensions grew between the Ryans and the other members of Clannad and they thought about splitting with the band, Nicky Ryan suggested to the dissatisfied young musician and singer Enya, who was his protégé, that she could make it as a solo artist if she came with them.

Suddenly it became Clannad against the Ryans and Enya. It was not a happy time for any of those concerned in the claustrophobic world of a touring band. The Ryans were faced with an ultimatum to 'back off' and allow the band to make the musical decisions or leave altogether.

They decided to split with Clannad, and Enya went with them. Her decision to 'foresake' the family in favour of the Ryans created a huge rift within the group and among the Brennan family.

'The whole Clannad involvement has been só distorted over time,' Enya said later. 'The fact is, at the time I took up with

Clannad, Nicky and Roma were managing them. It was Nicky who invited me to join the group. It was after Nicky and Roma ceased to be a part of Clannad that I left the group. I did not want to be part of the group without having them in charge, so I left and entrusted my future to Nicky and Roma, which obviously proved to be a very wise decision.'

'They turned to Enya and said – these are the very words that were said, "Enya, if you want to be a star you stay with us. If you want to be nobody, you go with the Ryans",' remembered Nicky Ryan. It was a stark choice and when Enya made her decision it opened up a gulf in the family that lasted for years.

'The split happened and Enya chose us. She felt she could see that for her personally, regardless of what happened afterwards, it was a dead end. So she entrusted the whole thing, her future, to us,' said Nicky Ryan.

'Here is a woman who, as a young girl, departed her family band Clannad amid a flurry of accusations and ultimatums, choosing to team up with the band's ousted manager and sound engineer, Nicky Ryan, and his wife Roma – a decision that remains as secretive and unfathomable now as it was virtually destructive to all concerned then,' wrote Tony Clayton-Lea at the beginning of a 1998 interview with the enigmatic Enya.

Enya who had gone away to boarding school in Milford College in Donegal at the age of twelve was an ethereal figure, but at the same time she had a tough Donegal streak that came from earning her own independence.

'I felt very protected and loved in the family and depended on other people to make decisions for me,' said Enya. 'But I went to boarding school at twelve and from that point became very independent.'

Although the Brennans were a strong family they were very different and ultimately Enya was a stranger in the band.

In her autobiography, published in 2000, Máire Brennan failed to spell out what exactly caused the split, and she largely glosses over the involvement of the Ryans in the departure of her younger sister.

'There was also a lot happening in other areas of my life,' she wrote. 'Even around my brothers, I could feel lonely, so I appreciated having Eithne on the road with us, but towards the end of the European tour there was a lot of tension between us all. We were exhausted, having been on the road too long, and were beginning to get on one another's nerves. It didn't help that I had a terrible temper and flared all too easily. Playing in a family band has many advantages, but it can often mean that when the going gets tough you take it out on each other with a liberty that only family can tolerate.

'I suppose it had always been difficult for Eithne. We loved what she brought to the band, but I know it was hard for her to infiltrate our years as a tightly knit nucleus. Musically, Ciarán and Pól had always been the creative force, and Noel, Pádraig and myself had then worked our own expression around them. It was a good formula that worked well. Inevitably, when Eithne joined us full time, she found it hard. She hadn't been part of the original song-collecting days and consequently didn't share our enthusiasm for the old songs. I suppose she always felt little more than a guest musician.

'As sisters we had always been close and talked about everything together, so I was sorry when the band business caused strain between us. One day, just after the tour, Eithne announced that she had decided to leave Clannad. She was going to pursue a solo career with Nicky Ryan as her manager. In the long term it turned out to be a good decision,' said Máire.

'She never really took to touring, nor felt part of the already established group, and two years later she departed causing a family rift that has only recently been healed,' wrote music journalist Neil McCormick about Enya in 2005 – over twenty years after she walked out on the band and her brothers and elder sister.

Enya, along with her managers Nicky and Roma Ryan, founded Aigle Music in September 1981. She left her family behind and moved in with the Ryans and their two young daughters, then living in a suburban house at Danieli Drive, Artane, Dublin, no longer in communication with her sister Moya and her brothers.

But for the young Enya it wasn't like a normal family row. She had been just a child in Donegal when Clannad started on their musical journey, and with touring and albums and the rock-star life that they led, she'd hardly seen much of them in the intervening years.

In her book Máire admits that the vow of silence that they took regarding the split has also caused them a lot of difficulty. 'There have been many damaging articles that have hurt my family deeply – stories about our relationships, particularly between myself and Enya. We resolved in the early days not to talk about our private lives but, especially in Enya's case, this has often led to more intrigue and false speculation. For an artist, it is the unfortunate consequence of being in the public eye, but what makes me really angry is the way the family inevitably bears the suffering.'

Initially it looked like the ultimatum Enya got from her family in Clannad was going to come true and it was Clannad who first found stardom with a hit record. After years of well-received folk albums Clannad made the big breakthrough into the pop charts when their theme from a BBC drama *Harry's Game* made it to No 5 in the British charts in 1983.

It had that multi-layered sound that would later become much more identified with Enya, but in fact she had nothing to do with it. It also had the obscure, repetitive lyrics which have become associated with her. A producer at the BBC became so concerned with the lyrics of the theme for *Harry's Game*, which had an IRA theme, that he hired a Gaelic translator to listen to them.

'Fol lol the doh fol the day

Fol the day fol the day' went the chorus.

'What does it mean?' enquired the BBC man.

'Nothing, it's nonsense,' answered the translator.

' 'Harry's Game' was done before Enya did the layering of voices and created what they call an 'ethereal' or 'haunted' sound,' says her sister Máire, and added, without a trace of irony, that there is a big difference between the two sisters: 'I write the words, Enya doesn't.'

The break-up of Clannad seems to have been the only trauma in Enya's life until the stalkers came creeping along the corridors of the castle that has come to represent the essence of Enya's mysterious music.

'Quite why she should attract such obsessive attention is something of a mystery. Enya has to be the world's most invisible star. Shy to the point of secretiveness, you never read about her in the gossip columns. She has never played a live concert and she seldom even seems to go out. When she made a rare excursion into the spotlight at the Oscars three years ago, she was delighted to meet Paul McCartney – but it was the former Beatle who approached her,' wrote another journalist who met her.

'Enya would never have dreamt of going up to him,' says her manager. 'She doesn't bother with any of that celebrity stuff and avoids it like the plague; she's very low profile.'

But there was no such attention for Enya when she started working on her first album in the garden shed in the Ryans' home. Released by the BBC in 1987, it featured the unique voice of Enya and her multi-layered music. A couple of very good Irish musicians, guitar player Arty McGlynn and the piper Liam O'Flynn played on it. But sales were sluggish and really never gave any indication of the phenomenon she would become.

Enya seemed destined to sink back into obscurity and the Ryans' back garden studio until the film-maker David Puttman used her music in an adaptation of *The Frog Princess* and introduced Enya and the Ryans to the BBC series *The Celts*.

The album was re-released as *The Celts* and it began the relentless climb that would make Enya among the world's best-selling musical artists.

'I started writing instrumentals but Roma pointed out they were very visual, so she started writing the lyrics,' Enya explained to an interviewer. 'Nicky had this idea of creating a wall of sound and started multi-tracking my voice. I do remember people saying to me, your music is not very commercial, how are you going to sell that?'

But in the end Enya didn't have to sell it. It sold itself. Her album *Watermark* in 1988 sold eight million copies and the song 'Orinoco Flow' was a huge hit. Another album *Day Without Rain* sold thirteen million copies. She didn't even have to do concerts to promote her albums.

Since then the money has flowed into the coffers of the three partners, Enya, Nicky Ryan and Roma Ryan, and put Enya onto the 'rich lists' so beloved of the Sunday newspapers.

But it hasn't been all plain sailing; the critics universally hate Enya, and the stalkers have a thing for her, her music and the romantic castle she inhabits on Killiney Hill.

Her music, according to the critics, is bland and her private life has always been shrouded in mystery. But why does she attract such attention from weirdos? Could it be the remote almost helpless quality which the tough Donegal singer has portrayed?

Early in her career a stalker bombarded her with letters and eventually stabbed himself when he could find no other way to get her attention and was thrown out of her father's pub in Donegal. But in 2005 she had a close brush with a very dangerous situation when a stalker broke into her castle and tied up her maid as he sought his very own private interview with the star. Enya realised something was afoot and locked herself in a 'safe' room and sounded a panic alarm. She could hear the stalker moving about the corridors of the castle trying to find her, but the intruder had fled before police arrived almost two hours later.

'You deal with it and you move on,' she said afterwards. 'Those things happen and for that moment it's not nice, but you have to put it behind you. Those kind of people have been there from day one,' she says. 'Regardless of how I live my life there are people who develop fixations that are not healthy. It could be a visual thing or it could be the music that they are drawn too. These people need help.'

There are many earnest websites out there dedicated to Enya and her music. 'The only thing Enya asked for in all her years as a musician is a bit of privacy, and that's the least that we fans can give her,' ends one unofficial website dedicated to her work.

But unlike many other family feuds there is a major difference to the row that blew up between Enya and Máire, Pól and Ciarán

161

in Clannad: ultimately they got over it. They got on with their lives and did not let it interfere with the family relationships that are so often damaged beyond repair in these dangerous situations.

'Tensions were created because we never answered any of the questions. If you're going to answer questions, people aren't going to believe you anyway,' contended Máire Brennan. 'The proof of the pudding is that Enya is my sister and I love her dearly and we get on really, really well. There's no way you'd get away with it in our family, anyway. She a wonderful aunt to my kids. We all go through troubled times on and off, but you get on with life, don't you?'

Pól had left Clannad many years before but in 2005 the original group got back together for the first time in fifteen years for three days of music, singing and dancing as part of the Earagail Arts Festival and to celebrate the life and times of their father Leo, their mother Baba, and the family contribution to the cultural life of Donegal, Ireland and, possibly, the world.

'Clannad, a ground-breaking group with album sales also running into millions, haven't had their full line-up on stage since around 1990. There was the lingering whiff of a row in the camp from when Enya famously left the band in the early 1980s. Despite these apparent obstacles there appeared in this year's Earagail Arts programme three events marking the Brennans' contribution to music in Donegal and well beyond,' reported *The Irish Times*.

'For star-gazers the only question was: would she or wouldn't she? Donegal, noted for a relaxed attitude to fame, just looked forward to three good nights.

'The issue of Enya's contribution was settled on the very first night – the concert by her mother Baba's choir Cór Mhuire in St Murphy's Church in Derrybeg. The programme noted simply that the five Brennan sisters – Máire (Moya), Deirdre, Enya, Olive agus Bridín – were to sing three hymns. There was no fanfare when Enya arrived up the aisle with her sisters midway through the concert. As rare superstar appearances go, they gave a new meaning to the term low-key.'

And low-key seems to be an exaggeration of the way Enya likes to keep it.

Chapter 8

Trouble at the Mill

Family gatherings such as the aftermath of a Holy Communion celebration can be dangerous occasions, as the Progressive Democrat TD for Longford Mae Sexton found out.

A child of her youngest sister Patricia made her first Holy Communion in St Mel's Cathedral and the family gathered afterwards in her sister's house in Farnagh, which stands on a hill overlooking the town of Longford.

As the night wore on the four sisters, Mae Sexton, Maureen O'Driscoll, Carmel Madden and Patricia Feeney got to talking about a piece of property their father owned in a laneway off Dublin Street in the town. It had once been the site of their father's bakery but now the family only owned a portion of the property known locally as The Shed.

For years it had been occupied by 'a close family friend' who ran a business there, but as the sisters sat around the kitchen table talking and having a drink that night concern was expressed that the tenant might eventually seek 'squatters' rights' when their father died. It was suggested that action should be taken to end the tenancy, although where the suggestion came from was to become a matter of dispute. According to Patricia Feeney this was 'Mae's notion' and that after Patricia brought up the subject of ownership of The Shed Mae 'began acting like a lunatic' and calling her 'a dangerous bitch'.

It was the beginning of a family feud that would have devastating consequences for the four daughters of Tommy Breaden and would split the family bitterly down the middle.

Tommy Breaden was a baker and property owner in the midland town. He was a short, dapper man with slicked-back hair who had his ups and downs in life. His bakery in Dublin Street, one of the main streets in the town, had once been well known, supplying most of the town of Longford with bread. Kids followed his vans shouting,

> *Breaden's bread*
> *kills a man dead,*
> *especially a man*
> *with a baldy head.*

Tommy Breaden had also been a local politician, serving for many years as a Fianna Fáil member of Longford Urban District Council, the local authority which ran the town.

The arrival of mass production and especially Pat the Baker, which was run by Pat Higgins, another local politician, in the nearby town of Granard, had closed his business and left Tommy Breaden bankrupt and badly in debt.

It was then that he became an important political ally and supporter of an up and coming young Fianna Fáil businessman called Albert Reynolds. The flashy Reynolds had made his money from dancehalls. He lived in a big house with a swimming pool on the outskirts of the town and always drove a fancy car. He had invested in local businesses, the most successful being C&D Petfoods which he eventually turned into a multimillion euro company.

Reynolds valued Breaden's knowledge of local politics and he gave him a job as a manager in his petfood factory. He also enlisted his aid as a trusted lieutenant as he began the long and torturous climb from local businessman to TD, minister and finally Taoiseach.

In the years that followed, as Albert Reynolds was off sorting out important matters like the peace process and leading the Fianna Fáil party, Tommy Breaden was back home keeping a close eye on the local constituency. As Albert Reynolds' 'man' in Longford his job was to sort out local problems and make sure what needed to be done was dealt with quickly and efficiently.

Breaden was a shrewd judge of what was going on and he wasn't afraid to tell Reynolds what needed to be done in his own back yard to keep his popularity ratings high.

When they first became friends Reynolds decided that owning his own newspaper would ensure that he could get his message across to the local electors. He bought *The Longford News*, the smaller-selling of the two newspapers in the county, from its brilliant but eccentric owner Vincent Gill.

Tommy Breaden's old bakery building was turned into the newspaper's office. It was in the draughty old bakery that the first editions of *The Longford News* under the new owner were turned out by a former circus bill-poster and hypnotist turned editor called Derek Cobbe. It was all hands to the pump in those early days with even Kathleen Reynolds, the glamorous wife of the businessman with political ambitions, helping out on the production line in the first few weeks.

At the back of the cavernous building was a laneway. If you

went up what was known as Breaden's Lane and through a gateway, you would find yourself walking through the back door of Bill Madden's pub.

In those days in the early 1970s Madden's pub was a typical local. Madden, who had once been in the army, was one of the great characters in the town. He had stools along the counter but the seating around the rest of the bar was old benches from railway carriages which he had acquired at the right price. His son Liam would one day marry Tommy Breaden's daughter Carmel.

Although Albert Reynolds eventually sold *The Longford News* newspaper Tommy Breaden had always retained a portion of the building. The Shed had an entrance on to the laneway which meandered along the back of Dublin Street.

Although of little consequence when property was cheap, it suddenly acquired quite some value with the steep rise in property prices. It also benefited when the government introduced incentives and tax breaks for urban renewal of run-down sites in the centre of many rural towns. Longford, one of the least prosperous midland towns, was one of the places which benefited greatly from this.

When Tommy Breaden retired from local politics he was succeeded in the family political dynasty in the early1990s by his daughter Mae.

According to local lore Mae Sexton, to use her married name, was very bitter about the way her father had been treated by both Albert Reynolds and Fianna Fáil. She always believed that they could have done more for him when his business got into difficulties and needed a helping hand.

'She hated Fianna Fáil,' said one local politician who knows and likes her. 'She has her own reasons and what can anyone say about that.'

So when she ran for a seat and was elected to the Longford Urban District Council in 1991 it was not for her father's party Fianna Fáil, but as an independent. The following year she ran in the general election as an independent with little success, but it was the beginning of the groundwork that would one day see her enter national politics – much to the surprise of the local political establishment.

Mae, who had watched her father for a long time, was a shrewd political operator. Within a few years she was elected the first chairwoman of Longford Urban District Council.

Her father was delighted with her success and on the night of her appointment he held a celebration dinner in the Longford Arms Hotel. Mae, married to local 'company representative' Tommy Sexton, sat at his right-hand side in the place of honour while her sisters and other members of the family were scattered around the table.

To mark the auspicious occasion he assured her at the dinner that night of his support and advice. Indeed he promised that it would be more than political advice he would give her. According to Mae Sexton, that night he promised her The Shed as a 'financial leg up' on the greasy political pole.

The Longford TD said that, of his seven children, she had an 'especially close relationship' with her father. She said it was easier for her because of her flexible schedule and their shared interest in local politics. She said that her late father tried all the time to pay her for the work she did for him in his last years, but she would never take anything.

'He decided to give me The Shed because he felt I needed the money, and the truth is I did,' she said.

But as she began to scale the political heights her father died in December 2001. The dispute with her sisters about ownership of The Shed really became a contentious issue in the family after the Holy Communion the year before. From then on things went from bad to worse.

'Since Daddy died I haven't talked to Carmel; about twice in two years,' said Mae Sexton. She said she was traumatised by the events the followed her father's death and the litigation that arose when her three sisters raised questions about her conduct regarding her father's affairs.

Because ownership of The Shed had been transferred to Mae by her father before he died it didn't appear in his will. It rankled with the sisters and they eventually launched legal proceedings against their sister Mae Sexton.

The sisters, Maureen O'Driscoll of Swords, Co Dublin, Patricia Feeney of Farnagh, Longford and Carmel Madden of Convent Road, Longford took a case under the Succession Act claiming that their late father Tommy Breaden failed in his moral duty to provide for them. Although he had given each of them bequests, they claimed The Shed was part of his estate and its value would have meant considerably more for each of his seven children.

They also sued the State Solicitor, Mark Connellan, who had drawn up the will, accusing him of failing to execute their father's will properly and leaving out a property in Co Cavan in which their father also had a financial interest.

Meanwhile Mae certainly rewarded her father's faith in her because after becoming chairwoman of the Longford Urban District Council she went on to confound the political pundits by being elected the first Progressive Democrat TD for the constituency of Longford/Roscommon in the general election of 2002.

Her election was one of those nail-biting encounters which

169

make election by proportional representation such a fascinating study. But her victory was spoiled on a personal level by the acrimony that had crept into her relationship with her three sisters.

They claimed that The Shed was only transferred to Mae as a means of terminating the long-term tenancy of the 'family friend' and should then have reverted to their father. They said their father was reluctant to ask the 'family friend' to give up his occupancy of the building and it was on this pretext that he transferred the title to his daughter. This, they said had only been a 'temporary little arrangement' – a phrase coined by Tommy Breaden's protégé Albert Reynolds to describe the coalition between Fianna Fáil and the Progressive Democrats – and that after the tenant left, the valuable property should have gone back into his estate to be divided equally among the seven children in the family when the father died.

When the case was heard in early 2006 at a sitting of the Circuit Court in Carrick-on-Shannon, Co Leitrim it was acrimonious and bitter. There were 276 documents lodged in court, including their father's detailed diaries.

Mae Sexton's barrister, Peter Bland, put it to the three complainent sisters that in the diaries he mentioned his daughter Mae more than all of the other sisters put together. But each of the sisters insisted that they were also close confidantes of their father and he made no distinction between any of them.

But after the Holy Communion night row Tommy Breaden, shrewd politician that he was, obviously anticipated the feud that would erupt in his family once he died. He wrote a final letter to his children, asking them to 'stay united' and more importantly, to help their sister Mae in her political career.

But his plea fell on deaf ears as far as Mae Sexton's three sisters were concerned. They went ahead with the bitter court case.

During the proceedings Judge Doirbhile Flanagan, who heard the evidence in the case, noted the 'level of acrimony' that existed between the warring sisters. At one point in the hearing she instructed the barristers for the two sides to 'keep the levels down in your spirited attacks on each other'.

Peter Bland accused Carmel's husband Liam Madden of being the prime motivator in the action against his sister-in-law.

'You take joy in litigation, don't you Mr Madden?'

Madden, an architect whose business is called Vitruvius Hibernicus after the famous architectural book by James Gandon, denied this. Although he had been involved in planning disputes, they had been professional encounters, he explained. Among these was a 'third party' appeal against the change of use of The Shed in Breaden's Lane from a store to a museum and offices.

Planning for the development was given by Longford Urban District Council in December 2001 – at the time Tommy Breaden died – and although the matter was appealed to An Bord Pleanála his appeal was dismissed and planning permission granted.

In court Mae Sexton's brother Jude backed up her version of events, saying that their father had promised her The Shed at the dinner. He said he had no interest in the family feud until he was told that the matter was going to be heard in open court.

'It was then that I felt it was my duty to come . . . a great injustice was being done,' he said in evidence. Another brother George did not attend the proceedings but the court was told that he was 'disgusted' that three of his sisters would embark on legal actions against the fourth.

In the end the judge decided that Mae Sexton was the rightful owner of The Shed but he gave costs in favour of her sisters.

Politicians are rarely stuck for words but when Mae Sexton

was asked about the effect of the court case on her life she said she was still so upset that she couldn't talk about it. It has hurt her deeply and divided her family to such an extent that she is just overcome when she thinks of it.

'I won,' she says, 'but it doesn't seem to matter all that much any more.'

◆ ◆ ◆ ◆

When an upmarket house auction took place a few years ago at Slane Castle, the seat of Lord Henry Mountcharles in Co Meath, it appeared on the surface that this was just another contents dispersal as the landed gentry tried to raise some hard cash to keep their vast estates ticking over for a few more years. But behind the sale of a rare private collection of 900 items of art, antiques and other family heirlooms accumulated over the centuries at Tempo Manor in Co Fermanagh, lay a bitter feud between Sir John Langham, sixteenth baronet of Castlebrooke and his mother the Dowager Lady Marion Langham, to give her her full title.

Tempo Manor is built on the site of an old castle of the Maguires and its 300-acre estate, where it is reputed that Maria Edgeworth set the first great novel in the English language *Castle Rackrent,* has been the ancestral home of the Langhams and their forbears for generations.

Ironically, the family estates survived war and strife for centuries only to descend into a bitter family feud just as peace was settling on the area once described as 'the dreary spires of Fermanagh' by Winston Churchill, who was a visitor to the manor.

The bitterness between the Langhams, mother and son, could be traced some believe to a row over the use of a large glasshouse in the grounds of the estate, but whatever provoked it the feelings certainly ran deep.

The seeds of the dispute that would lead to the dispersal of Tempo's grand contents went back more than a dozen years before the auction when Sir James Langham bequeathed Tempo Manor to his son John, while he was still alive, in order to avoid death duties.

In the same arrangement he left the contents of the house to his estranged wife Lady Marion. Although they were separated for many years at the time, they never divorced and he believed it was a fair division of his legacy.

Even before her husband died Lady Marion removed half the contents, antique mirrors, paintings, family portraits and brick-a-brack, to a house she had built on the estate, filling it from floor to ceiling with valuable artefacts.

During Sir James's lifetime relations between mother and son were tolerable, but when he died the will became a serious matter of contention between the two. Sir John duly inherited the title and his mother, Lady Marion, the contents of the house.

After the funeral it was all downhill for the Langhams as the family feud got fully into its stride.

In May 2004 Lady Marion returned to the manor and took the remaining contents leaving her son with just one possession in the big empty house – a portrait of his ancestor Sir John Langham, the first baronet, the adventurer who started the ancient dynasty. It hung over the chimney piece in the drawing room like an affront to the family honour.

The Dowager Lady Marion then announced that the treasure trove of family heirlooms would be sold at a day auction in Slane Castle, Co Meath the following September.

'It's a criminal thing to do and I really think it's out of spite that my mother decided to sell,' complained Sir John.

'My relationship with my mother has never been good since the time I got married,' he added. 'When my grandmother died she removed half the contents of the house. I offered her £500,000 for the remaining contents, but she declined because she wanted more money,' he said.

The bitterness really set in in the days leading up to the sale with Sir John vowing never to speak to his mother again.

'People might say that they are just things and that we should let them go but some things are historically important. It's a criminal thing to do. I will never forgive my mother for what she has done and I have kept all the inventories to make sure that future generations know exactly what happened.

'These things are more important to us than to anyone else and now it will be near impossible to get everything back together again,' he said before the sale.

When the new lord of the manor saw the prices his family treasures sold for he realised how modest a value he had put on them – there wasn't a hope in hell of ever getting the family silver back under the roof of Tempo Manor again.

Lady Langham denied that the sale was to finance her exotic travels with a new boyfriend.

'I do go around the world, but it's for work and business pays for it. The rest is my business,' she said haughtily.

She also defended her right to sell her own property, even if it was part of a collection that once adorned one of the most important and historical houses in the country.

'The sale is wrong, I know, but it's not my doing. I think he's like a naughty boy in his pram throwing out his toys because he's cross with mummy. He behaved stupidly and he should be more dignified and not say anything. All he's done for me is to get me more publicity. Bad publicity is still publicity.

'I am not ashamed of what I have done . . . I'm very pragmatic about things. If he doesn't talk to me, he doesn't. Life goes on. If you think about it, I first had a child who was born with brain damage. Then my other son broke his neck. And I still continued to live my life. You have to deal with the lot that's thrown at you. It's really his loss, not mine, and I continue to live my life and do my work.'

Although they both sat in the auction room at Slane Castle, in Co Meath, it was at different sides of the hall.

'John isn't having anything to do with me. It's very sad, I think you can get on better in life by actually talking,' said Lady Langham on the day of the auction, after they walked by each other without a word or a sideways glance.

She watched the bidding and witnessed her son trying to buy back paintings, furniture and historical items that had adorned the home he had lived in since he was a mere child.

But the sad part for Sir John Langham was that he just didn't have the money to hold on to much of the collection that came from his house.

'I bought a dozen of the family portraits back,' he said, 'most of them were more recent ones. I couldn't afford the early ones. It's very sad. Seeing your relatives going out in bubble wrap isn't particularly nice and now that they've been dispersed all over the place they'll never be brought together again.'

Following the sale Lady Marion Langham issued a brief statement.

'This sale marks the end of a sad chapter in the Langham family history and I very much hope that we can now move forward.'

Her son still wasn't impressed. She had more than a million in the bank while he was left with a great big empty house and a few family portraits rescued from his mother's fire sale.

◆　◆　◆　◆

It's hard to believe there could be so much blood, sweat and tears over Aran sweaters. But when it comes to family feuds they don't come much more intriguing and complicated than the many squabbles of the Kelleher family, owners of the multimillion conglomerate that started out as a simple knitwear shop beside Blarney Castle in north Cork.

Christy Kelleher, patriarch of the clan, had a simple but brilliant idea: sell Aran sweaters, Donegal tweed, Waterford Glass and other Irish goods to the thousands of Americans and other tourists who came each year to kiss the Blarney Stone at the famous castle, built in the fourteenth century by the McCarthys of Muskerry.

Christy Kelleher had the gift of the gab and a gift for business as well. Looking at the coachloads of tourists with nothing much to buy after leaving Killarney he decided to attract them to his new store by giving any coach drivers who stopped outside his store a ten per cent cut of what their clients bought while they were inside. It wasn't long before every tourist bus and coach passing through Munster was diverting to the Blarney Woollen Mills store.

Opened in 1966, it had a turnover of millions by the time Christy died in 1979 and handed it over to his large family and their spouses. But as the business grew so did the enmity within the family so that more than a decade later various members of the Kelleher family have turned up in the High Court in Dublin to take an action against one or other members of the family.

Christy Kelleher's seven children, Frank, Pat, Catherine (Freda), Marian, Kevin, Bernadette and Christy all went into their father's business. Apart from Christy Jr, they would all end up in some sort of family squabble in the years that followed.

Freda Hayes, the eldest of the Kelleher girls, became managing director in 1979 after her father's death and the hardworking family extended into Dublin, Cork, Killarney and other tourist locations bringing their brand of quality Irish produce for sale.

In time some of their spouses also joined the company, particularly Michael O'Gorman who was married to Marian Kelleher and Esther who was married to Frank Kelleher.

They took over another thriving tourist enterprise, Kilkenny Design, which had been a semi-state company. It had been doing very good business but losing money because of the way it was structured and its lack of commercial focus.

They also extended the empire with two hotels in the Blarney area, buying up a knitwear company, Donegal Knitwear, and launching the Club Tricot brand.

Then in 1993, after fourteen years at the helm, there was a boardroom coup against Freda. Amid considerable family acrimony, she left the company.

But Freda, a tough and astute businesswoman, didn't waste much time. Using the finances from the settlements and her intimate knowledge of the tourist business, she set up her own homeware company, Meadows & Byrne, in direct competition with the rest of the family in Blarney Woollen Mills and Kilkenny Design.

She eventually ended up with seven stores dotted around the

country – the flagship in Nassau Street, Dublin, just a stone's throw from the family firm.

Marian took over from her older sister and ran the company. During the next five years she doubled profits at the Blarney Woollen Mills and by 1998 turnover had increased to IR£46 million, a huge jump in sales for the various brands.

But then trouble erupted in the family again. This time three of the brothers wanted to get rid of fellow director Michael O'Gorman – Marian's husband. O'Gorman took a High Court injunction against them to stop himself being removed as a director and claimed that the next move would be to get rid of his wife.

Marian was joined by her sister Bernadette Nolan in the dispute, so the two sisters were now pitted against their three brothers, Pat, Frank and Kevin. The fourth brother, Christy, was not involved in any litigation or family feud.

The sisters then went to the High Court to block their sister-in-law Esther being brought onto the board to replace Michael O'Gorman.

The litigation was bitter and threatened to be prolonged until lawyers arrived at a settlement to split up the assets of Blarney Woollen Mills.

'The family rows over the management of the business made headlines a year ago this week but the seeds of the company's re-organisation were sown long before that,' said a report in the *Irish Examiner*. 'At the heart of the debacle is the competition for control of the board of directors at the County Cork company founded by the disputing siblings' late father, Christy Kelleher.

'One of the first signs of internal difficulties at the Blarney dynasty was the resignation of Freda Hayes as chief executive in

1993. Her departure was believed to be decided on after a series of disagreements.'

None of the family was prepared to say whether these were personal issues or if they related to the direction of the business and control of the growing number of companies within the Blarney Woollen Mills empire.

With Freda Hayes banished and running her own business, Meadows & Byrne, the remaining members of the family had to decide how to patch up their differences. In the end they agreed to split the company in two.

The remaining sisters, Marian O'Gorman and Bernadette Nolan, got the now profitable Kilkenny Design arm of the business with shops in Dublin and Kilkenny. The Blarney Woollen Mills side of the business, including a number of hotels, went to the brothers, Pat, Frank and Kevin.

Then, in a manoeuvre that nobody expected, Freda Hayes and her Meadows & Byrne chain made peace with her brothers and Blarney Woollen Mills in 2000. The two companies merged and she was appointed chairman, retaking her position at the helm of her father's empire.

One might think all this business infighting was enough for one family, but the disputes were not over yet.

In 2005 the Blarney Woollen Mills company was 'taken private' and re-registered in the British Virgin Islands so that it no longer had to make financial or other information public. The secretive Kelleher family, who resented much of the press coverage of the various family business disputes, always refused to make a public comment on their tangled internal affairs.

'As a private company we will be entitled to keep that [financial] information private,' said the chief financial officer of the multimillion euro business.

But they couldn't keep the lid on the disputes. In 2005 the warring Kellehers were back in the High Court with brother Kevin Kelleher taking out yet another injunction, this time against the Blarney Woollen Mills company to stop them terminating a concession licence agreement under which he operated in the Blarney Woollen Mills complex in Cork and seeking damages for breach of contract.

Kevin Kelleher's personal company Kellmorr Ltd operated a licensing agreement with Blarney Woollen Mills. Mr Kelleher admitted that he had been forced to reorganise and restructure his business. Then Blarney Woollen Mills sent him a letter serving notice of the group's intention to terminate the concession licence. Kelleher had outsourced manufacturing operations which had previously been carried out at the Blarney complex. However he successfully argued in court that the group's plans to terminate the licence agreement was, 'An opportunistic attempt to exploit a clause in the licence agreement about insolvent trading.'

In the end the matter was settled between the family and the Kellehers have got back to the various very profitable business ventures and avoided the litigation that made them one of the most talked about business families in the country.

Sometimes family disputes don't have all that much to do with money. Sometimes it's strictly personal, as when one sister steals another sister's boyfriend and then marries him.

The macabre case of the Parrott sisters in the nineteenth century is a classic case of obsession and a determination to exact revenge.

Angelica and Rosaleen Parrott lived at Shalardstown House near the Tipperary village of Clogheen. The suicide of their mother followed shortly afterwards by the death of their father Cadogan Parrott, may have slightly unhinged the sisters, but Angelica decided that no matter what the cost she would have revenge when her lover Dagan Ferritter left her for her sister Rosaleen, and married her in 1837.

As the elder daughter, Angelica had inherited the house and estate so after the marriage she closed up the house and went abroad where she met and fell in love with Count Nicholas Orloff. They were married in Russia and went to live in Paris. But there her ill-luck continued: her husband caught a chill and died.

Dressed in widow's black Countess Orloff returned to Shalardstown House, sacked all the servants but one, an old retainer called Creed, and lived as a recluse, never leaving the house and never inviting visitors to come to it.

Meanwhile her sister Rosaleen and her husband Dagan Ferritter had fallen on hard times. They lived in a small cabin outside the walls of the big house, but were not allowed in through the gates. Countess Orloff had given them a small allowance but she was determined that they would live out much of their lives in poverty and unhappiness.

Years passed as the younger sister waited for the countess to die so that she could get her share of the inheritance.

Then Angelica began a strange daily ritual. Each day at exactly three o'clock Countess Orloff's coach would drive out the gates of Shalardstown and tour the countryside for precisely one hour. Of course the curtains were drawn so nobody could see inside, but the daily ritual was as regular as clockwork and hanging from the carriage window was a jewel-encrusted riding whip, a wedding present from the count, which she always carried.

Years after this ritual began some locals in the tavern began to ridicule Dagan Ferritter about his lost inheritance. They told him he wasn't a man at all that he didn't confront his sister-in-law and demand to be treated properly. Goaded into action and backed up by some of the tavern crowd he marched up to the front door of the great house and demanded to see the aloof and reclusive Countess Orloff, as she had styled herself.

Creed, the old retainer, said she wasn't in. Pressured by the mob he finally broke down and told them an incredible story. The countess had been dead for eleven years, he said. On her instructions he had had her body embalmed and he had driven the corpse out each day in the carriage for eleven years to keep up the impression that she was still alive. It was all done to keep her younger sister Rosaleen and the lover who had spurned her from getting their hands on the wealth of Shalardstown House.

She knew that her death would leave the way open for them to get the inheritance so she spent her final year inventing the ritual that would keep up the pretence that she was alive.

The couple moved out of their cabin and into the big house. They even complied with a wish expressed in Countess Orloff's final letter that the trademark riding whip should be placed in a glass case in the hallway of the house.

The new master and mistress of Shalardstown didn't have much time to enjoy their inheritance, however. Within a year both were dead and locals believed from that moment on that the house was haunted by the ghost of the bitter and vengeful Angelica Parrott.

You always knew that the Gallagher brothers would work hard, play hard and, to quote one of their sons, fight like tinkers.

'It was all family . . . the punch-ups and fighting like gypsies and thieves,' says Peter Gallagher about his father and uncles.

They were hard Sligo men who started life with McAlpine's Fusiliers and ended up running a multimillion euro conglomerate that built houses in England and Ireland, developed land and owned various businesses that ranged from manufacturing locks to timber processing.

They might have driven around in Rolls Royce cars and lived in mansions but all bar one stayed true to their roots as Irish navvies until the end.

For the Gallaghers it was a mixture of national pride and making money. They were intensely loyal to their Irish roots and wanted to bring prosperity and jobs to the West which they had been forced to leave after a basic education because there was no work for them. But they also had a huge appetite for making money and using their political connections in the pursuit of a fast buck.

Few families have turned out such a group of colourful characters and the brothers' outing at the annual general meeting of the construction firm became the great yearly brawl of the business calendar as they aired their family dispute in public.

At any one time most of the brothers would be directors of the firm, but there was always one who had been turfed out and wanted to make mischief from the outside.

'The acrimony was vehement and public,' remembers one shareholder. 'The shareholders' meetings in the Shelbourne Hotel amounted to little more than slanging matches between Charles on the floor and his other brothers at the table.'

But the very public displays of family bitterness were also marked by private feuds, some of which were settled in the old-fashioned way.

'They were tough men. Charles did hit Pat – he said something so my father smacked him in the mouth. He was eating sausages for a week afterwards,' remembers Peter Gallagher about his father Charles and one of his uncles after a dispute flared up between them.

'It was the outsiders who really stirred it up; if they were left alone the brothers would have sorted it out among themselves, but it got very dirty in the end.'

There were seven brothers out of the fourteen Gallagher children who were born on a small farm near Moylough, Co Sligo. Pat Gallagher was the eldest of the brothers and after a very basic education he emigrated as a teenager and started working on the buildings in England in the hungry years of the Economic War. His brothers Matt, James, Hubert, Joe and Dan all followed in quick succession.

James, who became better known in later life as a Fianna Fáil TD, remembered leaving school at fourteen to work as a grocer's assistant in Ballaghadereen, Co Roscommon. At the age of nineteen he moved to Liverpool to join his brothers who were building bomb shelters and supplying materials for government construction contracts during the turbulent years of the Second World War.

'The Gallaghers made a fortune in wartime Britain,' says the writer and historian Ryle Dwyer. 'One of the brothers was deaf and the others used him to avoid conscription. When any of them were called up for military service the deaf brother would report for induction using the specific brother's name. Being deaf he was naturally rejected and nobody outside the family was any the wiser.'

As the war progressed and the contracts got bigger the Gallaghers gradually moved up the pecking order until they moved from Liverpool to London to form a myriad of Gallagher family firms.

They sent home money so that their younger brother Charles could get a good education in St Nathy's College in Ballaghadereen and do a degree in engineering in Trinity College Dublin – a far cry from the national school education the older members of the family received.

Charles said he had no memory of ever meeting his brother Matt until he was twenty years of age and Matt came home from England for a visit.

In 1947 Charles followed his brothers to England and joined the family firm, the Gallagher Group which had been founded by Matt. By now the Gallaghers were prospering in the post-war British economy, building houses, buying up land and beginning to carve out a niche for themselves in the tough unforgiving construction sector.

But Matt Gallagher considered himself a patriot and when the Irish Republic was declared in 1949 he was determined to go home and become a pioneer of the new Ireland.

He came back to Dublin and became a founder member of the Fianna Fáil organisation called Taca. Known as 'the men in the mohair suits' the members of Taca were wealthy businessmen, and particularly builders like himself, who would provide the financial muscle for Fianna Fáil. In return they would gain government contracts and have access to the corridors of power.

It was a neat arrangement for both sides, but eventually it would lead to the whiff of corruption that afflicted Fianna Fáil and led to all those tribunals that have given the party such a bad name.

Although he had founded the Gallagher Group, when he came back to Ireland Matt Gallagher cut his links with his brothers and went out on his own. He became a major player in the Irish property market and built an empire which his wayward son Patrick would eventually bring crashing down around him and who would end up in jail in Northern Ireland for his troubles. But all that would come later.

(Matt Gallagher remained aloof from the feuding among his brothers. His legacy to the Irish people was the Royal Hibernian Academy which he built at Ely Place in the centre of Dublin on the site of Oliver St John Gogarty's house and part of George Moore's garden. The original building was burnt down in 1916. He started building it in 1960, but it was still incomplete when he died in 1974 and the family finally finished it off in 1987, handing it over to the state as his memorial.)

James, who was the biggest shareholder in the family business, also returned to Ireland and became a Fianna Fáil TD for Sligo in 1961. It was the enmity between him and his youngest brother Charles which would lead to the destructive episodes that characterised the family gatherings. James and Charles never saw eye to eye in business or politics, although ironically both of them hero-worshipped their brother Matt.

In 1973 the Gallagher brothers had a number of construction companies between them. They gathered in Allied Irish Investment Bank in College Green to announce the flotation of their various interests in a new public company to be called Abbey Limited. Charles Gallagher, aged forty-six at the time, was appointed the managing director of the new company.

He moved back to Ireland and bought himself an imposing home called Inchacappa House near Ashford, Co Wicklow and settled down to run the business. He was the overall boss with responsibility for construction in both Ireland and Britain.

Meanwhile James gave up politics to concentrate on building up the business. He was to look after the non-building interests, which included timber processing, building supply firms and a lock manufacturing company.

Charles was a pragmatic businessman. After two years of hard slog as chairman of the group he realised that they were effectively running a company with two arms, an English arm and an Irish arm. He was running the profitable house-building business in England, but his brother James was losing money in Irish ventures that seemed to have been opened for political rather than business reasons. They were valuable assets to the local communities in the West – but they were losing money for the company.

A close look at the balance sheet told Charles that the Irish arm was costing the company a fortune but when he tried to persuade his brothers James and Patrick to close some of the loss-making Irish operations they stymied his every move.

He got fed up with it and in 1975 he resigned as managing director and returned to England to concentrate on the building and development business there.

His brothers were so annoyed that they booted him off the board of Abbey altogether.

After heated exchanges he held on to his shareholding in Abbey but he started up a rival house-building company called Matthew Homes, named after his adored older brother.

The contrast between the Irish and English branches of the family could hardly have been more different. James Gallagher was a tough Republican who returned to politics and was re-elected to the Dáil in 1977, calling for the repeal of the Offences Against the State Act which was used by Jack Lynch's government to crack down on IRA terrorism. It was such an extreme position that his running mate Ray McSharry disassociated himself from it.

In contrast, Charles joined the Conservative Party in Britain and as a construction magnate was on friendly terms with the upcoming leader of the party, Margaret Thatcher.

With the success of Matthew Homes, Charles Gallagher began to prosper in the same proportion that Abbey began to decline. The company's annual meeting descended into chaos, with the brothers shouting and abusing each other and even getting down to fisticuffs.

'The reasons for the share price decline were two-fold,' wrote one business analyst. 'The company's Irish interests were weak and the brothers fought – with an intensity that only families are capable of.'

It was an astute observation. The poor shareholders watching from the wings could only throw up their hands in horror at the activities of the warring Gallaghers.

Then James Gallagher died suddenly at the age of sixty-three in Cyprus where he had business interests. His brother Patrick, now in his seventies became chairman. But things just could not continue as they were.

In 1985, a decade after he was booted out, Charles Gallagher was reappointed to the board of Abbey and became chairman with the support of James's two sons – Seamus, who was involved in the family business, and Donal who was a barrister.

Old Pat Gallagher could not bear to have his brother back in charge of the family firm and he opposed the new regime. But he was out-voted at board level and after he was defeated he was thrown off the board himself.

Bitter and disillusioned he joined forces with another

construction company, the British firm French Kier, to launch a hostile bid to wrest control of Abbey from his brother Charles.

After an acrimonious bidding war the attempt failed and Patrick Gallagher sold his shares in Abbey. Charles Gallagher was now the undisputed leader of the clan.

'You just sort of stood there and listened to them – nobody had the intelligence to sort of stand up and say, let's bring this to a halt,' said Charles's son Peter Gallagher of the family feud.

Though his father and uncles may have 'fought like tinkers', he and his cousins all got on very well together, he said.

When Charles Gallagher died, his son Charles became the chairman of what is now Abbey plc. Charles is very much of the English branch of the family and is based outside London although the company is listed on the Irish stock exchange.

At one AGM he made reference to his opposition to monetary union (the introduction of the euro) taking a very Conservative position and saying that it was likely to force Europe into recession. He was wrong, of course – the opposite happened. But luckily he had retained the company's land bank in Ireland and so he was able to avail of the construction boom that has continued unabated in Ireland for the last decade.

While he runs the company from England, his younger brother Peter sits in his elegant home near Enniskerry outside Dublin playing down the family feud that once consumed the Gallagher brothers. But Peter does wonder why he has never been asked to join the board of Abbey himself.

Maybe there is a second generation feud waiting to flare in the Gallagher family to bring a bit of life back to the dull world of bricks and mortar.

◆ ◆ ◆ ◆

Money doesn't always buy happiness, according to the old saying. In the case of the O'Flynn family it pitted a once happy and united family against one another in an intriguing planning dispute that had its origins in the old family home.

Kilcrea is located in 'the fertile valley of the River Bride about fifteen kilometres west of Cork city' and a short distance from the picturesque village of Aherla. It is good tillage farming country, 'well wooded with short ribbons of bungalows and houses' on the small rural roads that criss-cross the fields and hedgerows.

This is an ancient place with Kilcrea Abbey on one side and the ruined Norman tower-house Kilcrea Castle nearby. It is also where the O'Flynn family farmed a substantial and profitable holding.

When Michael O'Flynn and his brother John left the family farm and moved to Cork city they went into the construction business. They had their good times and bad, but by the 1990s they were emerging as the biggest developers in Cork and among the wealthiest businessmen in Ireland.

Michael O'Flynn liked to stay well away from the limelight and it was only when he emerged as a major international player in the property business that people began to take an interest in his affairs.

As well as building huge swathes of suburban Cork, O'Flynn became a substantial investor in property in both Ireland and England. In one major deal his investment company, Tiger Developments, spent €485 million on property portfolios along with the investment arm of Goodbody stockbrokers.

Michael O'Flynn and his wife Joan decided to build themselves a mansion befitting a construction magnate and they could think of no better place to locate this grand new home than at Kilcrea, among the rolling acres where Michael had grown up.

They already had a large house in the area, but they went to his parents who had 'a large holding' at Kilcrea and bought a ninety-acre portion of the family farm to build their new home.

But this was to be no ordinary house. 'The proposed development consists of the formation of a serpentine avenue leading from the minor road to an east-facing, two-storey, nine-bay breakfront house in a mid-nineteenth century neo-classical style,' said the planners' report. The O'Flynns were building themselves a 10,000 square foot mansion (890 square metres) in the style of the great Palladian mansion built by the ascendancy in previous centuries.

'The west front has projecting wings that partially enclose a parking court for ten cars,' wrote the planner, John O'Donnell. 'One of the wings contains, at first-floor level, a small office and apartment.' There was also a 'comprehensive landscape master plan' to enclose the house in trees, leaving it open 'to a prospect from the east front'.

There was only one fly in the ointment. Across the fields lived Michael O'Flynn's brother Larry, his wife Eileen and their sons Martin and Adrian. They didn't like the idea of a huge mansion going up beside them and dwarfing the other houses in the area.

When plans for Michael and Joan O'Flynn's dream house were lodged, an objection was received from Eileen O'Flynn, their sister-in-law.

However, the plan was given the go ahead by Cork County Council (with twenty conditions) so they objected to the national planning authority An Bord Pleanála. Larry did not join his wife in this objection or appeal, but he did enter his own 'observation' which in effect opposed his brother's grand design.

The observation and the objection from Larry O'Flynn and his wife Eileen claimed that his brother did not have any 'housing need', that the grand entrance would 'invade their peace and privacy', that it would have a negative impact on the area and that it would 'dwarf and devalue' their own property.

They also claimed that it was out of scale with the area and would destroy the rural nature of the place and worse still it would be an 'eyesore' from the local historic monument Kilcrea Abbey which is open to visitors and tourists.

They proposed a new entrance, but Michael O'Flynn argued that it would split his ninety-acre farm in two 'and possibly make headlights more visible' from the road as he sat in his new drawing room.

Of course Michael O'Flynn said he had a need to live in a house – and a man of his wealth and standing needed a big house at that. He also said that it was not located within an area of scenic significance and that with the different levels in the hilly rural terrain it would 'not impact on the historic monuments' in the area.

'The design and landscaping in the proposed development have due regard to the rural context,' he argued.

'The applicants' proposal is a grand project which should be considered on its merits,' said the inspector for An Bord Pleanála, John O'Donnell. After outlining a number of defects in the submission he felt that while Michael O'Flynn was a local he already had a substantial house in the area and didn't need to build a new mansion for himself and his family. In his decision of June 2004 the planning inspector recommended that Michael O'Flynn's grand design should be turned down.

However his view was not endorsed by the planning appeals board and Michael O'Flynn got permission to go ahead with his mansion providing he met certain conditions regarding the landscaping of the area.

'An Bord Pleanála has overruled a decision by its own inspector and granted Mr O'Flynn permission to build the mansion, which will be one of the largest private residences ever built in Co Cork,' said the report in the *Irish Examiner*.

Among the conditions laid down was that the new O'Flynn mansion should be occupied by the family 'or their immediate heirs' for seven years and that they should abide by the landscaping plan submitted and agreed by the planning authority.

The house was built and it seemed that was the end of the story and the bitter family feud that had engulfed the O'Flynns for several years.

Far from it.

Larry and Eileen O'Flynn believed Michael and Joan O'Flynn had not complied with the landscaping conditions imposed. They brought a civil case against them to Cork Circuit Court where it was due to be heard by Judge Patrick Moran.

Before Judge Moran could hear the evidence Michael O'Flynn dropped a bombshell. 'Cork multimillionaire Michael O'Flynn has made an application to Judge Moran seeking not to have the judge hear the planning case because of what he claims is a perception of bias,' wrote Ralph Riegel who covered the case.

The claim of bias arose because Michael O'Flynn's construction company had been fined €200,000 by Judge Moran in another court case arising from the death of a nine-year-old boy who had been playing on one of the construction company's building sites.

As a result of his judgement in that case O'Flynn objected to the same judge hearing the family 'planning wrangle' under Section 160 of the Planning Act, brought against him by his brother and his brother's family.

The property developer's counsel Mr Sean Lynch BL stressed that his client was concerned about 'the perception of bias' rather than anything he felt the judge had done wrong. However Judge Moran believed that the property magnate had 'not been very fair' to him in papers submitted to the court. In seventeen years on the bench as a judge he had never before faced a suggestion of bias, he said.

'The tenor of the affidavit [by Mr Michael O'Flynn] is one of, shall we say, not very fair to the person at the receiving end of it – that is myself,' said the slightly miffed judge.

The judge will shortly make a decision as to whether he will or will not hear the planning dispute involving the two O'Flynn families.

Chapter 9

Old Lover

Father Conmee, walking, thought of his little book *Old Times in the Barony* and of the book that might be written about jesuit houses and of Mary Rochfort, daughter of lord Molesworth, first countess of Belvedere.

A listless lady, no more young, walked alone the shore of lough Ennel, Mary, first countess of Belvedere, listlessly walking in the evening, not startled when an otter plunged. Who could know the truth? Not the jealous lord Belvedere and not her confessor if she had not committed adultery fully, *eiaculatio seminis inter vas naturale mulieris*, with her husband's brother? She would half confess if she had not all sinned as women did. Only God knew and she and he, her husband's brother.

From *Ulysses* by James Joyce.

All that remains today are a few stone steps that led to the grand front entrance of Dunboden Park a once magnificent house which was forever marked by the evil of the man who owned it, Robert Rochfort, the first Earl of Belvedere.

These last reminders of Dunboden Park lie deep in the heart of the Irish midlands, not perhaps the most romantic setting for a well-remembered love affair that turned to savage retribution and tragedy, but in the manner of his time Robert Rochfort's father, George, carved a great romantic house from amid the soggy land on the edge of the great Bog of Allen.

Now a stud farm, its high walls, well kept and mended, run ribbon-like for several miles enclosing Dunboden and its mysteries even to this day. Through tall thick beech trees you can see a ruined gate lodge and the walled garden, but the house is long gone, leaving only the story of the cruel Lord Belvedere and the infidelity of his beautiful wife, Mary.

The Rochfort family settled on these lands after the Battle of the Boyne when the victorious King William rewarded his generals with parcels of land for their services in putting his rival King James to flight and subduing the papist Irish.

Out of this flat plain at Gaulstown, which is near the modern village of Rochfortbridge in Co Westmeath, George Rochfort carved out his own Anglo-Irish dream. He erected a grand house, 'two storey over basement with a five bay front and side election, porch with engaged columns, entablatures over windows', according to the great architectural historian Mark Bence-Jones.

He built the high walls to enclose his grand estate. He planted thousands of oak and beech trees to hide his great house from the prying eyes of the half-starved peasantry. He laid out formal gardens where peacocks strutted, and built ornamental canals for boating with the important visitors who came from London, Dublin and the other great outposts of the empire to pay homage to his wealth, power and influence.

In Gaulstown George Rochfort created his own little bit of the great empire that his sovereign was beginning to assemble around the world. He owned thousands of acres of good land stretching from Rochfortbridge down to the shores of Lough Ennel near Mullingar.

In a generation George Rochfort's three sons would spread out from Dunboden, building a series of great houses at a time of great poverty and deprivation in Ireland. As was the custom the eldest son, Robert, was given Dunboden. The second son, Arthur, got Bellfield, another great estate which is marked today by a ruined gate lodge and the remains of an old walled garden. The third son, George, built a house called Rochfort and later renamed it Tudenham. The ruined hulk of the house still stands by the lakeshore outside Mullingar.

Robert married young but his wife soon died. Then he set his eyes on the beautiful sixteen-year-old daughter of Richard Molesworth of Dublin.

One of the great advantages of living where he did was that he had a great house and estate for entertaining the nobility in grand style, but he was within easy striking distance of Dublin, parliament and the fashionable set who were at the height of their powers, building the grand squares of Georgian Dublin.

Rochfort, described as a 'handsome rogue' according to accounts of the day, had a keen eye for the ladies and it was at a ball in Dublin that he first set eyes on Mary Molesworth, eldest daughter of the prolific third Viscount.

Richard Molesworth had been the King's Ambassador at the Court of Denmark and had inherited several thousand acres of land in Co Meath. He was a war hero who had been ADC to the Duke of Marlborough at the Battle of Ramillies and had saved Marlborough's life during this bloody encounter with the French.

After his service to the crown he retired to Ireland where he lived a fine life, drinking and carousing, fathering bastards and giving his name to a once elegant little street that carries it to this day.

He was also a financial speculator and he lost most of his family fortune in the notorious South Sea Bubble, an investment mania akin to the dot.com drama of the late 1990s. Lord Molesworth, who would officially father ten children (nine daughters and a son) by his two wives, was in rather impecunious circumstances when his beautiful young daughter, Mary, married Robert Rochfort on August 1, 1736.

Rochfort loved her, according to accounts, but he was a cruel and passionate man. In quick succession the young bride had four children. Jane, the first-born, was a huge disappointment to the ambitious Rochfort, who wanted a son and heir at the first attempt.

He soon succeeded, however; his second child he christened in his own name, Robert. He asked his good friend, King George II to stand as his godfather.

Although the king did not travel to Dunboden for the ceremony he did his friend the honour of accepting the invitation and dispatched one of his trusty court favourites to stand as proxy.

As well as his mansion at Dunboden, Rochfort then began building a beautiful Italianate mansion called Belvedere – Beautiful House. It was surprisingly small but stunning in the architectural detail such as ceilings and plasterwork and built less then ten miles from his family seat, the grand but plain-looking Dunboden. Belvedere was to be his fishing lodge where he could escape from the cares of office and bring his mistresses. The house stands on a hill looking out over Lough Ennell, much appreciated for its natural beauty at the time.

But in currying favour with King George II at his court in London and making himself the centre of attention for the ladies, Rochfort had been neglecting his wife. In the evenings her carriage used to leave Dunboden and drive along the rutted road to Bellfield, the home of her husband's brother, Arthur, about three miles away. With Robert far away in London it wasn't long before these visits turned to love and Mary began a passionate affair with Arthur.

Everything was fine as long as her husband remained at the court of St James where he was much in demand and could rub shoulders with more important people. A fashionable figure in London, he took a string of mistresses and as the Member of Parliament for the 'rotten borough' of Westmeath was a man of importance and standing.

But Rochfort, a naturally suspicious man, would on occasion suddenly return to Dunboden 'to chastise everyone about him' according to contemporary reports. He was not foolish and he realised that it was from his estates that he derived the income which allowed him to live the high life in Dublin and London. He was careful enough to make sure that his estates were properly run and his tenants were paying their rents. He had spies and informers to make sure he was well versed in what was going on.

And so in time he learned of the affair between his wife and his brother.

'At the last post several letters from Ireland began an account of a most unhappy affair that lately passed in Dublin,' wrote an old gossip John Percival, Lord Edgemont in his diaries. 'Robert Rochfort of that kingdom, who some years ago married a daughter of Richard Viscount Molesworth for love, she being very handsome though no fortune, and used her in the tenderest manner, was privately informed that she cohabited unlawfully with his younger brother. Upon which he put the question to her and she with much consummate impudence admitted the fact, adding that her last child was with him and that she had no pleasure with any man like that she had with him.'

Loose morals were not uncommon in Georgian Ireland but for a wife to admit that she was having an affair with her husband's brother and that the brother was the father of her last child was quite unusual.

Mary, not yet thirty, and Arthur were lucky to escape with their lives.

'My lord thereupon locked her up . . . and in his rage took a charged pistol with him with the intention to find his brother and shoot him, but that very night he (Arthur) went on board a ship and sailed to England where he now lives concealed if not fled abroad,' according to Edgemont.

Robert Rochfort was a powerful enemy and was determined to have his revenge on his brother and his wife.

'He then went to Lord Molesworth and telling him his unfortunate case, asked his advice what he should do. My Lord (Molesworth) replied that he might do what he pleased; that having committed such a crime as incest and confess it, he should have no concern about Mary because she was only his bastard by his wife before he married her. Rochfort resolved to be divorced, is now prosecuting her as an adulteress. We are told that when separated she will be transported to the West Indies as a vagabond.'

But fate intervened to save Mary Molesworth from white slavery. King George II decided to reward Rochfort for his services to the crown and made him Viscount Bellfield. Knowing that a case for 'criminal conversation' against his brother (up to quite recently a man could sue his wife's lover for damages) would lead to a huge scandal and the public humiliation that his wife and brother were having an affair, he decided to drop the case and the divorce proceedings that he intended to take.

Instead he locked Mary up in Gaulstown, forbidding her any contact with the outside world. She was confined to the house and gardens of the great estate. When her daughter, Jane, married Brindsley, the second Earl of Lanesborough from another rich and powerful Anglo-Irish family in 1754, Rochfort even forbade her to attend the marriage or see her eldest daughter on her wedding day.

She was walled up in her prison while her husband moved his household to his new home in Belvedere on the shores of Lough Ennel. He only visited the house at Gaulstown on rare occasions to ensure that his security arrangements were in place and his servants were carrying out his wishes to keep his wife in solitary confinement.

Robert's brother George's house was also on the shores of Lough Ennel. Robert was so jealous that his brother might see him or his mistresses walking in the grounds of Belvedere that he built the Jealous Walls, a great big folly to shield his house and garden from the prying eyes of his brother.

In the year 1756 Robert Rochfort received further rewards for his loyal service and his good friend George II elevated him further in the nobility by appointing him the first Lord Belvedere.

While the new Lord Belvedere squandered his great fortune on mistresses and high living in London, Dublin and Belvedere, his faithless wife languished in Dunboden confined to a life of loneliness and misery.

She made one desperate attempt to escape and made it as far

as Dublin and the house of her father in what is now Molesworth Street. But he refused to let her in.

'Go back to your husband,' he ordered and within twenty-four hours she was back in Gaulstown where she would remain for years to come.

The cruel Lord Belvedere now curtailed her freedom still further and she wasn't even allowed visits by her children. When she went walking in the gardens a servant had to walk in front of her ringing a bell, in case her husband might be on the estate and have to meet with her.

The unfortunate Arthur, whether through love or homesickness, returned to Ireland in 1759 and made his way back to Westmeath and his own house at Bellfield. Instead of a welcome, he was immediately arrested on the orders of his brother, who was now in charge of the army in Ireland, and charged with the crime of 'criminal conversation' for having an affair with his brother's wife.

He lost the case and was fined £20,000, an enormous sum at the time and many millions in today's money. With his estate already confiscated by his brother Robert he couldn't pay the fine and so was clapped in irons and taken off to jail. He spent the rest of his life in the Marshalsea, the debtor's prison in Dublin, where he died in dreadful conditions, never seeing his lover or their child again. Lord Belvedere gave a whole new meaning to the term 'family feud'.

Meanwhile he continued to live the high life in Belvedere, ignoring the plight of his broken wife living in fear and confinement just miles away. While Robert Rochfort, Lord Belvedere was enjoying his trysts, his wife was turning into an old woman long before her time.

The Earl of Belvedere was now one of the most important men in Ireland and was rewarded further by his patron, King George II with the title of Master General of the Irish Army in 1764. Although he was known as 'The Wicked Earl' for his treatment of his wife, Lord Belvedere was also renowned for the beauty of his home Belvedere with its fine ornamental plaster, its grand gardens and its beautiful demesne, planted with trees and shrubs imported from all over the world.

The first Lord Belvedere died in 1774, almost bankrupt. Despite his high position in Irish society he had squandered the fortune left to him by his father.

After he passed on his son Robert released his mother after almost thirty-one years of captivity and loneliness.

He was horrified to find that she had acquired 'a wild, scared, unearthly look, whilst the tones of her voice, which hardly exceeded a whisper, were harsh, agitated and uneven.'

Mary Molesworth couldn't bear to spend another night at Dunboden and fled immediately to live with her daughter, the Countess of Lanesborough in her grand home Belvedere House (now Belvedere College) in Dublin. She had the appearance of a very old woman, yet she was only fifty-nine years of age.

The story of Lord Belvedere and his cruelty to his wife was never forgotten. Among others to immortalise her plight was James Joyce, a pupil of Belvedere College, in that short passage from *Ulysses*.

The second Lord Belvedere sold Dunboden to pay his father's huge debts and moved to Belvedere. But ill luck followed the family. His son Robert, the third Lord Belvedere, was known locally as 'Bobby Bawn', 'the cruellest landlord in Westmeath' and was murdered in 1798. The Belvedere title became extinct in 1816.

The new owners of Dunboden, the Coopers, were a kindly family and model landlords. During the Famine they helped out the poor and the starving and they employed a huge staff when there was no other work in that part of the country.

Yet there was something in the folk memory that forever marked the house as a cruel and unforgiving place. On the first Sunday of May, 1923, when most of the hostilities which had marked the War of Independence and the Civil War had ended, a group of masked men arrived at the great front door of Dunboden with paraffin-soaked rags and cans of petrol. They ordered the last of the Coopers out of the house in their night attire and then set the imposing house on fire.

'Within minutes the house was ablaze, smoke ascending high into the morning sky. My mother and father, who were newly wed at the time, stood on the top of a nearby hill, on their way home from first Mass, and watched its firey demise. It burned for hours. Its floors fell in and its staircases glowed through the smoke-blackened glass of its windows. Finally, the roof gave way and collapsed into the inferno. Nothing was left but the shell and two tall chimneys that still stand like penitent arms, raised to heaven for forgiveness,' wrote Patrick A Galvin in his memoir of the house and its history.

Thankfully no such fate befell Belvedere House, which still stands on a hill overlooking the beauty of Lough Ennel. Part of the Jealous Wall that Lord Belvedere built to shield himself from the prying eyes of his younger brother George were blown down in a great storm a few years ago. The contents of the house, including furniture and portraits of the Belvederes, were sold and scattered by its last private owner Rex Beaumont in the 1980s. But the house with its small though beautiful rooms still stands as a monument to the cruelty and beauty of that gilded age.

Chapter 10

The Fianna Fáil Family

PJ Mara, the legendary spin doctor, was having a drink in the Visitors Bar in Leinster House when a reporter shuffled over to him with the burning question of the day.

'Who did pay for Brian Lenihan's liver?' he enquired.

Brian Lenihan was Tánaiste under Charles Haughey. After a long and liberal relationship with whiskey he had been flown to the Mayo Clinic in the United States in the government jet to undergo a liver transplant. When the hospital enquired who would be paying the enormous bill they were told it would be 'taken care of'.

It fell to Lenihan's long-time friend Charles Haughey to put the word out among the party's well-heeled supporters that they were expected to make a donation 'to the cause'. It was a matter of honour to be asked and a refusal was not countenanced.

Much later the issue of how Brian Lenihan's hospital bill had been settled became the subject of a public investigation by the Moriarty Tribunal, which was trying to establish who gave Charlie Haughey all his money and, more importantly, what he did for them in return for this largess.

'The family,' replied PJ Mara to the question of who paid for Brian Lenihan's liver transplant.

'The Lenihan family? They didn't have the money for that,' replied the hack.

'The F-A-M-I-L-Y,' said PJ Mara for a second time, drawing himself up like a Mafia Don and putting on his best Italian-American accent.

He meant the Fianna Fáil family.

Nothing typifies the Fianna Fáil family more than the mysterious, almost Masonic organisation from which the current Taoiseach, Bertie Ahern, derives his power.

Built around St Luke's, a suburban redbrick house in Drumcondra on the outskirts of Dublin, the smooth-running constituency organisation has effectively kept Mr Ahern in high office for more than a decade.

It is here he planned his strategy to take control of Fianna Fáil. It is here that his close political confidants meet, away from the prying eyes of other politicians and the avaricious press. It is here the deals are done that ensure Bertie Ahern stays where he is as long as he wishes.

St Luke's is also a hot-bed of intrigue and power games, with a legendary cast of characters, male and female. Only the enigmatic Bertie Ahern controls all the tentacles emanating from St Luke's, tentacles that burrow into the underbelly of Irish society.

To quote Charles Haughey, who took the young politician under his wing and invited Ahern to the influential 'Saturday mornings' in his Gandon mansion, Abbeville, he is, 'The most skilful, most devious, most cunning of them all.'

Bertie Ahern appears disinterested in business success or

social standing unlike his predecessor Albert Reynolds, or money and privilege like his mentor Charles J Haughey, who aspired to the life of a country squire with his fine mansion, his horses, his holiday island and his mistress.

Amiable though he is, Ahern has never been 'one of the boys'. Yet the wily son of a farm manager from Drumcondra has been in power longer than any Taoiseach, apart from the founder of his party Eamon de Valera. Nobody, it seems, knows who he really is.

Political observers believe that his legendary detachment is a result of his cosy political set up in St Luke's which takes care of his 'backyard' and leaves him free to run the party and the country knowing that his base is secure and the trusted few will tell him what he really needs to hear and not what they think he wants to hear. It is a small coterie of people he trusts deeply who call to his office there and tell him what's really going on and what should be done about it.

Observers have noted that only rarely does he visit the Members Bar in Dáil Éireann to meet up with TDs in an informal setting, and he almost never goes to the Visitors Bar where many politicians and senators like to hang out with journalists, businessmen and lobbyists if only to find out 'what they're saying about us'.

Instead he returns to 'the family' in St Luke's, his constituency office, to find out what way the wind is blowing.

He has an almost set routine, working there all day Saturday before going to one of the local pubs, Fagan's, Kennedy's or the Tolka House, for a few drinks with his pals. He follows the same routine on a Sunday except when there's a football match on in Croke Park, or Dublin are playing within striking distance. Around Christmas when the rest of the country is lazing about or enjoying the racing, Bertie is pottering around St Luke's, finding things to do and according to some reports, even answering the telephone to constituents looking to have some mundane issue taken care of.

It is a ritual that seems detached from his gracious office in Government Buildings on Merrion Street or the other great edifices like Farmleigh which he could avail of for a cosy weekend whenever he felt a need to be pampered. Bertie Ahern likes St Luke's so much that he met the British Prime Minister Tony Blair there and then took him across the road to his local for a pint of Guinness.

For a man who hasn't really had a family life since entering politics, St Luke's is home. It's where many of the big decisions are taken and where a lot of people believe the real power resides. It is also a place of alliances and feuds of constant bickering. But 'Bertie' as he's known stands aloof from it all.

'From the outside, the house is a smart but modest redbrick building set back at a jaunty angle from one of Dublin's busiest traffic routes linking the airport to the city centre. Constituents and regular travellers on the Drumcondra road can often monitor the Taoiseach's attendance by the presence or absence of a black shiny Mercedes car parked outside.

'There is a constituency office and a private office on either side of the large entrance hall and stairwell. There is a bar just to the rear of these which is used for occasional entertaining for periodic constituency organisation cheese-and-wine evenings. It is principally this bar that gives the place its quaint, country-hotel aspect. The pumps on the bar counter include his own favourite trademark tipple, Bass,' wrote John Downing in his book *Bertie Ahern: A Political Biography*.

But the description hardly captures the power and intrigue that lies within and which gives the place such myth-making power in

Fianna Fáil.

St Luke's was bought by a group of trusted businessmen for Bertie Ahern when his marriage to his wife Miriam broke up in 1986 during his year as Lord Mayor of Dublin. It was ready and waiting when he came out of the Mansion House where he had spent one of the most formative years of his political life, building up a power base among the political and business community during the twelve months as the public face of Ireland's capital city.

The job of Lord Mayor is what you make it. Bertie Ahern was the politician who made the most of it in the last twenty-five years, schmoozing with the great and the good and getting his picture in the paper almost daily.

It was a year when he seemed to be at his most relaxed, mixing with Dubliners in easy familiarity and marking his territory as a future party leader. It was a perfect launching pad for that steep political climb and having St Luke's up and running when he left the Mansion House was a master stroke.

What passes for a 'constituency office' is rather more opulent than the redbrick semi-detached house would indicate. Upstairs there is a rather well-appointed apartment: a bathroom with gold taps and under-floor heating, and some nice touches with regard to furnishing which would indicate the hand of Celia Larkin, later to emerge as a style guru in her own right.

It was an unknown Dublin solicitor and friend of Ahern's called Gerald M Brennan who put together the trustee agreement by which a group of businessmen and friends of Ahern, some of them in the construction business, agreed to buy, refurbish and fund St Luke's.

Under the terms of the trusteeship Bertie Ahern would have the use of the building and facilities for his lifetime in politics and only afterwards, when he had retired altogether, would it revert to his political party, Fianna Fáil.

Of the trustees three of the four, Tim Collins, Des Richardson and Joe Burke, went on to become millionaires and members of important state boards and in the process they also paved the way for Bertie Ahern to take power in Fianna Fáil and eventually see himself as Taoiseach. It was a neat deal.

Intriguingly Gerry Brennan, his trusted legal advisor and friend, committed suicide on May 24, 1997, just days before Bertie Ahern won the election that has put him in power for a decade. By then St Luke's was established as the power base of the new Fianna Fáil and some of its main 'fixers'.

A great deal had happened in his public and private life in the meantime. As close observers noted, as well as intrigue St Luke's was also a place of romance. A central figure was a tough Finglas girl called Celia Larkin who over the years would become the power behind the throne and the subject of countless newspaper headlines.

Becoming Lord Mayor of Dublin in 1986 was the springboard the young Dublin politician Bertie Ahern needed to make his mark on the party and the country, and he intended to take full advantage of it. The Mansion House is a gracious building on Dawson Street in the city centre and with a crippling schedule of meetings, receptions, dinners and social events it is an ideal base for the city's Lord Mayor.

But there was another consideration. Bertie and his wife Miriam (Kelly) had two young daughters to care for. Initially the family intended to move from their house in a middle-class development in Malahide, Co Dublin and into the Mansion House as a unit, but after a few weeks Miriam Ahern realised that she wasn't seeing much of her husband anyway and the place was totally unsuited to family life and the needs of her two girls who needed to be closer to Malahide, their schools and their friends.

Being Lord Mayor meant that you got a keg of Guinness as a gift from the brewery every week, and political friends, associates and hangers-on expected to be invited in to drink it. It often meant raucous late nights and Miriam Ahern didn't like the strange environment which put her and her family on public display. After a short time she moved back to the family home in Malahide leaving the young Lord Mayor a free hand in the city.

One photographer who was sent to the Mansion House on a job remembers hearing voices raised in anger coming from a room off the hallway. It was a member of Miriam's family pleading with Bertie to 'come home' to his wife and family, that the life he was leading could only end in trouble and a family dispute.

But by then there was no turning back.

'When he became Lord Mayor the relationship with Celia began to become noticeable,' said one observer. 'People began to notice them out socially and realised that for her it was more than just the job.'

'The plain reality was that Bertie was never home and when he got home Miriam's family were in situ, keeping her company. It was no way to keep a marriage going. Like many marriages in politics and other walks of life, one partner got careless and that led to the collapse of the relationship. At that stage Celia was not involved,' a close friend, Tony Kett, is quoted as saying in the book *Bertie Ahern, Taoiseach and Peacemaker* by Ken Whelan and Eugene Masterson.

When his year as Lord Mayor came to an end Bertie Ahern didn't move back into the family home in Malahide, but into

St Luke's which had been renovated by his builder friends. Celia Larkin was working downstairs as his 'constituency secretary'. His marriage was over and his relationship with Celia began in earnest. And would eventually become part of the legend of St Luke's.

The break-up of the Aherns' marriage was a bitter affair and despite his own strong old-style Catholic religious convictions, he and Miriam eventually obtained a judicial separation, with the case taking four days when it was heard in Dolphin House, a family courthouse in the centre of Dublin.

Later Bertie admitted that they could have come to a much friendlier agreement had they not both consulted firms of lawyers to argue over the details of the settlement. News of the bitter court case and the hard-fought settlement soon spread around the Dublin media and legal circles and like all good stories it took on a life of its own.

'I know all the rumours and so do Celia and Miriam; I can do sweet nothing about these things,' said Bertie in his only public comment on those turbulent events in his personal life and the break-up of his marriage.

But even these remarks were clouded in controversy. He later claimed it was an 'off the record' comment to the two journalists who were writing a book about him and wanted to be 'briefed'. They disputed this version and said that he knew at the time that the interview was being taped and that the quotes would be attributed to him.

'You can sound me out till the cows come home: you'll find no Garda reports, no barring orders, nothing. I'll tell you there's not a whole many things in my life that I can 110 per cent swear on because I'm no more an angel than anyone else in this life, but of the barring orders there's zilch,' continued Mr Ahern.

'There were no guards ever involved, to Celia's house, to Malahide, when I was in Pinebrook before I was in Malahide, ever. There was no barring order of any kind; there were no threatened barring orders.

'There was never a hospital incident. Celia fell at a party and that was it. And the following day she went out and joked about it with Mary Harney. It is rubbish; you can march into the Mater yourself and you will find nothing.'

But it didn't stop the rumours spreading. The one rumour that was true, however, was that Bertie Ahern had found a new love.

Installed in St Luke's Celia Larkin was now indispensable in business and in his personal life. She was his eyes and ears in Drumcondra. When he was promoted to a job in the Department of Labour she went with him to an office in the department as constituency secretary, a government job that enables ministers to save their seats by looking after constituents as well as running the country. When he moved up the political ladder to the Department of Finance she followed after him, remaining an indispensable part of the Ahern 'machine'.

Bertie Ahern then began the process of acclimatising the general public to his 'situation'. Although it was well-known in politics and the media that Celia was his lover, it wasn't publicly written about and commentators steered clear of the issue. Then one night he went on the Pat Kenny Show and admitted, unprompted, that he was separated like many other fathers in modern Ireland. He was carefully preparing public opinion for what would follow.

On budget day when a minister brings his wife for the obligatory photograph, Bertie Ahern brought neither wife nor mistress. Instead he brought his growing daughters Georgina and Cecelia to pose with him and the minister's briefcase.

In 1992 Charles Haughey resigned as Taoiseach and leader of Fianna Fáil and it was expected that Bertie Ahern would challenge Albert Reynolds for the job. But there were whispers in the Dáil bar and around the corridors of power that TDs 'would want to know where their leader slept at night'. It was a clear reference to Ahern's marital status and in the end he didn't put his name forward at that time.

However, Albert Reynolds only lasted two years. He was brought down by the bungling of the Attorney General's office in failing to proceed with a case against a paedophile priest, Fr Brendan Smith. It was a complicated affair and Bertie Ahern, a cool head in a crisis, did not rally to Reynolds' side when he was badly needed. Maybe it was his legendary detachment, maybe he wasn't part of the inner circle, or maybe he knew the government was falling apart and it would provide him with the perfect opportunity to take control of Fianna Fáil.

As he stood aloof, the Reynolds' administration crumbled in contradictions and confusion.

Bertie Ahern was the natural successor and when he was appointed leader of Fianna Fáil in 1994, his lover Celia Larkin was sitting quietly unnoticed in the hotel room where he gave his first press conference. Her status as 'First Lady' was raised as an issue by the tabloid journalist Paddy Clancy drawing boos from some of Ahern's supporters in the room.

Many of the journalists present were equally unhappy that the issue of the Taoiseach's mistress had been publicly aired, because now they knew their bosses back in the newspaper head offices would want stories about Celia and her place in the Ahern household. They didn't relish having to write them. The old taboo about politicians and their private lives was breaking down and there was a lot of discomfort, in politics and journalism, about it.

Unlike Britain where the private indiscretions of politicians are big news there is something of a stand-off between the political establishment and the media in Ireland. Journalists need an excuse to cross the line into a politician's private life. A politician who makes moral pronouncements while conducting an affair is a perfect example. Then it becomes 'in the public interest' – or to put it another way, the perfect excuse – to write about them.

It's an arrangement that suits both sides. Some politicians in Leinster House are notorious womanisers, but they manage to get away with it because they keep their opinions on morality very much to themselves.

'Most journalists who are privy to the political world could name a number of senior politicians who have had, or are having sexual relations with women who are not their wives,' said the reporter Katie Hannon in her book *The Naked Politician*.

She also quoted Bertie Ahern on how difficult marriage can be for a person in public life.

'It just makes it hard. I remember when I said that somebody said it depends on how you organise it . . . But it's a hard thing to do for anybody and I think anyone who goes right through it [political life] without a problem has done very well.'

The pixie-faced Celia was bound to be noticed sooner or later, especially when she took over a plush office in Government Buildings and a state salary of IR£36,000 a year.

Then in November 1994, in a move calculated to cement her position as the leader's consort, she was by Bertie Ahern's side when he formally took over as president of Fianna Fáil from Albert Reynolds at a glittering party dinner in the Burlington Hotel in Dublin.

A few jaws dropped, some of the old guard who stood for the moral values of the Ireland of de Valera were scandalised, but most of the men in the mohair suits took a pragmatic view: a man's private life was his own affair.

The prying eyes of the media were new firmly trained in Celia's direction, but with Fianna Fáil in opposition there was no real opportunity to bring the private life of Bertie and Celia into the public domain.

So Celia Larkin played a low-key role in Bertie Ahern's public life as leader of the opposition and it seemed her profile would all but disappear when, after the 1997 election, he became Taoiseach.

There was no mention of Celia and although she was sitting in the public gallery when the great moment arrived she was largely ignored, either because people didn't notice her or because she wanted to keep it that way.

It was said that Padraig Flynn, who would not have been a political ally of Bertie Ahern, and his wife had to rescue her and bring her along to the party that followed Ahern's elevation to leader of the country.

Celia Larkin's rise seemed to mirror that of her lover, Bertie. When he became Taoiseach she was appointed 'special advisor' at a salary of over IR£75,000. It was quite a step up in the pecking order. The girl who had started in St Luke's addressing envelopes was now a force to be reckoned with.

She seemed to take high office in her stride and she already knew her way around the corridors of power. When it came to sharing out offices for the new administration she knew the system better than most and got herself allocated a grand big office in Government Buildings that had once belonged to the Labour Party leader, Dick Spring when he was Tánaiste.

Some people felt she was getting a bit above herself: a constituency 'secretary', as they dismissively called her, lording it around Government Buildings was not done. But Celia threw her head back and ignored the begrudgers.

Later on it would become much harder for her, but in those early days she was determined to show anyone who was interested that she was a tough lady who was able to look after herself. Maybe that's why she appealed to Bertie Ahern. She never looked back, she never complained and when it all ended in tears she did not, like Terry Keane, turn around and 'tell all' for money, despite getting plenty of offers.

It would take another four years before Celia Larkin's name first appeared on an official government invite – to a dinner to be hosted by the Taoiseach for the President of the United States, Bill Clinton and his wife Hillary, in Dublin Castle.

Until that day the 'serious media' largely ignored her presence as the new face of modern Ireland. When questions were asked about her status they were met with cold official silence. The era of the Taoiseach's 'partner' had arrived.

But in the years that followed, St Luke's would be a battleground between the old order, led by friends of Bertie Ahern from his early years, and the new order, led by Celia Larkin. There was a marked difference in both style and substance.

The old guard, who were sometimes known as 'The Drumcondra Mafia' because they hung around the local pubs in the constituency with Bertie from the days when he was a tousled-haired young fellah in an anorak, may have started off supporting Fianna Fáil but now they were fiercely loyal to just one man, their local TD. As he rose through the ranks they prospered but they had little time for the trappings of the new 'style guru' who came among them.

On the other hand Celia Larkin learned very quickly that on

the national and international stage on which she now found herself, style counted for far more than substance.

As Ahern began to dress and act like a leader rather than someone coming from a Dubs football encounter, he was being pulled in different directions by the old and the new factions. According to observers, this led to a deep-seated feud in St Luke's between the two sides and various stories and tit-bits were leaked to the newspapers aimed at damaging one or other of the factions.

It quickly became a matter of which side you chose and a young politician called Royston Brady would eventually find out that just because you appeared to be the 'chosen one' did not automatically mean you got the support of the organisation.

Celia Larkin had been replaced as constituency enforcer by her understudy Cyprian Brady, an unlikely named individual who idolised Bertie Ahern and hitched his own political ambitions to his hero by running his Drumcondra operation from the back room in St Luke's.

While Celia had left all that behind she understood the value of knowing what was happening 'on the ground' and so she had groomed her own informants to watch over St Luke's and the intricate political goings-on behind closed doors. One of them was a young county councillor called Royston Brady whom she had taken under her wing. Big and brash, he too idolised Bertie Ahern and had set his sights on following in his footsteps. He was also the brother of Cyprian Brady, so he had access to both sides of St Luke's.

In time he would become the shining star of Drumcondra, but like all bright stars his would eventually burst in a blaze of glory only to dissolve in a cloud of media dust. Royston Brady talked too much, something his hero was always careful to avoid.

In the hotbed of rumour and intrigue surrounding St Luke's

the various factions were vying for position and power and a word out of place could spell disaster.

By now Celia was undisputedly Ireland's First Lady standing by Bertie Ahern's side at state events in Buckingham Palace, the White House, Sydney, the Great Wall of China and other far-flung destinations where the leader's presence was required.

As she travelled around the globe by government jet at the tax-payers' expense some of the more conservative clerics, Catholic and Protestant, began to be uneasy about how she had acquired the status of First Lady without actually being the Taoiseach's wife, or being elected to anything.

It was an invitation to a government event to celebrate the elevation of the ascetic and distant Catholic Archbishop of Dublin, Desmond Connell, to the rank of cardinal which caused the most controversy. The invite, coming as it did from 'The Taoiseach and Celia Larkin', left the cardinal embarrassed and displeased.

It was left to the editor of the *Church of Ireland Gazette* to thunder against this slight to the most senior cleric in the country, a man who had long promoted the sanctity of marriage. There was such a political and media furore that on the night of the reception in the State Apartment in Dublin Castle, Celia Larkin was not in the official line-up to greet the elderly churchman of profoundly conservative views.

By 1999 Celia Larkin, who was now on first name terms with Cherie Blair and Hillary Clinton and had remodelled Bertie Ahern into a reasonably elegant man, was no longer content with her role in life. She decided to give up her state-paid job as the Taoiseach's constituency secretary and leave politics, where she had spent her formative years.

She embarked on a new venture, a beauty salon intriguingly

called Beauty at the Blue Door. Etched into the glass panel on the doorway was her romantic take on life and love.

> *You may only be*
> *One person in this*
> *World but for someone*
> *You are the world.*

By now, however, there was a coolness creeping into the one person in her world, Bertie Ahern. Each summer he spends the best part of August in Kerry with his daughters and during his holidays one year Celia Larkin got a little jealous and started ringing the rather splendid Great Southern Hotel at Parknasilla at odd hours of the night demanding to be put through to him. She was in America at the time and may have been homesick or simply confused about the time, but it didn't go down very well.

Celia also knew that he was never going to divorce his wife, Miriam, and marry her – he had been cornered into saying it in interviews. There were a few embarrassing skirmishes. There was an occasion at the Galway Races when the Taoiseach and Celia Larkin made the mistake of going into a jewellery shop accompanied by a band of photographers. It was teasing on a grand scale, but it backfired badly.

By the summer of 2003 it was all over, although neither of them wanted to admit it and kept up the pretence that there was still a relationship.

Asked by gossip columnist Jason O'Callaghan if they still had a relationship Bertie Ahern answered, 'As far as I know we do, I slept with her last night.'

It all seemed a little undignified for the head of a country to have to justify himself in such a way.

As the 'on/off' stories circulated in the newspapers a trusted aide of Mr Ahern rang a Dublin newsroom to inform them that the two would be dining together at the elegant Shanahan's Restaurant on St Stephen's Green. They did, but they were distant and everybody knew they were simply doing it to keep up appearances.

The battle for Bertie also centred on St Luke's. Celia Larkin built up an alliance with Royston Brady to try to protect herself, but it was generally agreed that the 'Drumcondra Mafia' never liked her and couldn't wait to see the back of her.

Despite the romantic coolness and the political intrigue his constituency organisation St Luke's was prospering. Bertie Ahern seems to have learned the same lesson as a New York character called Professor Seagull who funded his lifestyle by holding an annual ball – in aid of himself. The St Luke's operation is run by the funds raised at an opulent dinner held each year in the Royal Hospital Kilmainham for the O'Donovan Rossa cumann of Fianna Fáil. The reality is that it is Bertie's annual fundraiser.

The dinner is attended by representatives of big business and builders and developers who take tables at €500 a head for the privilege of rubbing shoulders with Bertie. The price of an admission ticket is just below the amount that must be declared to the Standards in Public Office as a 'political donation' and attendance is by invitation only.

Those seeking an open door to the most powerful figure in the country come to pay tribute and all the proceeds go to paying for a full-time staff, the upkeep of St Luke's and the considerable expense of running the best-oiled political machine ever seen in this country.

Two people who were among the prominent figures with an open door to St Luke's were the oddly named brothers, Cyprian and Royston Brady. Cyprian was a favourite of Bertie and Royston a trusted confidant of his lover, Celia Larkin.

But as events would prove brothers can also fall out, especially in the heady mix of sex, politics and money surrounding St Luke's.

The brotherly love between the Bradys would end up in a bitter row and at one time it seemed that judiciously placed 'leaks' were aimed at ruining the careers of them both. These 'leaks' were coming from sources very close to St Luke's.

From a young age Cyprian Brady, the serious-looking and elder of the two Brady brothers, got involved in the political organisation of Bertie Ahern TD, when he was the rising star of Fianna Fáil. Cyprian was the perfect 'ward boss' running St Luke's efficiently, smoothing the way for Ahern, ironing out any difficulties he might have at local level. When he was appointed a senator by his mentor he became the eyes and ears of the Fianna Fáil leader, making sure that his boss was well-informed at national and local level.

His brother Royston, tall, good-looking and ambitious, a man with the common touch was elected to Dublin City Council and seemed destined to rise effortlessly to the top. He even seemed to be following in his hero's footsteps. He was appointed Lord Mayor in 2003 and appeared perfectly placed to enter the European Parliament as a highly paid MEP at the election which came just as his term of office was ending.

With the European election campaign underway in 2004 there were two Fianna Fáil candidates in Dublin and they were like chalk and cheese.

On the Southside was the patrician figure of Eoin Ryan, whose grandfather had been a founder member of the party and a Minister for Finance and whose father had been a senator and prominent businessman. The family had prospered in politics and in life and their political affiliations certainly hadn't hampered their progress. But Eoin Ryan, a Blackrock College boy and graduate of UCD, had not found favour with Ahern. Maybe it was his upbringing or the ease with which he seemed to achieve his objectives. Maybe the tough northsider detected a hint of arrogance in the likeable southsider.

Though capable and ambitious with a successful start as a junior minister who had tackled the drugs issue in Dublin, Ryan was demoted in a government reshuffle after the 2002 election. It was a clear message that Bertie Ahern, the New Fianna Fáil, didn't like the old crowd or their hangers-on.

Royston Brady, on the other hand, came from a working-class Northside Dublin background. His father had been a taxi driver and while the family had been party supporters, anything he got in politics he got for himself, with the support of the St Luke's organisation.

As Lord Mayor he was selected to run with Eoin Ryan on the party ticket for the European elections in the Dublin constituency.

There was a fair amount of Southside v Northside snobbishness associated with the election campaign. Royston Brady was regarded by many as uncultured and ignorant in the subtle art of national politics, while Eoin Ryan was seen as the 'party man' with real ability which had not been recognised.

But the irony of the situation was that all the opinion polls indicated that Royston Brady was by far the more popular candidate of the two, and barring a disaster he would win the seat. Added to that Bertie Ahern and Celia Larkin were determined that he would take the seat in the European parliament as a snub to the old guard. There was no room in St Luke's for the privileged elite who dominated the party. They used their considerable influence to ensure that big business and big money poured into the Royston Brady campaign. Senior party figures loyal to Ahern were drafted in to shore up the campaign.

But what some people forgot was that in the complicated world of St Luke's Royston Brady was 'Celia's candidate' and because of the bad feeling that existed between the new and the old guard he didn't get the backing of the hard-nosed campaigners who ran the 'Bertie Ahern' machine. Indeed they went out of their way to help the 'Southside' candidate Eoin Ryan just to spite Celia. When he held a major fundraising event in Croke Park, the so-called Drumcondra Mafia ensured that all the tables were full. It was their way of letting Celia Larkin know where the real power lay.

In politics disaster is never lurking very far away. In an interview with the writer Joe Jackson in the early stages of the campaign Royston Brady, Lord Mayor of Dublin, told a strange story from his childhood. He said that on the night of the Dublin bombings in 1974 in which thirty-four people had been killed by Loyalist paramilitaries – believed to be in collusion with undercover British security agents – his father's taxi had been hijacked by the escaping bombers and his father had been dumped in the Dublin Mountains as the gang made their getaway.

The article was published in the *Sunday Independent* but seemed to pass without comment. Then a couple of weeks later as the campaign went into overdrive the families of the Dublin bombing victims, a powerful lobby who were seeking a public inquiry into the events of thirty years before, began to ask awkward questions.

They said that the story of Mr Brady senior as a crucial witness to these events had never been documented before. They asked why he had not been called to give evidence at the inquiry in the aftermath of the bombing conducted by Judge Ronan Keane.

They also wanted to know why Royston Brady had not come forward to a more recent inquiry conducted by Judge Henry Barron, a member of the Supreme Court, and given testimony that could have a crucial bearing on what happened that night when the bombers brought carnage to the streets of Dublin.

Why, they wanted to know, had he never gone to the police with this vital information?

The story was taken up by the *Evening Herald* newspaper and suddenly Royston Brady was on the run. At first he defended the story, saying it was true, but when he was informed there was no evidence to back up his version of events he said it was 'a family story' that had been told by his father and which he had no reason to disbelieve.

As the story turned into a political disaster for the Royston Brady campaign he appealed to his brother Cyprian to step forward and come to his defence by confirming the details he had given in the interview.

But his brother Senator Cyprian Brady did not come forward. With Royston Brady under siege there was a deafening silence from St Luke's.

Effectively Royston was left on a limb, twisting in the wind. What rankled most was that he had been abandoned by his own brother. How could that have happened? According to some political observers it was very simple: Cyprian Brady didn't want to help out his brother because a year earlier he felt he had been snubbed by Royston.

The high point of Royston Brady's year as Lord Mayor of Dublin had been his marriage. He was the first Lord Mayor in years to be married while in office and he chose to use the trappings of the city, the ancient Lord Mayor's carriage and the Mansion House as the focal point for his fairy-tale wedding to his bride Michele McConalogue. But such was the importance of the big occasion that children were not invited – and that meant that the children of his brother Cyprian were excluded from the celebration. From such small things family feuds arise.

Young and relatively inexperienced, Royston Brady took the wrong option when the crisis arose in his election campaign. Instead of confronting the issue he cut and ran. In the dying days of the campaign his organisation effectively fell apart as he fled from the media and failed to deal with the story.

It was devastating for the young and politically ambitious politician who had just handed back his chain of office of Lord Mayor. On the night of the count Eoin Ryan confounded the earlier opinion polls and was elected Fianna Fáil MEP for Dublin. Still holding his seat in the Dáil he was destined to be a very wealthy man, even if he only lasted the five-year term in office.

Royston Brady was so devastated that he couldn't even bring himself to appear at the announcement of the election results in the RDS in Dublin. This breach of etiquette was considered almost as bad as the faux pas he had already committed with the story of his father and the bombings.

As the dust settled it emerged that Royston Brady's father's taxi had indeed been hijacked after a bombing – but it wasn't the night of the Dublin/Monaghan bombings as he had said. It was a different bombing outside Liberty Hall two years earlier, in 1972, in which two busmen had been killed. It was an understandable mistake; he had only been a young boy at the time and did not have a very good grasp of recent Irish history.

By then Royston Brady's political career was in ruins. So was his relationship with his brother Cyprian.

To try to revive his political fortunes two years later Royston Brady sought to get a nomination for the next general election on the same ticket as the Taoiseach, Bertie Ahern. But Cyprian was having none of it: he had already put his name forward and was duly nominated as the faithful servant to the Master of St Luke's.

Soon after, questions began to be asked about a trip to Egypt which Cyprian and Royston had made with a businessman friend – but which Cyprian had never declared.

The trip in October 2002 was organised by the Egyptian businessman Mahmoud Rahim who was based in Dublin and had invited Cyprian and Royston Brady to visit his country. Cyprian Brady had not made a declaration of this 'gift' as he is obliged to do as a senator under the Standards in Public Office rules. As there were only three of them involved it seems odd that details of it were leaked to the media. Senator Brady countered by saying that it was purely a recreational trip and Mr Rahim organised the business-class flights and a stay in a five-star hotel. He said hc had fully reimbursed his host at a later stage for the cost of the flights.

'So I went for four days, it was purely recreational. I am very careful and I checked everything. Mahmoud is a family friend. I gave Mahmoud the money as had been agreed.'

But his version of events was contradicted by Royston who said that Cyprian organised the trip and it was paid for by the Egyptian businessman. He insists neither of them paid back Rahim for the all-expenses four days.

'As everyone knows Cyprian still has his Communion money. There wasn't much recreation on the trip. They seemed to be conducting business and I was sorry I went on it afterwards.'

Cyprian Brady was puzzled about why his brother would

contradict his version of events.

'I don't really know. All I can say is that after last week [the constituency nomination] there are a lot of annoyed people out there. It's quite sad. You can choose your friends, but your family is your family,' he told the newspaper *Ireland On Sunday*.

In a way that's what made St Luke's so important to Bertie Ahern, they weren't a family, they just acted like one. In the five trustees of St Luke's Bertie Ahern got men of vision but also of complete loyalty to his cause. The men who set up St Luke's would ensure that Bertie Ahern never had to worry about money, and some of them prospered in the process too.

The least well known was Jimmy Keane, a local 'ward boss' who was a friend of Bertie Ahern's and a good man at guiding him through the labyrinthine world of local politics. He remained a largely anonymous figure as did another trustee, Jimmy Reilly whom Keane replaced as trustee when Reilly died.

But the other three trustees of St Luke's went on to become millionaires and prosper from the contributions out of the public purse.

Des Richardson, a wealthy businessman who sold his Foxrock mansion in May 2006 for more than €3 million would later become Fianna Fáil's chief fundraiser. He was also appointed a director of Aer Lingus as a reward for his loyalty to Bertie Ahern and for his contribution to the foundation and running of St Luke's.

Joe Burke, a small building contractor, was 'a close friend' of Bertie Ahern from the early days. When Bertie Ahern wanted someone to 'take a look' at something he would designate Joe Burke. It was in this way that Burke got entangled with the whole planning saga of developer Tom Gilmartin which ended up before the Flood/Mahon Tribunal looking at payments to politicians from developers.

He also had some troubles in his personal life when he split up with his wife, but the most notorious episode in his career was what became known as 'the Sheedy Affair'. Philip Sheedy, an architect, had killed a young mother when driving while drunk. He was sentenced to four years in jail with a review of the sentence after two years. Representations were made to Bertie Ahern to see if Sheedy could be put on day release from prison. Ahern passed the query on to his private secretary who asked the private secretary of the Minister for Justice, 'What's the story?'

Joe Burke, who knew Sheedy through his work in the building business and had used him to get work done, visited him in Shelton Abbey, an open prison in Wicklow.

Coincidentally Philip Sheedy's sister met Judge Hugh O'Flaherty, among the most senior judicial figures in the country, as he was walking near his home in Herbert Park. She asked him about her brother.

Then matters got complicated. Sheedy was released after just nine months of his sentence, because of his mental condition. The victim's family was never told and the judge who had presided over the original trial did not hear the review of the case, which was handled by a newly appointed High Court judge, Mr Cyril Kelly. When details of the Sheedy Affair became public, two senior judges, Judge Hugh O'Flaherty of the Supreme Court and Judge Cyril Kelly of the High Court, had to resign.

The pressure was such that Joe Burke had to issue a statement to the media through his solicitors.

'I wish to state that media reports and comments which attempt to link me to the way in which Philip Sheedy's case was dealt with by the courts are wholly unfounded, devoid of any substance whatsoever and deeply hurtful to me and my family.

'My connection with Philip Sheedy was based on work he did as an architect. A member of his family contacted my office seeking a character reference for court proceedings which I was happy to supply. I had no contact thereafter in relation to this case and do not know if the character reference was ever used. My visit to Philip Sheedy in jail on October 14, 1998, was a purely personal gesture and had nothing to do with his subsequent release.'

He went on to say, 'My long-standing friendship with the Taoiseach, which is public knowledge, has absolutely no connection with the Sheedy controversy. I am in the same position as any other member of the public in not knowing or understanding why Philip Sheedy was released. His release came as a surprise to me. It has absolutely nothing to do with me or with my friendship with the Taoiseach.'

Was he protesting too much? Some people wondered why a close associate of the Taoiseach and two senior judges should go to such lengths to help a convicted drunk driver avoid part of his sentence. The question was never satisfactorily answered.

But Joe Burke continued to prosper. He was appointed a member of the influential Dublin Port Company and rose to executive chairman, earning himself a fat salary and a sleek Jaguar car for his loyal service.

The most intriguing of the trustees, however, was the fourth, the 'fixer' Tim Collins, a close friend of Mr Ahern. In time Collins made a fortune from 'getting people together' in massive property deals and pocketing a sizeable percentage of the profit. Of all of the St Luke's trustees he was the closest personal friend of Bertie Ahern. They went back a long long way.

For Tim Collins the appointment of Bertie Ahern as Minister for Labour was the beginning of a career that would make him very rich, give him an introduction to some very important people and make him only slightly infamous.

Until it went into liquidation, Collins ran a company called Pilgrim & Associates which was a loosely based business of architects and interior designers. He had been in the tiling business himself and over the years had got to know builders and architects. When Pilgrim Associates was formed his job title was marketing manager – but the fancy term didn't disguise the real job, which he later explained was getting out there and bringing in the business.

Having his friend Bertie Ahern in the office of the Ministry of Labour proved to be fortuitous as well as profitable. At the time, the Department of Labour were searching for a site to build a new headquarters for the state training agency for the catering business, CERT. The new minister, Bertie Ahern, had ideas for a site, which just happened to be in Amiens Street in his own constituency. (It is now the headquarters of Bord Fáilte.)

A prestigious firm of architects, Arthur Gibney & Partners, was employed to design the new multimillion pound headquarters and after a tendering process the contract to build the new headquarters was assigned to a good Fianna Fáil contractor Bernard McNamara.

Then 'most unusually', according to those in the business, Pilgrim & Associates – Tim Collins's company – was 'parachuted' into the job with a lucrative contract as a second architectural firm on the contract.

'My function was to get clients in, bearing in mind that at the time it was difficult trying to get people in and to get business out and get on with it,' Collins would say later. But with a helping hand from his friend Bertie Ahern, the minister, he had no trouble at all in getting a slice of the action when the new CERT headquarters was being built.

Only much later, when there were serious problems with the building, did things start to get very nasty.

The new semi-state headquarters was built on the banks of the Tolka River in the north inner city. After an unusual amount of rain the river behind the building flooded, ruining the basement. As insurance companies, surveyors and other investigators went in to assess the damage, other defects were found in the building. Various experts eventually calculated that when all the costs were taken into account the bill to put the job right would be about IR£1 million – and CERT, the stage agency involved, asked the insurance company to pick up the tab.

However, a tough North Dublin solicitor acting for the insurance company decided to play hard ball when the matter came for settlement several years later – by which time Bertie Ahern, the rising star of Irish politics, had moved on to the Department of Finance and then to the Taoiseach's office.

'The then minister responsible for the hotel and catering industry was Mr Bertie Ahern, now the Prime Minister of Ireland,' the British insurance company was told by its Dublin lawyer in a letter stamped 'private and confidential'.

'The appointment of the architect was unusual in that two architects were appointed, Messrs. Pilgrim & Associates and Arthur Gibney & Partners. It is interesting to note that they are now in liquidation and apparently they were uninsured. The Principals of Pilgrim & Associates were Mr Tim Collins and Mr Tim Roe, the former being a close political associate of Mr Ahern, already referred to.

'Various meetings and discussions have taken place as and between the parties,' the insurance firm was told. 'CERT have been aggressive in maintaining their claim but to counteract their moral high ground the potential of a political scandal counterbalances the righteous position they maintain,' he advised.

The directors of CERT, mostly political appointees, were told in no uncertain terms that if they pursued their claim Bertie Ahern would be dragged into the mess through his good friend Tim Collins and things would get very dirty.

In the end the litigation which could have cost over IR£1 million was settled for IR£45,000 (plus IR£50,000 in costs) rather than going to court where the names of Bertie Ahern, Tim Collins and St Luke's would have drawn a lot of attention from the media and other quarters.

Interestingly Des Richardson was also a director of Pilgrim & Associates.

Mr Collins then got involved in land dealings for the powerful McCann family who control the public company Fyffes, one of the biggest fruit distributors in the world. Collins was involved in the acquisition of Airlee Stud in Lucan for Neil McCann. With each deal he would get a 'finder's' fee of between ten and twelve per cent of the price of the land he was brokering. In that way Tim Collins became a central figure in the saga of the 'Battle of the Boyne' site on the outskirts of Dublin.

The site had originally belonged to the Coddington family but after their grand house was burnt down during the Troubles the family decided to sell the estate. At the time, the government and the Minister for Foreign Affairs, David Andrews, was interested in acquiring the site because of its historical associations with the famous battle between King William and King James which changed the course of Irish and British history. But before they could do anything, in December 1997 the McCann family had stepped in and acquired the 700-acre site for IR£2.7 million through a company of theirs called Deep River.

About a month later, in January 1998, the site was offered to the Office of Public Works because of its historical significance. An interdepartmental committee met to discuss buying the land from the McCanns in March 1998 but nothing much happened after that. The OPW got a valuation of between IR£4 million and IR£7 million as the cost of buying the site. Then in February 1999 the Department of the Taoiseach got involved.

'It was through the Taoiseach's office that we were approached first,' revealed Mr Barry Murphy, Chairman of the Office of Public Works. The first approach, he said, was informal, but a formal meeting took place with the Taoiseach's office on March 3, 1999.

Less than eighteen months after the land was first mentioned to the OPW, it bought Deep River for IR£7.8 million – a tidy profit of IR£5.1 million for the already very wealthy McCann family and without having to spend a cent on the deal.

Interestingly enough the Taoiseach's close friend Tim Collins, who had brokered the deal between the McCann family and the state walked away with a commission of over IR£600,000 for himself.

Even better, the deal was structured so that the state bought the company Deep River instead of simply buying the land and so the McCanns avoided paying almost IR£1 million in capital gains tax and stamp duty on the profits of the sale.

Asked was he directed to purchase this land Mr Murphy of the OPW replied, 'The correct answer to that is that the government asked us to.'

At the same time a close associate of Tim Collins in a series of separate land deals was Frank Dunlop, a former government press secretary turned 'fixer', who now says his job at the time was to bribe county councillors to rezone land around Dublin for big builders and developers.

Tim Collins and Joe Burke were also involved with another developer, Tom Gilmartin who was prepared to lash around huge sums of cash to develop sites at Bachelors Walk in Dublin City Centre and Quarryvale, a shopping centre he hoped to build at Blanchardstown on the outskirts of Dublin.

Gilmartin, originally from Co Sligo, had been living and operating in Britain for many years. He said he didn't know the Dublin market and to smooth his way with politicians he employed Frank Dunlop. Oddly enough Joe Burke was also involved as an intermediary between Gilmartin and the Taoiseach, Bertie Ahern.

During Tribunal hearings Mr Tim Collins insisted, 'I am not a political person.' But one of the tribunal judges, probing his relationship to the Taoiseach, said, 'Mr Collins, I get the impression you are not being forthcoming with us.'

Meantime, Bertie Ahern now described his close friend Tim Collins as a 'local person' and later as 'someone I know outside of politics'.

Although he was a serious individual in property-dealing in Dublin at that time and made a huge fortune, Tim Collins claimed the only reason he went to Frank Dunlop when he was dealing in land was because he had read about him in the newspapers.

It seemed an odd kind of statement given that the brash Dunlop had been involved with Jack Lynch and Charlie Haughey, and for years had been on the fringes of Fianna Fáil and knew many of the main players personally.

The three main trustees of St Luke's certainly prospered as part of Bertie's 'golden' inner circle. Like Des Richardson and Joe Burke, Tim Collins was rewarded for his services with a job on a government state agency. He was appointed to the board of Córas Trachtála but he resigned before investigations were made into his land dealings.

For some people St Luke's was about romance and being close to the centre of the Taoiseach's world. But for others it was obviously a means to make connections and oil the wheels of commerce.

Through it all one man remained aloof and untouched: the Taoiseach Bertie Ahern.

Charlie Haughey was right.

Chapter 11

The Crock of Gold

One bright sunny morning the sheriff arrived at the front gates of Chesterfield, a palatial estate at Cross Avenue near Blackrock, Co Dublin. Set in nine acres of gardens and pastures, the grand house, its gardens, tennis courts and swimming pool, sat like an oasis in the midst of suburban Dublin.

But the sheriff, arriving to collect a bank debt and armed with a court order had no interest in such things. As he drove through the big iron gates and up the long winding avenue shaded by tall beech and oak trees his car was followed up to the house by a large truck.

His job that morning was to seize as many goods as he could from the house to pay the mounting debts of the owner, Tom Roche Sr, one of Dublin's best-known businessmen and an individual most people presumed was rich beyond his wildest dreams.

The sheriff, acting on instructions from creditors, expected to take away grand antiques, valuable paintings and family treasures accumulated by one of the Ireland's wealthiest individuals. This was a man, after all, who had made several fortunes. He had created Cement Roadstone Holdings (CRH), built Ireland's first toll bridge and in the process made millions. Of course he also had his failures, a grandiose plan to put a huge cavern under Dublin bay to store gas being one that cost him more than a million pounds.

Tom Roche was a restless man, bristling with ambitious energy and consumed by a ferocious will to create great things from concrete and stone, and along the way accumulate vast amounts of wealth.

It wasn't just money, it was creating businesses that interested him. In doing this he got involved in various schemes with members of his family, one of which would eventually lead to a feud that would haunt him to his deathbed.

Tom Roche hadn't always had money and maybe that was the reason he was such a driven man. He was no more than a boy when his father, a civil servant, died and left the family virtually penniless. His mother had to sell the family home and move from posh, genteel Sandymount in Dublin 4 to the much poorer and tougher neighbourhood of Inchicore on the other side of the city. Tom, who was at school in Blackrock College, then one of the country's top fee-paying schools, had to leave after the Inter Cert to, as he said himself, 'go grubbing for pennies'.

'I was ambitious, even as a youngster. I wanted to build something, no matter what,' he told Ivor Kenny in a rare interview. 'The trigger for all that was a small business for which my mother paid £250. It consisted of a yard where we stored coal and a machine with which we made concrete blocks. My brother, Donal, who joined me in the business, left school even earlier than me, at age fifteen. He's been the steadying influence when I strayed too far from the sensible path.'

By the time the Second World War started less than a decade later, he and his brother had four trucks on the road.

Roche had little interest in formal education. 'You could put it this way: one day I was at school and the next I had a shovel in my hand and I was delighted. My mother set an example. I think that may be common in Irish mothers. My father really died too soon to have influence,' he said.

As well as making and selling blocks he collected coal from the docks, put it into bags and then drove around his old middle-class neighbourhood in Dublin 4 selling the fuel to friends of his mother and father who wanted to help the family out in their time of need.

From this small yard came a company called Castle Sand and eventually Roadstone, and in 1970 he merged it with the much bigger Irish Cement to create Cement Roadstone Holdings, which is now known as CRH.

It was a tricky deal because his company was much smaller than the one he wanted to take over. But like an inspired deal-maker he played 'the green card' and enlisted the help of his political connections – one Charles J Haughey just happened to be Minister for Finance at the time. The state insurance company Irish Life Assurance owned ten per cent of both Roadstone and Irish Cement and after they 'favoured' the deal proposed by Roche the new conglomerate emerged. Its first chairman was Sean Lemass, an inveterate gambler, former Taoiseach and father-in-law of Tom Roche's political pal Charles Haughey.

Roche was a tough taskmaster and later regretted how 'callous' he had been to some of the men who worked for him. He never liked sitting in an office and even when he was running a corporation like CRH he would insist on going out to the company quarries and if he didn't like the way things were being run he would sack whoever was in charge.

'He was a very difficult man. He was brilliant all right, but he was hotheaded and you have to remember these were hard times and when someone was sacked like that it had a terrible effect on their families. There weren't jobs to be picked up like there are today,' remembers a company executive.

But Roche came up the hard way and he never lost that hard edge that he had to develop as a teenager. He didn't like being 'chairman' ensconced in a boardroom when he could be on the ground interfering in the business.

'Once the merger was in place it became a corporation and had to be run on formal lines, and that did not suit me at all,' he said.

As the company he had created grew he often questioned the layers of managers and accountants it began to accumulate. 'Does it help to sell stone?' he wondered.

The money Tom Roche made along the way allowed him to buy Chesterfield from an old established Dublin business family, the Bradburys. In many ways Roche was a symbol of a new Ireland with its new money and its pretensions. The boy from the coal yard taking up residence in the grand home of an old Protestant business dynasty typified the new era and the new business class ascendancy.

But Tom Roche was not fully satisfied with the huge company he had created. He wasn't satisfied with the big house and demesne that he owned on the outskirts of Dublin. He wasn't satisfied with the trappings of wealth, power and privilege that it gave him. He wasn't even satisfied with the access it provided to the highest office of the land.

Tom Roche was always looking for another scheme to make money, for himself and for his family. It was what made him so successful, but it was also what precipitated his downfall.

He was involved in various companies with his family, so when Tom Roche's son-in-law Michael Wymes, who was married to his daughter Eleanor, came to him with yet another business proposition that would make an enormous amount of money Tom Roche thought nothing of plunging a fortune into the new venture.

The new boom was mining and an opportunity to get in on the ground floor presented itself. Michael Wymes and Tom Roche pounced on it.

Wymes, the son of a former commissioner of the Gardaí, and an Irish international basketball player, had qualified in University College Dublin as a veterinary surgeon and later as a barrister. His real interest, however, was business and he believed the opportunity of a lifetime had just presented itself to him.

Back when Michael Wymes was going to school in the 1950s children were taught in their geography lessons that there were no minerals in Ireland. There might be a few grains of gold in the Avoca River or deep in the Sperrin Mountains but the rest of the island was worthless. We might as well accept that the rich fertile soil that propped up agriculture was the country's greatest resource. The teachers were wrong, dead wrong.

In the early 1970s a geological survey caused an international sensation. The largest zinc ore body in Europe was discovered on the banks of the River Blackwater at Nevinstown outside Navan, Co Meath on the lands of a farmer called Patrick Wright. What would become crucial to the whole saga in the years that followed was that Mr Wright owned both the lands and the mineral rights, which was an unusual situation in the area.

There were various stories about how the discovery was made but Pat Hughes, Ireland's best-known mining expert and head of the Canadian-owned Tara Exploration and Development, stepped in to try to buy the lands. While these negotiations were in progress Tara discovered that this was just the tip of the iceberg. There was a wonderful seam of zinc around Navan and they bought up as much land as they could from local farmers. However, on these lands the mineral rights were not owned by the landowners, but by the Irish government. It would take four years of negotiations and court proceedings before Tara would finally get the go-ahead to open their mine.

In the meantime, negotiations continued with Farmer Wright about acquiring his land on the other side of the Blackwater which contained zinc deposits worth an estimated £200 million at the time. But the farmer was a cautious man and he was also in a stronger position than all the other landowners because he owned the mineral rights. Suspicious about the price he was being offered by 'the Canadians', he discussed the matter with his family doctor, Dr Paddy Randles. As it happens, Randles was married to Michael Wymes's sister and she communicated the news of the find to her brother, the vet, lawyer and businessman who lived nearby on a farm in Dardistown, Co Meath.

Michael Wymes quickly realised the significance of the information and he knew that if he acted quickly there was a lot of money to be made out of it. His father-in-law had both the money and the connections. Where could they go wrong?

It was all very Irish with family entanglements and local connections, and the international mining moguls who ran Tara Mines were very bitter over the way they believed Wymes and Roche were allowed to gazump them out of the find, aided and abetted by the Irish state.

The third partner in the venture was John A Wood, a wealthy 'merchant prince' from Cork who had a building supply business and was a friend of Tom Roche.

On March 18, 1971, they established a company to buy the Wright farm and set up a rival mining operation to Tara Mines. The Wright family would get ten per cent of the company for free and the other three families, the Wymeses, the Roches and the Woods, would put up the money and get an equal share of the business.

In a fit of optimism the company was named after an Irish racehorse, Bula, which had just carried off the famous Champion Hurdle steeplechase at the Cheltenham Races in England on St Patrick's Day. The new owners of Bula believed they had found the famous crock of gold within sight of the historic Hill of Tara.

Tara Mines appealed to the government and the courts, claiming that they had been effectively gazumped in the deal. But their protests fell on deaf cars.

Both sides entered into a bitter confrontation that would cost millions, lead to the longest and most complex court case in Irish legal history and eventually leave the fortunes of its founding families teetering on the brink of disaster.

In those early days in the mid-1970s life seemed to be a bed of roses as the three horsemen of Bula looked forward to the fortune that they just had to extract from the ground. And everyone, it seemed, wanted a piece of the action. The Labour Party, long advocates of state control of natural resources, just happened to be in a coalition government with Fine Gael at the time. To prove an ideological point in 1976 the Minister for Industry and Commerce, Justin Keating, insisted on the state splashing out £9,540,000 of the taxpayers' money to buy a forty-nine per cent stake in Bula from Tom Roche, Michael Wymes and the Wood family.

It cost almost £10 million for a green field farm on the banks of the Blackwater – and this at a time of austerity under the government of Liam Cosgrave where the Minister for Finance, Ritchie Ryan, was known as 'Ritchie Ruin, Minister for Hardship'.

The government was not the only organisation infected with enthusiasm. The banks were falling over themselves to get a share of the action. As the money flowed, Michael Wymes bought himself a new home, The Hermitage, a period property behind high walls directly across the road from his father-in-law's estate on Cross Avenue, the leafy road that links Booterstown and Blackrock. He also started looking around for a country estate befitting a mining magnate.

He had no problem raising the finance to purchase a Palladian mansion called Bective House in Co Meath, with hundreds of acres of land, two miles of cut-stone walls and salmon rights along the River Boyne which is the boundary of the property.

According to the architectural historian Bence-Jones, Bective is 'a plain two-storey house built in 1790 with good staircase hall.' The house was the childhood home of the writer James Stern, long-forgotten author of *The Heartless Land*, who came from a family of Anglo-German bankers and was a friend of James Joyce. And, we're told (in the early seventies) it was 'recently bought by Tower Cement Ltd'.

It seems rather unromantic that a Palladian pile should end up in the ownership of a cement company, but of course all the grand Irish houses were built by clever businessmen.

'Anticipating the mine would be opening shortly, Wymes himself bought the nearby Bective House, a Palladian mansion, for around £500,000. On the associated farm he raises Charolais cattle and has produced several prize-winning bulls,' said an *Irish Times* profile writer of the young and ambitious businessman.

Warming to the theme the writer told readers that Wymes, the country squire, stocked the 370 acres of lush farmland and groves of timber with pheasant and employed a gamekeeper. 'He took to his country squire role like a cat takes to cream,' he wrote.

When the first of three tranches of government money came through in 1978-79, Wymes was a millionaire. He would hold on to the house through thick and thin in the difficult years that followed, a feat that left many of his detractors scratching their heads in amusement and admiration as he doggedly spent years fighting over the carcase of Bula mines in the Four Courts in Dublin.

The one thing Wymes never produced was zinc. There were ten million tonnes of it sitting under the good green sod of Wright's farm but there were powerful interests determined that it would never come out of the ground.

Michael Wymes's vision was for an opencast mine, which could be brought into operation quickly and cheaply. It would also allow Bula to sell zinc ore on the international markets more cheaply than its rival across the River Blackwater, Tara Mines, which had the added expense of sinking mine shafts to bring its lode to the surface.

But Wymes's plan could not be considered environmentally friendly, even in those far-off days of 1979, and Meath County Council refused to give it planning permission. Among the main objectors were the rivals on the other side of the river.

Wymes believed they were carrying out a vendetta against him with the objective of forcing him to sell the Wright farm back to them.

At exactly the same time as the planning permission was refused, Tara Mines offered to buy Bula, a move that would end the feud between the two firms and leave the Wymes, Roche,

Wood and Wright families with a handsome profit. But personal animosity had now built to such a pitch between Wymes and Brendan Hynes, who had taken over from Pat Hughes at Tara, that he turned the deal down flat.

Wymes reapplied for planning permission to get the mining operation going. He was turned down again. The planning process turned into an interminable struggle. Various Ministers for Energy from different governments with different political agendas got involved along the way.

Unlike other mining operations the directors of Bula had not borrowed a huge amount of money to get the mine up and running. Their borrowings were about £5 million. But there was no sign of the mine opening and interest rates were high. Interest alone was costing the company about £5,000 a day – an enormous sum at the time.

The worst part of it, from their point of view, was that in their enthusiasm for the mine and in their belief that it would make them a vast fortune they each had given personal guarantees against the loans. Tom Roche had put his home and his family fortune on the line. But as the days, weeks and months passed, there was no mine, no ore coming out of the ground and no money coming back to pay the loans.

As he looked out over his estate in Blackrock the man who had left school at sixteen to become a coal carter in the Dublin docks and had walked away from CRH with over a million pounds could only watch helplessly as his fortune drained away.

'The interminable delays experienced in trying to bring the mine into production left Bula Ltd with liabilities approaching £27 million, due to the rolling up of interest on a relatively low base of borrowings. Some £9 million of Bula's loans were arranged on foot of personal guarantees from the directors,' wrote

Des Crowley in the *Sunday Press*.

These would eventualy rise to a staggering £60 million.

Each week the banks, the revenue and other assorted creditors began another process in the courts to recover their money.

The Northern Bank Finance Corporation got a judgement against the Bula directors for £3.9 million. Another bank was after them for £900,000 and the Revenue Commissioners said they were owed £300,000. Out in the country Michael Wymes's opulent estate was under siege, with the sheriff for Co Meath seizing his herd of pedigree Charolais cattle and carrying them off to be sold to the highest bidder.

By the early 1980s John A Wood had died and his son Richard was brought in to replace him. Tom Roche had also brought his son, Tom Roche Jr, into the firm to help get the mining operation off the ground. But Michael Wymes was the driving force behind the project.

Eventually in 1983 Bula got planning permission to open its mine. It began to look for finance to finally exploit the £200 million worth of ore under the ground at Navan. But already badly burned, the banks and financial institutions wanted the men behind Bula to pump money into the company to show 'good faith'.

At the same time, the government was conducting separate negotiations to sell its shareholding in Bula to Tara Mines. When these failed and the banks closed in, Wymes resigned as a director of Bula.

A consortium of banks, owed £15.5 million, appointed the well-known Dublin accountant Laurence Crowley as receiver, and he effectively took over with a mission to sell the business and try to recoup as much as he could for the banks and other creditors.

Michael Wymes wasn't going to allow that, however, and

began a legal action to stop the sale. He sued Tara Mines, the state and various government departments who were implicated in the mine.

In taking the legal proceedings that would go on for the next thirty years Michael Wymes entered into another deal with Tom Roche Sr. The Roche family would finance the litigation, but Wymes, a trained barrister, would do the groundwork, employ solicitors and barristers and appear in court. It would be his case and he would devote most of the rest of his life to it, although he didn't know that at the time.

In some ways it was a master stroke. Once the legal proceedings began, all the money that was owed became tangled up in the litigation, and the creditors could not come after them until it was resolved.

Wymes was, said one of the judges who heard the long-running legal arguments he advanced, 'a man obsessed' and an 'eccentric and difficult' person, who heeded neither advice nor caution in his bid to claim what he believed was rightfully his and what had been taken from him in a giant conspiracy that nobody but he fully understood.

In the years that followed, the turns and twists of what became known as the Bula Saga continued to be a constant factor in Irish business.

'Mr Wymes had indulged in and was a master of interminable nit-picking, legalistic and antagonistic correspondence with all and sundry and especially with the Minister and his Department with whom he should have been seeking good relations,' said a report in *The Irish Times*. 'It was very strange that there appeared to have been a complete failure on the part of Bula personnel and especially Mr Wymes to appreciate the cost of time and borrowed money.'

At the same time, Michael Wymes was telling his creditors down in the High Court that he no longer had any income. He said that since resigning from Bula he didn't have any wages and he had no assets outside the state. He admitted that he lost £468,000 on 'commodity trading' the year after he got the first cheque from the Irish government.

Tom Roche Sr felt under such enormous pressure around this time that he was about to accept an offer of just £500,000 for his beloved Chesterfield from the hotelier PV Doyle. Wymes pleaded with him not to sell and he didn't.

When the house and estate in Blackrock was finally sold many years later it made the highest price ever paid for a private home in Dublin – a record that stands to this day.

'Bula Mines was a mistake,' Tom Roche told Ivor Kenny in an interview that he refused to have published during his lifetime, 'because there were too many bits in it that would hurt people. I was tempted by the piratical aspects and the romance of it,' he continued. 'There were a few times when I could have got out, but I hadn't the final say. All the assets I had were sucked into it.'

What he didn't say, however, was that he had taken about £5 million out of Bula and an associated oil exploration company – and put them to very good use.

Tom Roche Sr and his son had already embarked on yet another business venture, this time with considerably more success. They were the main driving force behind a new company called National Toll Roads (NTR) which had come up with the notion of building the country's first toll bridge joining up Ringsend on the south side of Dublin and the Point Depot on the north side of the Liffey. The new bridge would allow drivers trying to get from one side of the city to the other to avoid the long and tedious journey through the clogged-up city centre.

It was an idea Roche had first entertained in the late 1970s but only became a reality one bright October day in 1984 when the Taoiseach of the day, Garret Fitzgerald, officially opened the first toll bridge in Ireland. Standing proudly by his side with a thin smile on his hatchet-like face, was the buccaneering businessman, Tom Roche Sr.

The new bridge was like owning a bank. Tom Roche and his son, Tom Jr, would do more than simply revive the family fortunes. National Toll Roads would make Tom Roche Jr one of the wealthiest individuals in the state and when he married PV Doyle's daughter Anne he would enter into an alliance that also saw him play a central role in the family fortunes of the Doyle hotels.

Brian Trench, in an article for the *Sunday Tribune* the day the East Link toll bridge opened, wrote 'It is a very private business empire, almost entirely run by members of the Roche family or by those who married into it.

'Their personal and social lives revolve around the large home of Tom Roche Sr with its several acres of gardens and a swimming pool.

'At sixty-eight, Tom Roche is one of Ireland's most powerful, but least-known businessmen. He is also the kind of businessman who likes to get involved in all the minute details of his projects. While the bridge across the Liffey was still only a fantasy, he was knocking on doors in Ringsend persuading local people it would not upset them and offering bathrooms, porches and community facilities in return for any inconvenience caused.'

Indeed Roche, thin and hardy with slicked-back hair and a wide smile, often sat in the toll booth taking money from motorists in those early days of the new venture. The man with the big estate in Blackrock would sit there on a Sunday evening so that he could keep in touch with his customers and let his employees know that he wasn't above doing the work.

Within a few years the bridge had paid for itself and he embarked on a second toll bridge, the Westlink, running over the Liffey on the west side of Dublin and linking the two ends of the M50 motorway. To aid his progress in this venture Tom Roche paid 'consultancy fees' of £74,000 to the colourfully corrupt politician Liam Lawlor TD, who would later go to jail for obstruction of the Planning Tribunal and die in a tragic car accident on a mysterious business trip to Russia.

But Tom Roche was used to dealing with people who could grease the wheels of commerce. He even handed an envelope with £10,000 in cash to the city manager in charge of planning, George Redmond, to 'hurry things up' so that the bridge would meet its construction deadline of 1987. (Indeed he often privately regretted not attempting to 'buy' planning permission in the early days of Bula.)

National Toll Roads went on to become one of the most profitable businesses in Ireland and the huge profits it generates have been invested in property, waste management, green electricity and other diverse businesses.

But while he was smiling for the photographers and reviving his fortunes with the toll bridges the dark shadow of Bula mines was hanging over Tom Roche and his grand home and even his family fortune. The interminable litigation was costing astronomical sums – and year after year the interest kept rising on the original borrowing.

Then in 1992 Michael Wymes got a telex message from his father-in-law to say that Roche was pulling the plug on the long-running court proceedings. When they met face to face Tom Roche Sr asked Michael Wymes to take a smaller share of a settlement if one could be arrived at. Wymes was puzzled, until he discovered that his father-in-law had already reached a profitable settlement if the legal proceedings were dropped and Bula was buried.

Wymes was incensed: Roche would come out with his debts settled and cash in the bank. Wymes would be ruined.

Michael Wymes found himself isolated. But more than that, not only was he cut off from the funding that Tom Roche had provided to carry on the litigation, but his case seemed irretrievably damaged because one of the major partners was pulling out.

The two men never spoke again.

There was no attempt made to hide the bitterness that crept into the relationship between them. A new set of legal proceedings began with Michael Wymes pursuing his father-in-law and his family through the courts.

It wasn't just business, it was also family. When Eleanor Roche's niece was getting married, neither she nor her husband Michael Wymes were invited to the wedding. The once close-knit family now found that the ties were broken and the relationships, business and social, began to fall apart.

Tom Roche was an autocratic man. He knew that the deal he was trying to do would have saved the Roche family fortune, but left his son-in-law with nothing. He put his own interests first – he was a businessman after all. But it had a terrible effect on his daughter Eleanor and the family feud has never been settled.

Michael Wymes heard many years later that in old age Roche Sr wanted to lift the telephone to try to heal the feud, but he just couldn't bring himself to make that call.

'What I look to in times of trial is a depth of inner strength that I can call on,' said Roche about the period. 'I think it originated in my mother. Fortunately, I can call on mental reserves. I don't need alcohol or pills. I think it also had its origin in the fact that I was grubbing for pennies when I was young.'

The city sheriff never did take anything from his estate at Chesterfield in Blackrock that fateful day in the mid-1980s. The phone rang and legend has it that when it was handed to the sheriff's man, Charlie Haughey, the most powerful politician of the day, was on the other end of the line. He asked in a firm and forceful manner that Mr Roche be given the time he needed to sort out his financial affairs and everything would come good in the end.

Roche was given the time and he did make a second fortune, but for the rest of his life he remained financially crippled by his foray into mining.

In 1995 Tom Roche made a present of IR£222,204 to each of his three daughters, Eleanor, Maura and Claire. It was his legacy to them and a considerable fortune back then, but nothing to what he would have been able to give them had he not become embroiled in the Bula saga. His mission to give something to his daughters accomplished, he handed over the reins of the family business to his son Tom Jr.

But while his toll bridge business was again making millions for the Roche family the feud that began over the Bula mine was far from over. The spectre of the mine continued to haunt the old man, even in his twilight years.

The guarantees he had given in 1978, 1980, 1981 and 1982 against the loans had never been paid and prior to his death the Ulster Investment Bank issued bankruptcy proceedings against Tom Roche Sr to recover their money.

The Northern Bank Finance Corporation also demanded €11.9 million from his estate. The Ulster Bank claimed they were owed €2.9 million and a further €3 million was owed in legal costs to the various banks and financial institutions over 'proceedings which have been ongoing for twenty years'.

Tom Roche Sr died on July 8, 1999. In keeping with his fierce privacy, symbolised by the tall trees behind the walls of Chesterfield, his funeral was a quiet affair attended only by close friends invited by the family. It was over before his death was publicly announced.

'An intensely private man he was far more at ease at the coalface than in the boardroom,' said the obituary writer.

He left Chesterfield in his will to his granddaughter Michelle, the daughter of Tom Roche Jr. The rest of his estate he left to his daughters Maura Tierney, Eleanor Wymes and Claire Fleming. He had €8,000 in a Bank of Ireland account and €19.81 in a savings account in the same bank in Montrose.

When all the figures were totted up by the accountants, Thomas Celestine Roche, who appeared to be one of the richest men in the country and was certainly one of the most adventurous businessmen of his generation, died insolvent with debts of €15,600,000.

It was all down to that moment when he had been tempted by the prospect of untold riches by the side of the Blackwater.

'It will be necessary for the executors to sell the leasehold premises [Chesterfield] bequeathed to the deceased's granddaughter, Ms Michelle Roche, and the total net proceeds of sale must be applied by the executors to the debt due to this bank,' the solicitors Arthur Cox advised

By 2003 it seemed that Michael Wymes had come to the end of the line when he lost a Supreme Court challenge to the sale of Bula Ltd to Tara Mines, thirty-two years after the company was originally established. But neither the Bula dispute nor the family feud was over, by a long shot.

The happy families that had once been a feature of life when Tom Roche and his wife Florence were alive and Chesterfield was the centre of the family social scene were no longer. In fact it was Chesterfield that would become the subject of a bitter confrontation between Tom Roche Jr and his sister Eleanor. The pressure of years of litigation led to the separation of Eleanor and Michael Wymes and Eleanor Roche left the Bective Estate in Co Meath and moved back to Dublin. Not to any ordinary part of the city, however. When Eleanor Roche drives out of her home in an upmarket housing development off Booterstown Avenue in South Dublin, she sees the tall trees and the boundary wall of Chesterfield, the home where she grew up, on the other side of the road. And a few hundred yards away are the fine wrought-iron gates closed against her.

In 2004 Tom Roche Jr sold Chesterfield to a developer, Myles Crofton, for €47 million. It was the highest price ever paid for a private family home in Dublin. But then on November 30 of the same year, when the deal was about to close, a snag arose and the huge business deal had to be put on hold. Eleanor Roche was laying claim to part of the estate, citing it as part of her inheritance.

Then Tom Roche Jr issued proceedings in the High Court in December against his sister seeking a declaration that she had no beneficial interest in Chesterfield. Some of the papers in the case were 'among the most bitter correspondence it has been my misfortune to read', said Judge Peter Kelly who was presiding over the case.

When it came before him in the Commercial Division of the High Court he adjourned the matter for a couple of days to ascertain exactly what her claim was.

To complicate matters further Eleanor Roche had handed over power of attorney to her son, Michael Wymes Jr.

'Mr David Barniville, for Mr Roche, said the sale was due to close on November 30 and had now been deferred. The purchasers had agreed to a revised closing date, but that was dependent on the claim being made on behalf of Ms Roche against the purchasers being withdrawn or the matter decided by the court,' went a report of the court proceedings.

In the following days the bitterness deepened when Michael Wymes Jr wrote to Myles Crofton saying they had nothing against him and were not seeking to hold him liable for what happened to Chesterfield.

'Mr Wymes Jr had last Tuesday night telephoned Roche and indicated that in principle he felt they could agree to a declaration which would allow the sale to proceed but which preserved his mother's claim against Mr Roche. However yesterday morning Mr Roche had received a text from Mr Wymes that it might be better if the matter was dealt with by the court,' said the court reports.

As if that wasn't complicated enough Wymes Jr, suffering from stress-related illnesses, then signed himself into a London psychiatric hospital. His mother Eleanor had also been taken to hospital suffering from stress as a result of the family feud over Chesterfield.

Then, in the days leading up to Christmas, Eleanor Roche made a declaration to the High Court renouncing her claim to her childhood home. The sale of Chesterfield went ahead.

But the litigation among the Roche and the Wymes families wasn't over yet. After settling his case with his sister, Tom Roche Jr issued legal proceedings against his estranged brother-in-law Michael Wymes, founder of Bula and owner of Bective House in Co Meath. The story had turned the full circle.

In early 2006 Tom Roche lodged a multimillion euro suit

against his former brother-in-law and business partner to recover a portion of the money he had invested in Bula. It seems the feud has some way to go, because Michael Wymes is adamant that the case will be defended.

The bitterness remains. But of course that's what family feuds are all about. In the end the whispered deal that the rainbow over Wright's farm near Navan, Co Meath would lead one family to the crock of gold proved to be an expensive and painful illusion. The family of Tom Roche Sr prospered, but in the process the family fell apart and the bitter legacy of the feud remains.

Still, Michael Wymes had something to smile about as he faced into yet another family legal battle. He put his beloved estate, Bective House and demesne, on the market in 2006 and sold it for €13 million.

It might not be the pot of gold at the end of the rainbow, but it's not a bad consolation prize.

IRISH CRIMES OF PASSION
Liam Collins

CRIME IS PERILOUS.
CRIME AND PASSION
ARE A LETHAL COCKTAIL.

Picture the beautiful temptress who buys her own grave, then lures her lover to a dramatic death scene in her bedroom . . .

. . . the husband who goes through his wife's mobile phone messages and unleashes a rage that not only leads to her murder but wipes out an entire family . . .

. . . or the coward brooding in a love triangle who hires a ruthless killer to murder his pregnant wife.

They are all here in the hidden Ireland, where ordinary men and women suddenly get caught up in that deadly moment when crime and passion collide – with fatal consequences.

Liam Collins investigates these tragic cases where love, lust, desire and jealousy twist and contort in a spiral of madness.

'These stories illustrate how a moment of madness can lead to a lifetime of misery.'
Paul Williams, Crime Writer

FOOT IN MOUTH
FAMOUS IRISH POLITICAL GAFFES
Shane Coleman

The history of the Irish State has never been told in quite this way! *Foot in Mouth – Famous Irish Political Gaffes* recounts the gaffes that rocked governments, shocked public opinion and mocked accepted uses of the English language.

A fascinating account of our politicians' moments of madness that leaves the reader wondering how our elected leaders can mess up so badly . . . so consistently.

- Pee Flynn's musing on the *Late Late Show* on life on a measly income (how will he pay for that third housekeeper?)
- Jack Lynch's memory loss concerning two British agents
- *That* Fine Gael Ard Fheis
- The PDs excessive housekeeping (let's dump these sensitive financial records in this skip!)
- De Valera's notorious response to the death of Hitler
- Paddy Donegan's 'thundering disgrace' comments

Over 70 gaffes are relayed in full cringe-making detail.
Gaffers are not a new breed and the gaffes in this book are prime examples of how politicians have been sticking their feet in their mouths for years!

TRUE CRIME

BLOODY EVIDENCE
Michael Sheridan

Killers do not have to prove their innocence.

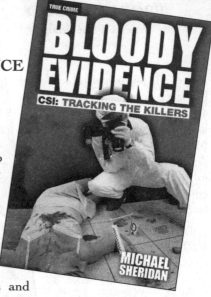

It is the burden of others to prove their guilt beyond any reasonable doubt. Detection, crime-scene investigation and forensic science have evolved hugely as killers become increasingly aware of the need to cover their tracks and destroy evidence.

Murder has become an epidemic in Ireland and the patterns, methods and motives mirror the progress of this disease in other countries. Bestselling author Michael Sheridan illustrates the complex nature of a murder investigation by exploring modern and well-established techniques of detection through a number of cases, such as the horrific Black Dahlia murder in which the victim was cut in half and drained of blood; the bizarre murder of six-year-old JonBenet Ramsey, which ten years on has hit world headlines again; or the savage West of Ireland murder of teenager Siobhán Hynes.

FROZEN BLOOD
Michael Sheridan

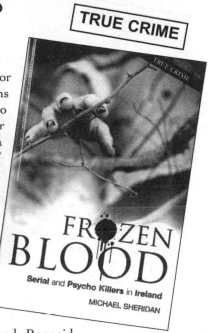

TRUE CRIME

Murder is an unspeakable horror but even more sickening depths are reached by serial and psycho killers. Best-selling author Michael Sheridan describes a distinct and brutal pattern of killing women which has emerged in Ireland, one used by psycho sex killers.

To powerful and disturbing effect, **Frozen Blood** examines the circumstances surrounding the murder and disappearance of several women. Young women such as Phyllis Murphy, who was raped and viciously killed, and Raonaid Murray, who was brutally attacked with a six-inch kitchen knife, murdered by men who have no inhibitions or feelings of remorse.

Why does an innocent child turn into a depraved killer? What are the common denominators among the tiny percentage of people who savagely kill? Why do they do what they do? Tracing the horrifying phenomenon of psychotic sex killers, **Frozen Blood** provides terrifying profiles of killers active in Ireland.

According to the experts, 'In the history of psychotic and serial killing it is unknown for the participants to cease killing voluntarily.' Although men such as John Crerar and Mark Nash are currently behind bars, it is only a matter of time before they are released: men who will live in our community once more; men who will live among us.

TRUE CRIME

TEARS OF BLOOD
Michael Sheridan

Murder and unlawful killing are now so common in Ireland that they no longer command headline attention. A daily perusal of the papers will provide dreadful details of killings. These details, the cases and the trials are publicly aired and then the media move on to the next story. But as best-selling author Michael Sheridan discovers, the effects of murder and killing are far-reaching for the families and relatives of the victims.

Through interviews with the families left behind and by researching inquest files and postmortem reports, the author reconstructs the crimes and exposes the horrific acts of merciless killers such as Noel Hogan, the Ian Huntley of Ireland; Peter Whelan; Anthony Kiely and Thomas Murray. Killers and murderers constantly lie about the crime; the facts do not.

Chronicling the devastating effects on the families of the victims, who include Lorraine O'Connor, Nichola Sweeney, Bernadette Connolly and Nancy Nolan, **Tears of Blood** – provides a unique and heart-rending insight into the aftermath of murder.

ERINDIPITY
David Kenny

Erindipity – The Irish Miscellany is like that Irish stew your mad granny used to make after she'd cleared out the back of the cupboard. Each time you dip your spoon in, out comes something unexpected.

Ever wondered:

- how many teeth Richard Harris lost to get nominated for an Oscar?
- when an Enya record was used in a multi-billion dollar heist?
- where's the place you're most likely to get a puck in the gob?
- how long it takes to re-feather a chicken in Dalkey?
- where's the smelliest-smelling place?
- what's the largest amount of ice cream lost at sea?

It's all here, crammed into 125 rambling 'essays' – the good, the bad, the extremes of Ireland – that will amuse, educate, annoy and misguide you in equal measure. Everything, in fact, you ever wanted to know about Ireland but didn't quite get around to asking.

David Kenny has been a journalist for the past 23 years and worked with the Irish Press Group, the Evening News and RTÉ television before joining the Evening Herald where he occupies the position of Senior Associate Editor. He is also the author of the bestselling The Little Buke of Dublin, Or How To Be A Real Dub. He is married and lives in Dalkey, Co Dublin.

GREAT GAA MOMENTS 2006
Finbarr McCarthy

Great GAA Moments 2006
recalls the stories that made the
headlines, reveals the drama
behind the scenes and captures
the colour and excitement of the
big match days at both club and
county level.

- The Omagh Brawl – that
  infamous opening match
  of the Allianz National
  Football League: Dublin
  v Tyrone
- Celebrations of the
  'West's Awake' as both Club Champions
  travelled back across the Shannon on St Patrick's Day
- The retirement of a hurling legend before the start of the
  Guinness Hurling Championship
- The claiming of another victim by the 'Blood Sub' rule in
  the Kildare v Offaly match
- Those managers who won't be back in 2007 – and the
  reasons why
- The clash of the best football teams in the provincial finals,
  including Cork v Kerry (Munster), Dublin v Offaly
  (Leinster), Galway v Mayo (Connacht) and Armagh v
  Donegal (Ulster)
- The excitement of a Tipperary v Cork Camogie Final
- The epic battle between Kilkenny, Limerick, Cork and
  Tipperary to become Hurling Champions 2006 was packed
  with unforgettable GAA events. This book contains them
  all, accompanied by superb action shots from on the field
  illustrating another spectacular season in Gaelic sport.